Not Weeded
BHS 4/05

89515

ENGLISH THEORIES OF
Economic Fluctuations
1815-1848

NUMBER 598
COLUMBIA STUDIES IN THE SOCIAL SCIENCES
EDITED BY THE FACULTY OF POLITICAL SCIENCE
OF COLUMBIA UNIVERSITY

ENGLISH THEORIES
OF
Economic Fluctuations
1815-1848

BY ROBERT G. LINK

AMS PRESS
NEW YORK

The Columbia Studies in the Social Sciences (formerly the Studies in History, Economics, and Public Law) is a series edited by the Faculty of Political Science of Columbia University and published by Columbia University Press for the purpose of making available scholarly studies produced within the Faculty.

Reprinted with the permission of Columbia University Press
From the edition of 1959, New York
First AMS EDITION published, 1968
Manufactured in the United States of America

Library of Congress Catalogue Card Number: 68-54282

AMS PRESS, INC.
New York, N.Y. 10003

To

Edith Murr Link

Preface

THIS STUDY is designed to fill in part a gap in the existing histories of economic thought, a gap which seems to have given rise to a widespread underestimation of the realism and relevance of economics in England in the period from the end of the Napoleonic Wars through 1848. To this end the works of six economists have been examined. Thomas Robert Malthus, Thomas Tooke, and John Stuart Mill are well known, but the other three writers, Thomas Attwood, Thomas Joplin, and James Wilson, have received relatively little attention. In each case an attempt has been made to present sympathetically the ideas of the writer, without unduly obscuring the force and violence necessary for an intelligible rationalization by modern standards. The uses to which the theories were put in analyzing contemporary economic fluctuations, as well as the policy recommendations advanced, are also described.

Originally the study was submitted in 1953 for the Ph.D. degree at Columbia University. No attempt has been made to undertake extensive revisions since the latter part of 1952, although changes have been made wherever the original version seemed unclear.

A number of books and articles have appeared since 1952 which would have deserved mention had they been available at the time. Of these the most interesting deal, not with the theories of the period, but with the economic fluctuations themselves. *The Growth and Fluctuation of the British Economy, 1790-1850* by Arthur D. Gayer, W. W. Rostow, and Anna Jacobson Schwartz is particularly notable: the reader who compares their conclusions with the theories advanced in 1815-48 will surely find striking similarities. R. C. O. Matthews' *A Study in Trade-Cycle History*, an intensive analysis of the fluctuations between 1833 and 1842, is also noteworthy.

Studies of contemporary theories include Joseph Schumpeter's *History of Economic Analysis*, which provides a useful corrective to the prevailing neglect of theories of economic fluctuations in general histories of doctrine. Of perhaps greater interest are the articles in *Economica*, "Classical Monetary Theory" by G. S. Becker and W. J. Baumol (November, 1952) and "Dichotomies of the Pricing Process in Economic Theory" (May, 1954) by Don Patinkin; in these articles, as in Patinkin's *Money, Interest, and Prices*, the assumptions of classical economics have been dealt with at a higher level of generality than is attempted in this book.

Special acknowledgments are due to Professors Arthur F. Burns and Joseph Dorfman whose comments and criticisms contributed to the present study. To Edith Murr Link the author owes a debt that is both personal and intellectual.

ROBERT G. LINK

New York City
November, 1958

Contents

INTRODUCTION *1*

THOMAS ATTWOOD *6*
1. EXPANSION, CONTRACTION, AND NATURAL REMEDIES *8*
2. MONETARY MISMANAGEMENT *13*
3. THE REMEDY *19*
4. THE GOLD STANDARD *31*
5. CONCLUSION *33*

THOMAS ROBERT MALTHUS *36*
1. WEALTH *37*
2. FULL EMPLOYMENT AND THE ACCUMULATION OF CAPITAL *41*
3. UNEMPLOYMENT AND THE ACCUMULATION OF CAPITAL *44*
4. EFFECTUAL DEMAND *53*
5. PROSPERITY AND DEPRESSION *59*
6. POLICY *65*
7. CONCLUSION *70*

THOMAS JOPLIN *73*
1. SAVINGS AND EXPENDITURE *74*
2. INTERNATIONAL GOLD FLOWS *83*
3. APPLICATION *85*
4. POLICY AND REFORM *92*
5. CONCLUSION *99*

CONTENTS

JAMES WILSON — 103
1. FLUCTUATIONS IN THE PRICE OF CORN — 104
2. GENERAL FLUCTUATIONS — 107
3. RAILROAD OVERINVESTMENT — 114
4. INTERNATIONAL ASPECTS — 119
5. POLICY — 121
6. CONCLUSION — 123

THOMAS TOOKE — 127
1. ECONOMIC FLUCTUATIONS — 128
2. CURRENCY, MONEY, AND INTEREST RATES — 136
3. MITIGATION OF ECONOMIC FLUCTUATIONS — 142
4. CONCLUSION — 145

JOHN STUART MILL — 148
1. CONSUMPTION AND PRODUCTION — 149
2. COMMODITY SPECULATION AND THE CYCLE — 153
3. FIXED CAPITAL AND THE CYCLE — 161
4. POLICY — 168
5. CONCLUSION — 177

CONCLUSION — 180

NOTES — 189

BIBLIOGRAPHY — 211

INDEX — 223

ENGLISH THEORIES OF
Economic Fluctuations
1815-1848

Introduction

THE STUDY of economic fluctuations has occupied a prominent position in economics since the second decade of the twentieth century, and can be traced back to the writings of Juglar and Jevons. Beyond that its ancestry is none too clear. The present study is an attempt to determine how much was known about the subject, and to what extent and in what manner it was discussed, in England in the period between 1815 and 1848.

The use of the term "economic fluctuations" requires a brief explanation. Wesley Mitchell distinguished "business cycles" from "(1) changes in business conditions which occur between the dates of 'crises,' (2) fluctuations which affect a minor portion of the economic activities of a business community, (3) fluctuations which recur every year, and (4) the less definitely established secondary trends and 'long waves.' " In so far as possible "economic fluctuations" as used here includes both Mitchell's "business cycles" and changes in business conditions between crises, although at times it has been necessary to include some discussion of fluctuations that affect, at least directly, only a minor portion of national economic activity.[1]

Existing histories of economic thought are not wholly satisfactory in their treatment of the earlier theories of economic fluctuations. The standard general history usually neglects the subject altogether. The more specialized histories of monetary doctrine,[2] although concerned with fluctuations, present their material by topic, so that it is impossible to obtain a comprehensive picture of the thought of any particular writer: it is impossible to grasp the intensity of a writer's interest in fluctuations, the interrelations between ideas, the extent to which systematic theories were propounded, or the use that was made of such theories in interpreting actual fluctuations and in suggesting remedies. Moreover these works concentrate, quite naturally, upon monetary theories of economic fluctuations. Studies that have dealt specifically with theories of economic fluctuations in this period are relatively rare and are not sufficiently detailed to be satisfactory.[3]

This gap in knowledge is not the result of an absence of economic fluctuations in England in the early nineteenth century.[4] Rather it is related to the fact that the titles of books and pamphlets published at that time did not, as a rule, indicate that the author was concerned with economic fluctuations. The modern vocabulary of "business cycles," "trade cycles," and "industrial fluctuations" did not exist. But from behind titles that suggest a restatement of "principles of political economy," or appeals for currency reform or for the repeal of the corn laws, the discussion of economic fluctuations went on. Theories were propounded and remedies were proposed.

The present study is designed to examine these theories. Originally it was thought that the literature could be covered with a degree of completeness and that writers could be classified into schools. This proved to be overly ambitious. The writers were not, in many cases, clear enough to warrant the kind of generalization that is implied in such an arrangement. Instead it seemed desirable to be far less extensive in coverage and to provide a relatively intensive treatment of six writers who appeared to be of particular interest: Thomas Attwood, Thomas Robert Malthus, Thomas Joplin, James Wilson, Thomas Tooke, and John Stuart Mill. There may be other writers who are of greater interest than these six, but, on the basis of the research done, these appear to be the most significant.

All six of the writers considered published their major works bearing on economic fluctuations between 1815 and 1848. These boundary dates were chosen to cover the period from the end of the Napoleonic Wars to the gold discoveries of 1848 and 1852, thus excluding, in so far as possible, theories particularly connected with the war period and with the effects of the influx of gold from America and Australia. These dates have the further advantage of coinciding roughly with two landmarks in the history of doctrine, the publication of David Ricardo's *Principles of Political Economy and Taxation* in 1817 and of John Stuart Mill's *Principles of Political Economy* in 1848.

A study of the writers on economic fluctuations during this period must inevitably include Thomas Attwood. Despite neglect until very recently,[5] Attwood wrote extensively on this subject during 1816-28, these being the years in which his most important works were published. He was generally acknowledged to be the leader of the "Birmingham School" of economists, a group that was united in its demand for a money supply adequate to maintain prosperity. In Attwood's writings this view, combined with the cry of "full employment," obtains a full treatment.

The most important single work of Thomas Malthus in this area is the *Principles of Political Economy*, first published in 1820. As early as 1811 he had written on economic fluctuations; his last important article appeared in 1823. His theory can be labeled "underconsumptionist," and it has certain similarities to that of Attwood. Modern interest in Malthus derives from J. M. Keynes' biographical article and from his *General Theory*.[6] Partly as a result there has been some tendency to accept Malthus as an early forerunner of Keynes. Often, however, this impression seems to be the result of a too easy acceptance of particular phrases in Malthus, involving both a failure to analyze his whole system and a failure to recognize differences in the use of language: "saving" is a very ambiguous term.

With Thomas Joplin the immediate postwar years are past, his major works having been published between 1823 and 1844. Though Joplin is generally associated with the Currency School because of his early statement of the "currency principle,"[7] his views were actually much more complex. His theory of "savings" and "expenditures" and his use of the "natural" rate of interest are in many respects strikingly modern. Joplin's work in fact provides the closest approach, in this period, to the modern doctrines that relate the level of income to the relations between saving and investment. Joplin is far closer to Keynes than is Malthus.

James Wilson published his most important works in 1839, 1840, and 1847; but he also expressed his views through the (London) *Economist*, of which he was the founder in 1843 and the editor until his death in 1860. While Attwood, Malthus, and Joplin emphasized, in one way or another, the level of aggregate money demand, Wilson was primarily concerned with the influence of "real" factors upon the level of economic activity. He advanced several different, though related, theories. One was an agricultural theory, connected with the corn laws and based upon a cobweb effect arising from the delayed response of farmers to price changes. Another, developed to explain the effects of the railroad boom of the 1840s, was an overinvestment theory of expansion and upper turning points; it bears a striking resemblance to modern theories of overinvestment.

The most important works of Thomas Tooke, the fifth writer to be considered, appeared between 1823 and 1856. Tooke collected information both statistical and "historical," particularly in his *History of Prices*, which has been the source of much later writing upon economic fluctuations during this period. His own explanations placed considerable stress upon exogenous events and upon fluctuations in inventory investment.

John Stuart Mill's relevant publications start in 1824 and for present purposes end roughly with the publication of the *Principles* in 1848. The choice of the 1848 boundary date is indeed partly influenced by the fact that Mill's *Principles* reviewed many of the controversies that had occupied writers during the preceding thirty years. From another point of view Mill's comments upon economic fluctuations were the outstanding heritage that

INTRODUCTION

the following generation derived from this period. In his books and articles Mill attacked Attwood's theories, used the theory of inventory speculation as advanced by Tooke, and added some of the elements of an overinvestment theory in propounding his own interpretation of economic fluctuations. He had a fairly clear conception of endogenous forces operating to bring about a transition from one phase of the "commercial cycle" to another, without the intervention of exogenous events; the phases that he recognized were, however, somewhat unusual.

Thus we confine our attention to six writers who, tentatively at least, can be described as representing the attitudes toward economic fluctuations that were put forward in England during the period from 1815 to 1848.

Thomas Attwood

THOMAS ATTWOOD achieved, not fame, but a brief notoriety as a political economist.[1] Although he was by profession a Birmingham banker, his real fame arose from the role he played in the agitations of the early 1830s. Francis Place described Attwood in 1830 as "the most influential man in England," while John Stuart Mill, writing in 1833, spoke of him as "the organizer and leader of our late victorious struggle."[2] But in each case the reference was to Attwood's leadership of the Birmingham Political Union and to the part which he played in the passage of the Reform Bill of 1832, and not to his activities in the field of political economy.

Thus the same essay which included Mill's laudatory description was entitled "The Currency Juggle" and was devoted to a scathing attack upon Attwood's program for full employment through the creation of currency. This attack was echoed in Mill's *Principles* fifteen years later.[3] Earlier Ricardo had commented briefly: "His claims to infallibility have been sifted by Huskisson and myself, and I believe it will appear that he is no great master of the science."[4] Generally, moreover, he received less serious attention than Mill had vouchsafed. The *Economist* in the early 1840s treated his theories as a joke, using the term "Brummagem," meaning Birmingham or "counterfeit."[5]

One explanation for Attwood's failure as a purveyor of economic ideas, despite his great prestige as a political leader, may be found in the form in which he presented these ideas.

THOMAS ATTWOOD

His biographer states that he wrote some fifty pamphlets during his life.[6] None of the available pamphlets, some of which run to over 200 pages, purport to be more than tracts for the times. They were, in the field of written economics, analogues of the mass meetings before which Attwood spoke in support of Reform, or the Charter, or his own economic program. Moreover, the pamphlets were badly organized, repetitious, and sometimes internally contradictory. He described his method as follows:

> I have thus thrown together a variety of thoughts and opinions, desultory indeed, but such as I have neither leisure or disposition to economize and arrange.[7]

This was true of all his work.

Most of his efforts were engaged in a rather pathetic attempt to create, not an intellectual following, but the kind of mass support which would make his program of monetary reform a reality. He seems originally to have been a Tory and as late as 1828 he was enthusiastic about Wellington as Prime Minister. But his program fell upon unsympathetic ears. For this and possibly other reasons, he became a leader of the Reform movement, hoping that a wider suffrage would lead to acceptance of his program. When the enlarged suffrage of 1832 failed to do more than elect Attwood to Parliament, he turned to the Chartist movement.[8] He presented the Charter to Parliament in 1839. But at the same time the Chartist Convention denounced the "power and corrupting influence of paper money," and declared that the industrious classes have been

> defrauded by the fraudulent bits of paper, which our state tricksters dignify with the name of money and are at this moment being robbed by that system of three-fourth of their labour.[9]

This repudiation influenced Attwood's resignation from Parliament and his virtual retirement from public life.[10]

He did succeed in gathering about him a group of pamphleteers who agreed with the main points in his program. These writers were no more successful than Attwood and their names are, for the most part, even more obscure.[11]

In what follows the main ideas of Attwood relating to economic fluctuations are examined. The first section deals with his earliest efforts in this direction, in which he describes fluctuations whose turning points arise out of "natural remedies." The second section considers Attwood's more usual view that turning points are attributable to the monetary policies adopted by the government and the Bank of England. Section three treats the remedy for depression and the means by which full employment could be achieved and maintained. The fourth section shows how the gold standard was related to fluctuations and to Attwood's program. In the final section an attempt is made to compare Attwood with more modern economists who hold similar views.

1. EXPANSION, CONTRACTION, AND NATURAL REMEDIES

It is possible to distinguish two explanations of economic fluctuations in Attwood's writings. Both are identical in respect to the description of expansion and contraction. Differences appear, however, in the explanation of upper and lower turning points. In the first explanation Attwood suggested that there were "natural remedies" that would end and reverse any expansion or contraction. This theory appeared in his earlier pamphlets.[12] For the most part, however, he ignored these natural remedies and attributed turning points to the policies of the government and the Bank of England. In this section discussion is confined to two subjects: Attwood's description of the processes of expansion and contraction, and his exposition of "natural remedies."

Attwood was aware of the elementary accounting relations between production, income, and expenditure. Like the modern national income accountant, he asserted that these three items were equal:

I think I have before reminded you, that it is not possible to produce £10 worth of any one given article without occasioning thereby, either directly or indirectly, an equivalent consumption of all other articles. Thus a ton of iron is produced, say, for £8, and sold perhaps, for £12. The labourers of one kind or other receive the £8 as wages, which they immediately expend in consuming £8 worth of other articles; and the ironmaster receives the other £4 as profit, or royalty, which he also either expends or invests in consuming £4 worth of other articles, and thus production and consumption always keep pace with each other.[13]

Attwood was, however, particularly concerned with the influence of money expenditures upon the level of production.

As long as the flow of expenditures remains adequate, general overproduction is impossible, though particular articles can be temporarily redundant.[14] Declines in the flow of expenditures, such as that which occurred in 1813, tend to depress prices, and once a general price decline gets underway it feeds on itself, and results in a general contraction of economic activity.[15] Money incomes, real production, employment, and currency in circulation all shrink in the course of such a contraction. Some stress is placed on the behavior of currency, apparently defined to include coin, bank notes, bills of exchange, transfers, book debts, and checks.[16] The volume of bills of exchange in circulation shrinks because of the diminished value of the goods on which they are based and because falling prices reduce the number of acceptable bills. Bank note circulation declines both because of the reduction in the quantity of safe bills of exchange and because bankers lose confidence. Thus declining prices lead to a reduction in the quantity of money and this in turn leads to further reductions in prices. Reduced currency and reduced prices "act and react upon each other."[17] Moreover, currency tends to be hoarded under such conditions.[18]

At the same time as currency is shrinking and velocity of circulation falling, holders of stocks of goods throw unusually large supplies on the market, in expectation of being able to repurchase later at lower prices. Falling prices particularly affect those who have purchased goods on credit:

A slight fall in the monied value of stocks involves all those kind of persons in losses and ruin, and in order to avoid this, they rush the more earnestly into the market to dispose of their stocks, whilst there is a chance of securing their credit and solvency by so doing.[19]

But the losses of this group quickly extend to those who do not trade on credit.

Attwood also described the same process in terms of interactions between income and expenditure. The losses that result from a fall in price impoverish and alarm the nation, so that expenditures are reduced.

When prices fall, production is arrested until the expenses of production fall in an equal degree; and whilst production is thus arrested, *consumption* is also diminished; . . . the inducements to employ labour . . . are diminished, and the prices of labour fall. The consumption of labour is thus diminished, and the prices of property again fall, and again act in depressing labour, and in crippling production, until national wealth is destroyed, or a re-action is promoted by the pressure of inevitable famine.[20]

During this general contraction fixed plant may change hands as the original owners are forced to sell at a loss. Describing the contraction after 1825, Attwood testified:

Capital which was worth £100,000 has fallen in some cases down to £5,000; that £5,000 gets into new hands, and enables the new man to carry on the machinery and the trade till another failure drives him to sell it for £2,000; and so there seems no limit to the depression in progress.[21]

Attwood went on to admit that sometimes the "new men" might continue to do business without failure, but he insisted that they could not make profits.

While admitting that here and there output might increase during a period of failing prices, Attwood believed that in the country as a whole production declined.[22] Employment certainly fell. The important thing was the uneven, chaotic nature of the fall in prices.

If prices were to fall suddenly, and generally, and equally, in all things, *and if it was well understood, that the amount of debts and obligations were to fall in the same proportion, at the same time*, it is possible that such a fall might take place without arresting consumption and production, and in that case it would neither be injurious or beneficial in any degree, but when a fall of this kind takes place in an obscure and unknown way, first upon one article and then upon another, without any correspondent fall taking place upon debts and obligations, it has the effect of destroying all confidence in property, and all inducements to its production, or to the employment of labourers in any way.[23]

The reduced profits and actual losses that led to reduced employment and production were also due at least in part to relative stability of money wages. Attwood was never clear in his views about the behavior of real wage rates in contraction, but he did believe that at least at first money wage rates failed to decline to the same degree as prices.[24] In any case the laboring classes received less real annual income since unemployment increased.[25]

The explanation of the upturn was simple. In the process of contraction in which production declines and stocks of goods are reduced, supply is cut to such an extent that prices rise. In some unspecified way money expenditures fall less than production:

The general agricultural and mechanical produce of the country is so far diminished as to bear no proportion to the inevitable consumption of the country.[26]

When the stocks of both necessaries, and luxuries, and riches of all kinds, are greatly diminished, and when the labourers have little employment, and less wages for their subsistence, a reaction is promoted by the diminution of produce, thus restoring high prices.[27]

But this adjustment takes a "considerable period."

Attwood did not adopt any other endogenous explanation of the upturn, but he made some remarks before a Parliamentary committee that might have been developed into such an explanation. Attwood argued that, while production as a whole had fallen between 1825 and 1832, there was at least one exception: ironmasters allegedly found it possible to reduce their losses through investment in additional furnaces, thereby spreading their heavy fixed costs over a larger output. Presumably this argument was based on the lower cost of the new furnaces. Had he pursued this line of thought he might have concluded that a contraction, through its effects on costs and effort, created incentives to invest that might limit the extent of contraction and even lead to revival. But this Attwood did not do.[28]

Once prices had risen after a contraction of production which outran a contraction of demand—Attwood described the cumulative expansion in the same terms as he had applied to the cumulative contraction. Bank note circulation increases and confidence revives. Just as stocks of goods were thrown on the market when prices were falling, so now stocks are accumulated. At this period the re-accumulation of stocks goes on, and . . . [raises] prices higher than even the diminution of produce would otherwise require.[29]

The rise of prices increases both the inducement and the means of employing labor, so that both employment and wages rise. As a result the consumption of labor is increased, prices of property rise again, and both consumption and production increase together.[30]

Attwood had little to say about a "natural remedy" that might end the expansion process, and he cited no historical instances. The expansion may end, he says, when the stocks that have been accumulated become excessive in relation to "the necessary wants of the country."[31] After his first pamphlet there is no reference to any natural end to expansion.

Only one attempt was made by Attwood to apply an endogenous explanation to historical upturns in economic activity. This he did in connection with the contraction of 1813-17 and the revival of 1817. Attwood argued that the downturn in 1813, for which he provided several exogenous explanations, was first reflected in a slump in agricultural prices:

If the late contractive action upon currency struck agriculture one or two years before it acted upon manufactures, even when agriculture and manufactures had long been on a par of prices, and when there was no reason to expect that greater stocks of agricultural produce had been accumulated than of manufactures, it may be reasonably concluded that agricultural produce is more immediately exposed to the operation of such an action, and that a considerable interval is thus allowed before it is felt upon manufactures.[32]

The fall in agricultural prices had immediate effects on agricultural employment and production, and in time affected manufacturing activity, as lower farm incomes resulted in reduced expenditures upon manufactured goods. By 1817 Attwood was arguing that the "natural remedy" of contraction was already operating to raise agricultural prices. A fall in agricultural production, resulting from reduced agricultural incomes, had outrun the fall in demand for such produce. The main causes of the rise in farm prices

are to be found in the exhaustion of stocks, in the devastation and injured cultivation of the land, and in the renewal of stocks, which is now rapidly taking place. To either of these circumstances I will venture to attribute an effect upon the present state of the prices of grain.[33]

Since a revival of this kind does not immediately lead to increased expenditures by the agricultural sector, prosperity does not spread at once to manufacturing and real wages actually fall. Only with some delay does the agricultural prosperity lead to prosperity in manufacturing and to a rise in the demand for labor.[34]

The "natural remedies" disappeared rather quickly from Attwood's writings. In their place he substituted explanations of turning points that depended primarily upon the policies of the government and the Bank of England. But the conception of expansions and contractions that involved interactions between expenditures and incomes and between prices and the money supply, and that resulted in fluctuations in prices, production, and employment, was not modified in his later writings.

2. MONETARY MISMANAGEMENT

While Attwood sketched a "natural remedy" for contraction and expansion, he chose, in describing the history of economic fluctuations, to lay most stress upon the monetary policies of the government and the Bank of England.

Even in his earliest pamphlet, when he was most interested in natural remedies, he emphasized that the depression after 1813 was strongly influenced by diminished government taxation and expenditure, rather than by a natural remedy.[35] In this discussion Attwood made no distinction between balanced and unbalanced budgets. Instead he apparently argued on the assumption that government taxes and expenditures, held in balance, were both reduced to the same extent. Such a reduction transfers the power to employ labor from the government to the capitalists. Unemployment results since

> it would take at least one or two years before the capitalists of the country would find their property increased by the revulsion of these Taxes, and still longer before they would be disposed or enabled to increase their expenditure, so as to provide the same maintenance for labourers as had formerly been supplied through the channels of the taxes.[36]
>
> The sudden revulsion of monied capital . . . , which is thus thrown out of the channels through which it has been accustomed to act, renders that capital stationary or inactive for a certain time, before it finds new channels of action upon property and labour; and thus the circulation system receives a shock which produces a contractive action.[37]

Although Attwood condemned policies of economy and retrenchment, he preferred to lay the blame for the postwar depression on an act of omission of the Bank of England: an issue of additional bank notes could have offset the reduction in government expenditure and prevented a cumulative contraction.[38] Later he also added another cause of the depression: the Bullion Report which "first acted in breaking up the established relations between property and money, in the year 1810."[39] The year 1813 was the only turning point at which Attwood seemed to divide cause and responsibility.

The situation in October, 1816, was being described by 1818 in terms that ignored completely the "natural remedy" that Attwood had earlier found in reduced agricultural production. Money was scarce, prices had fallen, trade was stagnating, and either one-third or one-fourth of the laboring classes were unemployed. It actually seemed for the moment that the theory of surplus population was correct.

Revival, according to Attwood, came only in 1817 after the

government had borrowed large sums of money from the Bank of England and used the money to retire exchequer bills, presumably from the public. Special significance was attached to the fact that government borrowing was from the Bank, not from the public. The purchase of exchequer bills did not, however, have an immediate effect on employment or production, though to a certain extent it did prevent further depression in London. The operation supplied money to holders of exchequer bills, these consisting

principally of a set of retired and antiquated bankers and brokers, and of a set of retired and antiquated capitalists, who are neither willing nor able to take upon themselves the task of employing money in any productive purposes.[40]

Eventually the use of this money in the extension of loans, or in the purchase of existing national debt, forced down the rate of interest and raised the price of national funds. As a result, the more active members of the community, scattered throughout England, reaped windfall gains by sales of national stocks, and used the proceeds for expenditures on goods and labor. Rising prices set in motion a cumulative expansion.

Thousands of manufactories have again been set in motion. Foreign trade has risen with the home trade, and it is now evident to everyone, the period is rapidly approaching, when our apparent surplus population will have abundant employment.[41]

Rising prices, however, had consequences, connected with the redemption of notes in gold, that worried Attwood in the fall of 1817.[42] Rising commodity prices tended, he argued, to raise the price of bullion and so lead to the melting of coin into bullion either for export or for other purposes.[43] Thus part of the currency disappears, so that, if prosperity is to be maintained, some other form of currency must replace gold coin. Moreover, Attwood was afraid that the Bank would adopt the policies that had been current before the suspension of specie payments under the Restriction Act.

At one period, when the natural creations of gold coinage, occasioned by its low prices, have filled the country with a circulating medium, and carried prices as high as the employment of the labourers and the welfare of the country required; then the bank has come forward with its increased circulation, "giving its sum of more to what already had too much," and glutting the nation with diseased excitements.[44]

While at other periods, when coin was melted down,

the bank, also, instead of extending its issue of notes for the relief of the social body, has been obliged to contract those issues, thereby increasing the general lassitude and depression, and driving millions out of employment.[45]

Even with continued suspension, Attwood feared that any panic would lead to bullion hoarding and, at the same time, to diminished discounting and diminished note circulation.[46]

The fears that Attwood had expressed in 1817 were apparently confirmed by the recession of 1818. This recession he attributed to a reduction of note circulation, arguing that the full effects had not yet been felt:

I have no doubt but that the present Reduction which has taken place in the Amount of Bank of England notes will occasion in a short Time much more important Consequences on the Trade of Districts [Birmingham] than has been yet experienced. A further Reduction would of course carry those Effects further; it would produce a Reduction of Country Bank Paper and would occasion a Reduction also of the Deposits with the Country Bankers, which are generally to an Extent much beyond their notes in Circulation. It would cause the Country Bankers to withdraw the Accommodation they at present afford to the Manufacturers, and would occasion very considerable Distress.[47]

Further reduction in Bank of England circulation would mean a return to the conditions of 1816.

In May, 1819, the reports of the two committees of Parliament on resumption of specie payments were presented. In July of the same year Peel's Act was passed. This act, with some modification in 1821, provided for the resumption of specie payments. Restrictions on the export of coin and bullion were repealed and the Bank was required to pay its notes in gold bars, at rates which were, by May 1, 1821, to attain the old par of £3 17s. 10½d. per ounce of gold.[48]

These events were the basis for Attwood's charge in October, 1819, that Parliament had forced the nation into depression:

> No sooner did the Country thus begin to breathe from the exhaustion and intolerable sufferings of 1816; no sooner did the Capitalists of the Country venture to purchase property, and to employ their capital in productive purposes, than Parliament came forward, and arresting the beneficent measures of the Government, arbitrarily *reduced* the average circulation of the *legal tenders*.[49]

Attwood argued that the resumption committee reports, as well as Peel's Act, had had an adverse effect upon confidence. He further argued that the contraction of the currency and hence depression and unemployment were the inevitable result of the act, since under the prewar relationship between gold and the pound sterling it was impossible to maintain a price level adequate for full employment.[50] After 1819 Attwood's attacks on Peel's Act were unceasing.

Writing in February, 1825, Attwood admitted that, despite resumption, the country was prosperous. He argued, however, that his earlier predictions of disaster had been mistaken only because the government had ignored the implications of Peel's Act. The government and the Bank had, starting in 1822 (the year from which Attwood dated the revival), pursued a policy that increased the quantity of money and so raised prices and created prosperity. Aside from the emancipation of the South American states, which had led to greater exports from England and an inflow of gold that had, in the past, gone to Spain, all of the influences upon money supply stemmed from actions of the Bank or the government. The legalization of one pound notes for eleven years had been favorable to revival since these small notes were an important part of the currency. The government, moreover, had borrowed from the Bank to pay pensioners; Attwood noted that such borrowing had favorable effects that borrowing from the public would not have. Further stimulants were found in government-induced lending by the Bank, both to landowners and to the East India Company. Apparently of its own accord the Bank lent to fundholders on the security of consols, adopted a policy of discounting three months' bills, and reduced the discount rate from 5 per cent to 4 per cent. All of these measures acted to stimulate confidence and spending.[51]

By December, 1825, however, the situation had changed and "adversity" had replaced "prosperity." The expansion engendered by the monetary measures of the Bank and government had led to a reduction of exports and an increase in imports, the resulting deficit being financed by exports of gold. In August and September the Bank reacted to this loss of gold by selling exchequer bills and reducing the note circulation.[52] Money became scarce and debtors found it difficult to meet their obligations. The resulting panic only ended when the Bank reversed its policy and issued notes, but even this did not end the contraction.

The renewed purchases of Exchequer Bills by the Bank, and the [Bank's] loan of three millions to the Merchants and Manufacturers will certainly relieve the distress among those classes, for a short period. It will enable them to meet their engagements, and when this is done, they will take care not to contract any more. But it will not relieve the Mechanics. These unfortunate men will be thrown out of employment, and out of bread throughout the whole country.[53]

Attwood criticized the government for its temporizing policy. A decisive policy designed to maintain the gold standard would have forced prices down through monetary contraction and maintained them at a level preventing the export of gold. The preferred policy would, however, have involved note issues adequate for the maintenance of full employment and either devaluation or the abandonment of the gold standard. Instead the government had combined both policies so that prosperity has been followed by disaster.[54]

For Attwood the years from 1825 to 1832 were years of contraction and depression.[55] Writing in 1828, Attwood placed great emphasis on the lag between the relaxation of credit and prosperity. The circulation of the Bank was greater in 1828 than in 1825 and yet prosperity was not equal to that of 1825. Attwood argued that it had taken four years to achieve the prosperity of 1825, while only two years had elapsed since note issues were increased after the panic of 1825. Confidence had not revived. The low rate of interest only reflected this situation:

> The productive classes of the community are not willing to *borrow money*, the *use* of which is attended with little profit, and probably with loss. They rather prefer, as far as they can, to contract their own establishments, and to draw their capital from the employments of industry, in order to lend it to others upon good securities. They choose, if possible, to throw upon others a responsibility which they dare not undertake themselves.[56]

Thus, though a sudden contraction of currency reduces prices and activity, increased currency and a low rate of interest do not immediately stimulate activity.

To an increasing extent as time went on Attwood changed the emphasis of his argument. Whereas the earliest essays had described the effects of rising prices or falling prices, in the later essays Attwood placed more stress on a static comparison of high prices and low prices. The changes in burdens upon productive activity stemming from taxes and private obligations received his attention to an increasing extent. Discussions of the process of expansion and contraction became less extensive. In testimony given in 1832, Attwood could hardly be forced into the admission that rising prices would yield windfall profits to holders of inventories.[57] Attwood now argued that changes in the price level changed the distribution of real purchasing power. Low levels of prices gave the power to those who were inactive, who hoarded or lent, and at the same time gave insufficient incentive to the active portions of the population. Speaking in Birmingham in 1829, Attwood said: "It is the *bees*, the industrious classes, who suffer, whilst the *drones* have prosperity enough."[58]

3. THE REMEDY

While most writers in contemporary England recognized the existence of price and even employment fluctuations, Attwood was one of the most vociferous of those who demanded a government policy that would cure the evils of fluctuating prices and employment. "Employment," Attwood maintained, "is a right which a good citizen may claim of his country without any kind of degradation or obligation."[59]

Full Employment: The Goal. Attwood made a distinction between indigent persons who could not work and those who could. There would always be those who were unable to work as a result of sickness, childhood, old age, and misfortunes. These people were the only proper object of public and private charity, but if relief were so confined, the sums involved would be small and would shrink from year to year as the character of the population improved.[60] But all those who could work had the right to employment; charity, whether public or private, was neither a right, nor was it fair. Attwood distinguished two types of unemployment: frictional unemployment and general unemployment. General unemployment was the result of the mismanagement of the monetary system and could be eliminated by keeping the monetary circulation "on so ample a footing as shall create a greater demand for labour, than labour can possibly supply."[61] This problem was Attwood's chief concern.

He recognized, however, that in a changing world even the maintenance of adequate general demand for labor would not avoid all unemployment.

The improvements of society and the changes and fluctuations of fashion and of trade will, it is true, be continually precipitating thousands of unsuspecting individuals into comparative poverty and wretchedness.[62]

But if the monetary system were managed so as to maintain adequate general demand for labor, those who were unemployed as the result of such changes would always be reemployed in other trades. While he gave the impression that frictional unemployment was a rather negligible problem, Attwood did recommend that steps be taken to protect individuals who, through no fault of their own, were temporarily unemployed. "Public establishments" should be set up in which the unemployed could find work at two-thirds of the customary wage;

goods produced in these establishments would be sold to the public. The original capital would be provided by the government, but inspectors and overseers were to be given "a proper participation," thus insuring that production would take place.[63] In effect Attwood was proposing a major alteration in the English Poor Laws, which, as they operated around 1818, had three features to which he objected: first, the failure to distinguish between unemployables and the able-bodied unemployed; second, the existence of "outdoor" relief; and third, the failure to utilize "workhouses" for productive, as opposed to disciplinary activity.[64]

If such "public establishments" were unacceptable, Attwood suggested that applicants might be put to work on the construction of roads and churches. Whatever the expense, the object was not pecuniary, but rather a matter of arresting "misery and degradation."[65] The alterations in the Poor Laws were, however, to apply only to children as yet unborn, for the present generation had been brought up in the expectation that the existing system would be continued and any change would, therefore, involve a hardship.[66]

Of far greater importance, however, was the problem of general unemployment. Either because he considered that the "public establishments" would solve the problem of frictional unemployment or because he doubted its importance in periods of prosperity, Attwood concentrated his attention on the elimination of general unemployment.

The Problem of Increased Spending. Attwood argued that activity would rise if spending increased. Thus government frugality was condemned because it led to reduced government expenditure, while capitalists were slow to react in increasing their expenditures when taxes were reduced. Private frugality was condemned along with government frugality.

All relief is in vain that has not the effect of keeping up family expenditure, or of increasing national expenditure to an equal amount.[67]

When it came to positive remedies for unemployment, Attwood was reluctant to advocate direct government expenditure either upon goods or labor. An exception was made for temporary unemployment, and Attwood argued that the soldiers and sailors discharged at the end of the war should have been employed on public works until such time as "the country offered a demand for their labour."[68] Here it was unclear whether Attwood was seeking full employment, or whether he was advocating a large standing army and public works for their own sake, as a symbol of English glory.[69] Otherwise Attwood confined his remedy to more narrowly monetary measures.

Throughout his writings Attwood maintained that the correction of depression required "*a forced creation of additional currency*."[70] The more specific proposals varied with respect to two elements: first, what type of currency was to be created; second, how the additional currency was to be injected into public circulation.

In his earliest pamphlet, *The Remedy*, Attwood proposed that the currency be increased through issues of Bank of England notes. Starting with *Prosperity Restored* the emphasis shifted to some form of paper currency printed by the government, and variously labeled "national paper," "circulating exchequer bills," "national instruments," "certificates," or "debentures." The essential difficulty with Bank of England notes was Attwood's doubt over the willingness of the Bank to pursue proper policies. Even in *The Remedy* Attwood faced the possibility that the Bank might refuse to lend to the government, and he mentioned that government paper would then be the way out. In writing his lengthy letters to Vansittart and Liverpool, Attwood tended to cloak his plan in moderate terminology. Vansittart was exhorted to issue "circulating exchequer bills" bearing no interest[71] and Liverpool, two years later, got an even milder version based on Bank notes.[72] The clearest expression of this difficult terminological problem appeared in the *Observations*, where Attwood advocated the gradual issue of national paper to accustom the public to this new medium, while retaining Bank notes until this task of education was completed.[73] Aside from the question of confidence Attwood clearly preferred the more manageable national paper, under any name, to Bank notes or even coin.

If we rely upon these two latter, in the hour of peril, they will desert us. At the very period when we most need their assistance they will be withdrawn.[74]

Given the fact that some kind of currency was to be issued, the chief problem was the means by which the injection was to take place. Attwood distinguished loans by the Bank of England, loans by the government to merchants and manufacturers, loans by the government to landlords and capitalists, and purchases of national debt. Loans by the Bank, while desirable, particularly if made at low interest rates and for long periods,[75] were not so susceptible to management; moreover, Attwood distrusted the Bank.

The best and quickest remedy was found in direct government loans. To obtain the funds the government could either create paper or it could borrow. Any borrowing should be from the Bank, for borrowing from the public would only take away with one hand what was given out with the other; this was somewhat inconsistent with Attwood's view that monied capital was idle in depression.[76] In lending, the government would choose borrowers according to the nature of the economic situation. In *The Remedy*, published in 1816, when Attwood saw no sign of prosperity or returning prosperity in any sector of the economy, he recommended loans to landlords, merchants, and manufacturers.[77] On the other hand in *Prosperity Restored*, published in 1817, Attwood observed a rise in agricultural prices and preferred to dispense with special agricultural loans. The "poor mechanic" was worse off than ever as the result of rising food prices, Attwood argued; nothing would aid him

but an immediate issue of a sum of money to his employers; which shall occasion an immediate and correspondent reaction in manufactures and commerce, without waiting for the tedious operations of nature, which will indeed bring his relief in the end, but ere it arrives he will find his grave.[78]

But Attwood added that if depression was so severe as to make manufacturers and merchants unwilling to borrow, then loans should also be offered to landlords and capitalists generally.[79]

In his later works Attwood placed less emphasis on direct loans made on landed estates and on personal security, and more emphasis on the stimulation of spending by means of national debt purchases. In *The Remedy* Attwood had stated that the purchase of exchequer bills would serve, though not so effectively, the same purpose as direct loans.[80] In *Prosperity Restored* Attwood indicated that purchase of national debt was a desirable measure, but he feared that the effects would be relatively slow as compared to government loans.[81] Purchase of national debt, particularly purchase of exchequer bills, tended to create purchasing power among idle London capitalists who would use their funds for the purchase of other securities. Only very gradually would the abundance of money in the London money market spill over into the hands of the active classes who would purchase goods and hire labor.[82] On the other hand, when Attwood's attention shifted from an analysis of the process by which full employment would be reached, to the means by which full employment could be maintained, he also tended to place increased emphasis on the relatively flexible policy of buying and selling national debt.[83]

Attwood was, as a rule, quite certain that increased currency in the hands of the public would increase spending. Writing in 1816, he expressed the belief that the repayment of private debts with funds lent by the government would have immediate effects:

By the payment of these debts, the shopkeeper would become affluent, and would discharge his own debts to the manufacturer; who again, in his turn, would find his affluence and his confidence revived, and would be induced and enabled to take on his workmen, in order to execute those orders which the renewed prosperity of his connexions would occasion.[84]

Landlords who borrowed from the government would both repay debts and increase, or cease to diminish, their expenditures. A revival of confidence would follow automatically.

In 1819, however, the adverse effect on confidence of the proposed resumption of specie payments worried Attwood. He then demanded not only an increase in the currency but also measures that would ensure the continuance of an easy money policy. Thus in his second letter to Lord Liverpool, abandonment of gold convertibility for five years became a prerequisite to the confidence that would make the spending of newly created money a fact, instead of a mere possibility. At the same time Attwood warned that delay might so depress confidence as to make even this measure ineffective.[85] The creation of additional currency, if properly supported by the authorities, was still, however, the correct policy in any attempt to increase spending.

Effects on Employment and Prices. Given an initial increase in currency and a resulting rise in spending, Attwood maintained that a kind of multiplier process would result in secondary increases in spending, and that the ensuing expansion of business activity would lead, not only to higher prices and wages, but also to an increase in employment and output.

Attwood's description of the secondary effects was vivid:

An additional sum of money being once created, is immediately brought into action upon the property and industry of the country. The parties receiving it, in the first instance, immediately make purchases, or pay debts, or lend upon mortgage, to an equivalent amount. The second parties receiving it do the same, and so on until the whole of it reaches the labourers, and from them it necessarily reaches other parties, until having passed through a hundred channels and created a hundred markets it continues just as active in its operations as it was in the first moment of its creation.[86]

In the present state of the country it is probable that the million and a half of money so created, will pass and repass through the hands of labourers every three months; and in the mean while it will be furnishing intermediate markets between one description of capitalists and another, so that in reality it may be presumed, that the issue of this money will furnish six millions of additional wages to the labourers and mechanics in *one year* from its first issue, and probably at least thirty millions more additional markets to the capitalists and proprietors of stocks.[87]

In itself this passage can be reconciled with either a modified quantity theory, in which an increase in the money supply affects both prices and employment, or with a Keynesian multiplier analysis. Since, however, Attwood related the maintenance of a stable level of employment and prices to the money supply, rather than to spending *per se*, the more marked affinity of his analysis with a modified quantity theory seems clear.[88]

That the process of expansion involved an increase in both employment and real output was never in doubt, although there was some ambiguity about the exact sequence of events, and particularly about the timing of wage and price increases. In debating with William Cobbett in 1832, Attwood asserted:

The truth was that labour always rose in price quite as fast as the products of labour, for when new money created a new demand for the purchase and consumption of commodities, those commodities could not rise in price, so long as new labour could be brought into the market to increase the supply of them. The labour was therefore all called into employment before the commodities could rise, and in the very act of calling labour into employment, the price of labour must necessarily rise.[89]

Elsewhere, in giving testimony before a Parliamentary committee, he implied, however, that wages lagged behind prices:

The prices of property being raised by an increase of the circulation, a reward is obtained in the production of every article of industry, and that reward calls all labour into full employment. The productive powers of the nation being thus put upon the full stretch, a great mass of annual wealth is thus produced, and in the very act of production of that additional mass of commodities and wealth the consumption of such additional mass is itself effected whether in the shape of wages, profits or taxes.[90]

Attwood in fact seems to have cared very little about the exact sequence in which wages and prices rose: in debating with Cobbett he was, as a politician, presumably chiefly concerned with the presentation of his program in such a way as to emphasize that he was a friend of labor. In addition, two other factors blurred the distinction between wages and prices. In

Birmingham, with which Attwood was most familiar, the distinction between entrepreneur and laborer was often quite tenuous in this period.[91] Moreover, Attwood frequently argued in terms of a distinction between the active members of society, including both laborers and entrepreneurs, and rentiers; when real output rose and prices advanced, only rentiers and creditors suffered, while all other classes gained both because output was larger and because rentier claims were smaller. The crucial point to Attwood was not the sequence of wage and price changes, but rather the fact that both employment and output would rise as a result of the initial increase in the money supply and the subsequent repercussions.

The Maintenance of Full Employment. By emphasizing the process by which full employment might be reached, Attwood laid himself open to the charge that he was advocating a continuous rise in prices. And when he denied this, he was attacked for being illogical: his opponents were willing to admit that rising prices might stimulate activity, but denied that high prices provided any stimulus to production and employment that was not equally provided by low prices.

Attwood went so far in adjusting his arguments to meet this attack that his earlier analysis of the cumulative process almost disappeared. Thus the committee which heard evidence in 1832 on the Bank of England charter had great difficulty in making Attwood admit that rising prices could be an important reason for profit.

Q. Is not this the explanation of the effect of the depreciation of the value of money, that when a manufacturer is trading, not for money but for time, when the period of payment comes round, he pays for the article in a currency of less value than he stipulated for at the time when he made the bargain, and thus secures himself a profit?

Attwood first answered: "That is an effect, but is of little consequence to the manufacturer." Then he admitted that the profits so gained might be large if the stock of goods involved was large, and concluded by reiterating that high prices, and not necessarily rising prices, were sufficient for the maintenance of full employment:

> I consider that there would be a great profit to the holder of stocks in the action of depreciation, but when the action of the depreciation was completed, there would still remain the reasonable profits of industry, and the same inducements would continue to employ labour, as existed during the late depreciation.[92]

The real advantage of high prices arose from the fact that fixed charges became less burdensome: this applied both to taxes used to pay fundholders and to payments that were the result of borrowing from private creditors. With high prices the real resources of the creditor class were small, and those of the productive classes large. Profits were higher and provided both the means and the inducement for great activity and full employment.[93] The crucial role of fixed money payments found expression when Attwood wrote:

> It is only when high rents, high taxes, and high debts have been contracted with reference to *high prices*, that any mischief is found in *low prices*.[94]

Attwood felt that the payments on national debt contracted during the high prices of the Napoleonic Wars were, through the taxes they involved, a heavy burden on the economy.

Stable Full Employment. High prices being necessary to full employment, the chief problem then lay in discovering a criterion which the monetary authorities could use as a guide in maintaining full employment. Employment statistics were unavailable, and Attwood did not suggest the collection of such data. Instead he proposed various price criteria: the price of wheat, the price of agricultural labor, or the market rate of interest. Each supposedly provided a guide that would permit full employment—"a greater demand for labour than labour can possibly supply"—to be maintained.

The loans which were to achieve full employment in *Prosperity Restored* were to be repaid after three years. At that time, the use of the money was to depend on the price of wheat: if the average price of wheat was above 15 shillings a bushel, the money would be withdrawn from circulation; if below 15 shillings, it would be used to retire national debt.[95]

Later in the same book Attwood recommended an even more desirable standard, agricultural wages of 18 shillings per week:

> The price of agricultural labour is the best standard *or par* whereby to regulate the issue of bank notes or national paper, because it is more deeply connected with national prosperity, and is less exposed to foreign influence than any other that can be devised.[96]

Preferably the operation of the system was to be in the hands of commissioners who would either control the Bank of England or would operate with national paper of some sort.

> Returns would then be made weekly or monthly to the commissioners, from the proper officers in every county, and the commissioners would be obligated to increase or diminish their purchases of debt, or to make sales of the debt already purchased, according as those returns might require. If the par of agricultural labour was made 18s. per week, and I think it ought not to be made less, considering the circumstances of the country; then, when the returns showed that labour had a tendency to fall to 17s. 6d. or 17s. it would be evident that the demand for labour was not equal to the supply, and that it ought to be made so by the purchases of the commissioners, increasing the circulation until it was. And when the returns showed a tendency in labour to rise to 18s. 6d. or 19s. per week, then it would be evident that the demand for labour was greater than the supply; and if thought desirable to alter such a state as this, it would readily be effected by commissioners reducing the circulation by reselling proper portions of the debt which they had purchased.[97]

Under this rule, there would be no possibility that the commissioners would abuse their authority.

But the rule was quickly followed by a new consideration and a new criterion that made the discretionary power of the commissioners much greater. As long as there existed any currency other than that issued by the commissioners, there was a danger that fluctuations in such other currency, bank notes or coin circulation for instance, might influence employment and prices.

If other currency contracted, the effects would be slow, only gradually leading to a lower price of labor. In ignorance of the underlying situation the commissioners might fail to act; and, when they finally did act, a further delay was inevitable:

> Neither when we [the commissioners] have issued sufficient quantities of those instruments, will their effects in restoring the employment and price of labour be immediate, but they will necessarily be gradual, and require some months for their operation, and during this period, a great part of the labourers may be deprived of employment, and the productive powers of the country be seriously crippled.[98]

As a remedy for such difficulties Attwood suggested another "par" or "political barometer" that would prevent the "possibility of labour being thrown out of employment for any period, however short."[99] Attwood asserted that the London money market was more sensitive than the price of agricultural labor to expansions or contractions in the currency. Hence he proposed that there be a "par of money."

> As long as money could be readily obtained in the metropolis, on approved mortgages at 5 per cent. it would be sufficient evidence that no contractive action has taken place upon the currency there.[100]

This would, he argued, provide a temporary guide to operations involving purchase and sale of national debt. Attwood did not explain exactly how this par was to be used in conjunction with the permanent guide provided by the price of agricultural labor.[101]

Despite the concern over prices implied by the discussion of these criteria, there was some foundation for the charge that Attwood favored continually rising prices.[102] At times he explicitly defended a gradually rising price level. Since he also argued that annuitants could adjust to such a known rate of change in prices so as to avoid losses, the desirability of the program was not entirely clear.[103]

Attwood's confidence in any criteria for full employment seems to have suffered somewhat by 1832. When asked, "What is your test of full employment?" he answered only, "It is difficult to obtain an absolute test."[104] But at the same time he reiterated his belief that monetary expansion was desirable under some criteria of full employment.[105]

4. THE GOLD STANDARD

Attwood usually admitted that the gold standard was incompatible with his plan for full employment. From time to time, however, he did claim that full employment could be attained and maintained even if the "ancient standard" of £3 17s. 10½d. per ounce of gold were accepted. At one point he argued that any rise in the price of bullion above par, resulting from bank note issues, would create a premium on exports of British goods so that bullion would return to par.[106] A similarly optimistic conclusion was tentatively advanced in 1832. If prices rose in England, some gold might flow out, but this might not force a contraction of economic activity:

> I am not certain that it produces that reaction, because an increase of paper credit, and a greater confidence consequent upon its operation, would occasion a rise in prices throughout Europe; for, the nations being relieved from the extreme pressure that they now feel, would certainly raise the prices of their manufactures; and the quantity of bullion thrown out of England, perhaps one half of what now exists in England, would produce so much prosperity in foreign countries, that it would also assist in elevating their prices, and in enabling them to consume at high prices our manufactured goods in the same way as they do now at low prices.[107]

More usually, however, Attwood accepted the traditional opinion that higher prices would lead to a diminution of exports, an increase of imports, and a loss of gold. The "ancient standard" was condemned precisely because it forced the Bank to restrict its note issues and force down prices, so as not to lose gold. The gold standard under a fixed mint price of gold was condemned because it made the domestic economy subservient to conditions abroad. Attwood argued that under a gold standard unplanned fluctuations in currency occur: first, because of the direct loss of gold coin, and second, because of the effects of gold flows upon the behavior of the Bank of England.

Solutions to the problem of minimizing external influence on internal economic activity ranged from the relatively conservative policy of setting the price of gold at an equilibrium level after a period of restriction to an extreme proposal under which the pound would not be convertible into gold. The conservative scheme found expression in a letter writen to Lord Liverpool:

> It is only after we have seen several years of prosperity, and of peace, and open communication among Nations, that we can be competent to judge how far the tendency of Gold to fly off to other countries, may be counteracted by local circumstances at home; and whether £5 or £6 or £8 sterling to the Ounce of Gold, will enable a metallic coinage to create and support that abundance of the Circulating System, under which all the taxes, and debts and monied obligations of society have been formed.[108]

This policy still left England at the mercy of gold movements. Any temporary exportation of gold would lead to reduced note issue and depression, while any temporary importation would lead to an enlarged note issue and higher prices.

> A sudden and great elevation of prices is thus occasioned, which lasts just long enough to deceive the public mind, and to induce people to contract engagements on the strength of it. It then disappears from under their feet, and such engagements eventuate in their ruin.[109]

Such fluctuations were inevitable under any gold standard and were an evil since they made business a gamble. The only argument for a fixed gold price was the shock to habits and confidence that any other system might create.

The best plan would involve abandonment of the gold standard altogether.

> Contrast all the dangers, the changes, the fluctuations, the unjust ruin, the unjust aggrandizement, attendant upon a Metallic Standard, with the security, the certainty, the equality of prices and of values; the exemption from unjust losses, and from unjust gains; and the general stability of all profits and of all prosperity, which a *non-convertible* Paper

Currency presents.—Self-existent, self-dependent, liable to no foreign actions, entirely under our own control; contracting, expanding, or remaining fixed, according as the wants and exigencies of the community may require, a *non-convertible* Paper Currency presents every element of national security and happiness, without the possibility of injuring any one class of the community.[110]

The drawbacks seemed unimportant and were rarely discussed. Attwood noticed that foreign exchange transactions and foreign trade might be hampered if the sterling price of gold fluctuated freely, or even if the price were varied from time to time. But he argued that this was unimportant.

I cannot think it of much consequence to enter into this disquisition, because it is evidently of too trifling a character to be suffered to interfere with questions affecting the full employment of labour, and the preservation of vital interests. Foreigners never trouble their heads about us in alterations of regulations they make in their coins.—If no foreign exchanges could exist at all, and, indeed if all foreign trade were annihilated by the alteration of the coins, it would be no argument against such alteration, provided it were shown that by that alone could the prosperity of the country be restored.[111]

5. CONCLUSION

Despite the early description of fluctuations that involved "actions on property" or "natural remedies," it is fair to describe Attwood's theory of economic fluctuations as a monetary theory. Attwood thus has much in common with writers such as R. G. Hawtrey and differs from those who have been unimpressed with the role of money. The rate of interest, however, receives somewhat less attention, a view which is generally typical of a period when distinctions between the effects of interest rates and the effects of the availability of credit were not as sharply drawn as in some modern literature.[112] As in Hawtrey, the role of inventory investment in accentuating the violence of both expansion and contraction is emphasized. Investment in fixed capital is at best only mentioned, a neglect which was common until the railroad boom of the 1840s influenced economic thought. The interactions between income and expenditure, although not described in any detail, are reminiscent of most modern interpretations.

As far as policy goals are concerned, Attwood probably has more in common with the followers of J. M. Keynes than with any other modern writers. Most striking is the emphasis upon full employment as the overriding goal. Full employment, it may be noted, is defined as a situation in which there is "a greater demand for labour, than labour can possibly supply,"[113] which is strikingly similar to W. H. Beveridge's "more vacant jobs than unemployed men."[114]

Yet in several respects Attwood's approach to policy differs sharply from the Keynesian view. First, Attwood was much more optimistic about the efficacy of monetary policy than are many followers of Keynes. This may be because the economy of his day was more sensitive to monetary measures,[115] or it may be that the measures had not been tried. In fact Attwood himself, as we have seen, does express, particularly in his later writings, some doubts about the effectiveness of such policy. If monetary policy had been tried and found wanting, would he have turned to fiscal policy? He was aware, as were his contemporaries, that government expenditures could have a major influence on the level of employment and prices, even, he seems to say, when offset by taxes. One suspects that the step from monetary to fiscal policy would have been a small one, not taken merely because it seemed unnecessary.

The second difference arises out of the absence of employment statistics. Thus there was no immediate possibility of setting up a level of, say, 2 per cent unemployment as "full employment." It is odd, however, that he did not suggest the collection of such statistics. Instead he suggested as criteria the price of wheat, agricultural wages, and the market interest rate. Since his inflationary bias is obvious, it is probable that this was not a price or wage stabilization program and that, if the maintenance of an 18 shilling agricultural wage still left noticeable unemployment, the figure would have been adjusted upward.

The general attitude of Attwood toward the conflict between

domestic goals and fixed exchange rates is very similar to some modern opinion. Gold convertibility was to be sacrificed without a qualm, even if this implied the cessation of all international trade. His suggestions for discovery of an equilibrium price of gold during a period of inconvertibility after the war, a price that would be compatible with full employment, recall the discussions of the 1920s and 1940s. The favored suggestion, that exchange rates be left free to fluctuate, is still a subject of controversy today.

All of this adds up to the conclusion that Attwood would have been much more at home in today's economics than he was in the political economy of his time. But it also indicates the extent to which the differences between the economics of the classical period and the economics of today turn, not upon matters of fact or matters of analysis, but upon differences in goals.

It may be that Attwood's failure to put across his ideas is to be attributed to the poor presentation of his case. He may have made a mistake, tactically, in appealing to the general public, through political unions, pamphlets, and speeches. Possibly the conversion of one or two Benthamites would have done more to further his cause. But he was also handicapped by the fact that those classes which probably are most interested in full employment wielded far less influence in the politics of his age than they do in more recent times. Again, one suspects that lack of information concerning the extent and magnitude of the evil he was attacking weakened his case.[116] The growth of knowledge concerning fluctuations undoubtedly has played a part in making the general public more receptive to full employment programs.

Thomas Robert Malthus

THOMAS ROBERT MALTHUS was not a politician of the Attwood type.[1] A respected clergyman and a product of an eighteenth-century environment, he had early gained fame through his *Essay on Population*. Successive additions, incorporating extensive empirical material, had added to his influence in intellectual circles. The number of refutations that were written during his lifetime testify to his success.

Yet his attempt to convince the political economists of his day that general gluts were an important possibility was unsuccessful. Nor was he any more successful in his suggestion that government expenditures were the remedy for depression. These were issues upon which James Mill and Ricardo triumphed for many years.

No imputation of blind prejudice to his opponents can serve to explain this failure. Laissez-faire principles were merely principles to his opponents, to be violated if circumstances and analysis suggested that violation would benefit the nation. Nor was the defense of the landlords very important as far as either the glut theory or the recommendations for government expenditure were concerned, since his views might reasonably have been accepted by any class.

One must at least consider the possibility that there was some fundamental difficulty in the glut theory, some flaw that made it illogical and unreasonable to Malthus' contemporaries. Had he presented a clear and convincing case, his doctrine would have convinced even Ricardo, or, perhaps one should say, especially Ricardo. One difficulty is obvious from even a casual perusal of the *Principles of Political Economy*.[2] The author who had written so lucidly on population was now far from lucid. Examples used for illustrative purposes often seem to be beside the point, and, when relevant, are sometimes cut off before interesting and obvious problems have been considered. Significantly, Malthus never got around to revising the last part of the *Principles*, so that the first edition, dated 1820, and second, dated 1836, are practically identical so far as this subject is concerned. Today's reader has of course the great advantage of being able to view Malthus and his opponents in the light of Keynes' *General Theory*.

In this chapter we will first examine the concept of wealth as defined by Malthus. There is no major problem in this subject, though it is essential to an understanding of the later arguments. In section two we come upon the first difficulty. It is always hard to tell whether the arguments on the dangers resulting from saving apply to full employment or to unemployment situations. Actually Malthus seems to apply the doctrine to both types of situation, and it is convenient to treat the full employment argument in section two and postpone the more interesting unemployment argument to the succeeding sections.

The major issues between Ricardo and Malthus appear in sections three and four. There is some overlapping here for it is hard to separate, as Malthus tried to do, the discussion of effectual demand from the discussion of oversaving. The fifth section tries to show how Malthus used, or did not use, the theory of the *Principles* to interpret the period of war prosperity and the postwar stagnation. The sixth section deals with both the remedies that Malthus rejected and those that he accepted.

1. WEALTH

Malthus centered his discussion of economic fluctuations and growth around the concept of wealth. Since "wealth" is used in a sense which is uncommon today, an exposition of what Malthus meant is of importance.

Adam Smith had introduced his *Wealth of Nations* with a discussion indicating that by "wealth" he meant a flow of annual produce, the concept thus being similar to the modern term "income."[3] Malthus for the most part followed this precedent,[4] though he did not explicitly recognize a distinction between income and wealth, and sometimes confused the two concepts.

An important issue for Malthus was the question of the types of product that should be included in wealth. Wealth he defined as "material objects, useful or agreeable to man, which are voluntarily appropriated by individuals or nations."[5] Of particular importance is the limitation to material objects. Malthus sought a definition that would accord with common usage and, at the same time, would be useful. Thus he rejected the narrow definition of the Physiocrats as conflicting both with common usage and utility. On the other hand Lauderdale's broad definition of wealth as covering "all that man desires as useful and delightful to him" was also ruled out. This concept would, Malthus thought, make measurement and comparison impossible. Such intangibles as political and civil liberty would have to be included, and, as a result:

It would be impossible to form any judgment of the state of a country from the use of the terms rich or richer. A nation might be said to be increasing in wealth, when to all common eyes, and in all common language, it might be growing poorer. This would be the case according to the definition, if a diminution of the manufacturing and mercantile products had been balanced in the opinion of some persons by the gratifications derived from the intellectual attainments, and the various personal qualities and services of the inhabitants. But how is this balance to be ascertained? how is it possible to estimate the degree of wealth derived from these sources?[6]

Malthus rejected the proposal that immaterial objects be included only when exchange was involved, for he was unwilling to accept the paradox of excluding free services, such as instruction to a friend, while including the same services if hired.

A similar desire for consistency led to the rejection of the requirement that the material objects to be included in wealth must be exchanged. To exclude farm produce that was consumed on the farm would involve both inconsistency and a violation of ordinary usage. Farm produce so consumed could be valued, Malthus believed:

Of the quantity and quality of the material commodities here noticed it would not be difficult to make an inventory. Many household books indeed furnish one; and knowing pretty nearly the quantity and quality of such articles, a fair approximation to their value might be attained by estimating them according to the market prices of the district at the time.[7]

Thus Malthus adopted the criteria of material objects currently produced, and did not require that the objects be exchanged. While admitting that wealth, so defined, was not the only end of society, he felt that only this definition would avoid confusion and at the same time approximate to common usage.

There remained the problem of aggregating the diverse objects in such a way as to permit intertemporal and international comparisons. Malthus saw that the first step involved the use of values:

When we come to compare objects of different kinds, there is no other way of estimating the degree of wealth which the possession and enjoyment of them confer on the owner, than by the estimation in which they are respectively held, evinced by their respective exchangeable values.[8]

Estimates in money were, however, of limited usefulness, since the value of money changed over time. In practice Malthus almost ignored the question of intertemporal comparisons, despite the fact that most of his argument was concerned with such comparisons. Instead he discussed international comparisons and reached the conclusion that the money value of wealth divided by the money wage of standard labor would give a fairly good measure of wealth.[9]

The quantity of standard labour [wrote Malthus] which the whole yearly produce would exchange for, according to the actual money prices of labour and commodities at the time might be considered as an approximating estimate of the gross annual revenue of the country. . . .

Different countries tried in this way by the value of their produce, would in general answer very nearly to the estimates which would be formed of their relative wealth, by the most careful and intelligent observations.[10]

Malthus made no attempt to prepare such estimates.

This method of measuring wealth by the amount of labor commanded was admittedly rough. Thus Malthus noted that it was possible for the amount of labor commanded to increase, while the quantity of commodities (assumed here, apparently, to be homogeneous) actually diminished; in such cases wealth, apparently meaning a physical quantity of commodities, does not increase in the same proportion as the amount of labor commanded. On the other hand,

neither does it [wealth] increase in proportion to the mere quantity of what comes under the denomination of wealth, because the various articles of which this quantity is composed may not be so proportioned to the wants and powers of the society as to give them their proper value.[11]

Such a situation involves a diminution in the amount of labor commanded:

The wealth of the society would be most essentially impaired; that is, its wants would not be in any degree so well supplied as before.[12]

For Malthus' discussion of fluctuations and growth, it is important to notice that wealth, which he sometimes called gross annual produce, and which will here be called simply product, or output, was a concept similar to the income concepts expressed in constant prices that are in use today. At the same time only material objects are included, so that services rendered directly to consumers do not directly increase gross annual produce. The services of labor are in fact divided into two categories, productive labor which does produce wealth, and unproductive labor which renders only personal services and so does not produce wealth. This distinction played an important role in Malthus' theory.

2. FULL EMPLOYMENT AND THE ACCUMULATION OF CAPITAL

It has been said that Malthus, in his treatment of the "progress of wealth," was largely concerned with conditions of less than full employment.[13] However, in many passages Malthus completely ignored the condition of the labor market, yet was apparently willing to stand by his conclusions concerning the dangers of excessive saving and the desirability of high consumption. It is probable that failure to make explicit assumptions with respect to employment led to misunderstanding, and that, to interpret Malthus intelligibly, a distinction between full employment and unemployment conditions must be made. In this section Malthusian doctrine under conditions of full employment is examined in so far as it relates to the dangers of excessive saving.

Profits, particularly the rate of profit, play a crucial role in the theory. Malthus distinguished between the "limiting principle" of profits and the "regulating principle" of profits. The former was identical with Ricardo's theory: resting on the law of diminishing returns in agriculture, it detected a tendency for the rate of profit to fall eventually to a level that would prevent the further accumulation of capital and the further growth of population. But Malthus placed more emphasis upon the regulating principle, which he thought had been neglected by Ricardo. In essence Malthus argued that even in the absence of the limiting principle, there might be checks to profits and so to accumulation and the growth of wealth.

The argument was first stated by Malthus in his discussion of profits.

As capital and produce increased faster than labour, the profits of capital would fall, and if a progressive increase of capital and produce were to take place, while the population, by some hidden cause, were prevented from keeping pace with it, notwithstanding the fertility of the soil and the plenty of food, then profits would be gradually reduced, until, by successive reductions, the power and will to accumulate had ceased to operate; and this state of things might take place rapidly, if a great proportion of those who were engaged in personal services were rapidly converted by saving into productive labourers.[14]

This case subsumes an extreme example, which Malthus did not outline. Suppose that all labor is devoted to productive activity, and that the rate of profit is close to the minimum at which accumulation will cease. If, under such circumstances, saving takes place and the wages fund increases, then the real wage of labor will rise, while production cannot increase. It should be noted that saving here, and generally throughout Malthus' work, means capitalist abstention from consumption of produce, and that saving is automatically invested in productive labor. No question is raised about the passage from saving into investment, and investment always takes the form of the use of product from a previous period to pay productive labor, which in turn will produce a new product in the current period. With a fixed product and higher real wages, the result must be a lower profit-product ratio and hence a lower rate of profit.

Malthus argued that there was, in such a situation, no need for more capital: the "less than ordinary profits" indicated that capital was plentiful.[15] He also maintained that unemployment would develop. Apparently he visualized a contraction of the wages fund as a result of the reactions of capitalists to the lower rate of profit. Since Malthus assumed sticky wage rates,[16] this implied unemployment:

The conversion of revenue into capital pushed beyond a certain point must . . . throw the labouring classes out of employment.[17]

Having carried the argument this far, Malthus was content, for the most part, to ignore further repercussions.[18]

Ricardo accepted part of this reasoning, objected to other parts, and tried to go beyond the point at which Malthus had stopped. Ricardo denied that the "regulating principle" had been ignored in his *Principles* and admitted without qualification that, under the assumptions that Malthus made, profits would fall; his only comment on the phase of the argument that showed the fall in profits was the brief remark: "The labourers would have a monopoly, and the price of their labour would depend solely on the demand."[19] But when it came to the simultaneous glut of labor and capital, Ricardo parted company.

First of all, Ricardo refused to see much more than a temporary error in the situation outlined. If profits were too low, then a contraction of operations would take place, and, as a result, a fall in the wages fund. Assuming flexible wages, no contraction of output would result, but rather a fall in wages, which would restore profits to the necessary level.[20] An unchanged output would now go to an increased extent to capitalists, who by the very act of contracting the wages fund created a personal demand for that part of the product which labor could no longer purchase. This adjustment would restore the situation that had existed prior to the excessive saving. Malthus, however, objected to this reasoning, both because he could not accept the flexible wage premise, and because he questioned the expansion of capitalist demand for product. Moreover, any implication that the difficulty was merely temporary, he rejected.

Second, Ricardo refused to accept the assumption of a fixed population: the remedy, he stated, was an increase of population, which would of course permit growth of the wages fund without the rise in wages that would diminish profits and prevent further accumulation. It should be noted that changing the assumption of a fixed population to that of an infinitely elastic population is analytically very similar to removing the assumption of full employment and substituting an assumption of unemployment. In either case, increases in the wages fund can take place without any necessary rise in real wages or fall in the rate of profits, as long as diminishing returns are ignored. Malthus objected to Ricardo's change of assumptions on two grounds. First, the adjustment could not be so rapid as to make the difficulty temporary: population did not spring up overnight. And second, there still remained a fundamental difficulty even under conditions in which the supply of labor (whether because of unemployment or because of population growth) was completely elastic. This second difficulty turned on the role of demand under underemployment; this subject is postponed to sections three and four.

It is, however, well to note that Malthus' proposition about the importance of demand and the dangers of oversaving was valid enough for full employment conditions, given his assumptions. The proposition was in one sense quite acceptable to Ricardo: rapid accumulation with a fixed population could diminish profits. On the other hand, the difference in assumptions as to wage rates was more important. Ricardo, looking to a longer run perhaps, or else more impressed with the short-run flexibility of wages, could not visualize a consequent unemployment of labor, and more generally saw adjustments as taking place rapidly and smoothly.[21] Malthus stressed the inflexibility of wages and the fact that adjustment would take time. He was never altogether clear as to whether, given sufficient time and sufficient flexibility, a return to full employment would take place automatically.

3. UNEMPLOYMENT AND THE ACCUMULATION OF CAPITAL

Malthus believed that saving could also be dangerous under conditions of unemployment. His refusal to accept the Ricardian argument that, with an elastic population, there would be no reason for profits to fall, fits in with this view. For to assume the elasticity of population in the long run as Ricardo had done was equivalent to the assumption that additional labor could be obtained without a rise in real wages; thus, as we have seen, the long-run problem and the short-run unemployment problem tend to be rather similar. That oversaving was dangerous under conditions of unemployment came out with particular clarity when Malthus discussed postwar England: labor was out of work, yet wanted work, presumably, though he did not say so, at existing wage levels.[22]

The fundamentals of the argument under condition of unemployment were identical with those used in the argument concerning full employment. In real terms saving meant the diversion of commodities from capitalist consumption into a wages fund from which additional productive laborers would be paid; since unemployment existed, additional productive laborers could be hired. Then output would increase. But capitalists require a certain profit rate on advances, and in the absence of such a profit the additional output would not be justified from the capitalist point of view. Additions to output had to be sold for something more than the extra advances made to the labor involved in the production of such output. The added incomes paid to labor could not provide a return to capitalists that would give rise to the required profits: at best such incomes could only cover costs. Malthus said:

No one will ever employ capital merely for the sale of the demand occasioned by those who work for him. Unless they produce an excess of value above what they consume, which he either wants himself in kind, or which he can advantageously exchange for something which he desires, either for present or future use, it is quite obvious that his capital will not be employed in maintaining them.[23]

Though this applied to a single capitalist, Malthus clearly meant to apply the same argument to some aggregation of all capitalists. Thus the increase of wealth, or annual produce, required examination of the state of demand, for only demand, other than that arising from labor, could justify the maintenance of a given output or further increases in output.

An intelligible presentation of Malthus' theory must make use of the fact that he intended to carry over the apparatus involving supply and demand and costs, which he had used for analysis of individual commodity prices and output, to the analysis of (aggregate) wealth. The major difference on the cost side lies in the fact that the argument abstracts from the diminishing returns characteristic of agriculture. As in the case of full employment, the Ricardian position on effects of diminishing returns upon profits was accepted, but was not considered relevant to the problem that Malthus was treating. The relevant returns were those outside of agriculture and these Malthus seems to have thought of as constant: the smallest drop in the price of a manufactured article, when costs of production were just covered, would wipe out all production of the article.[24] It is, therefore, not unreasonable to assume constant returns to labor in discussing Malthus' theory of aggregate output.

Another problem arises from the two ways in which Malthus measures costs and demand. For short periods, the value of money being constant, Malthus was willing to measure costs and demand in money. Since the value of money was defined as the reciprocal of the money wage rate for standard labor, constant value of money meant a constant money wage rate. Over longer periods, the value of money might change and Malthus preferred to measure costs and demand in terms of laborers commanded, i.e., deflating money values by the money wage rate.[25] Much confusion arose from the decision to carry on the discussion in terms of labor commanded rather than in terms of money. Greater clarity can be achieved by assuming, as below, a constant value of money.

Once these two assumptions, constant returns to labor and constant value of money, have been adopted, a schedule can be drawn, probably without doing violence to Malthus' ideas, relating money labor costs to annual output (Q). This schedule is linear and passes through the origin; in Figure 1, where S represents aggregate costs (or spending) this schedule is represented by W. No question of a "full employment" level of output can be raised in connection with this schedule. The labor input implied in any level of output does not represent all the labor employed in the economy, since only productive labor is implicit in this schedule. Other labor may be employed unproductively, rendering personal services to landlords or capitalists; such services by definition cannot be included in annual output, i.e., in wealth. Expansion of output can come about either through employment of unemployed labor or through the diversion of unproductive labor to productive activity.

It is less easy to find in Malthus any justification for assumptions about necessary costs arising out of rent and profits. In fact, but for the special role which Malthus attributed to landlords as spenders, not as income earners, one would be strongly tempted to exclude them completely from the analysis. For want of any other assumption, and in order to complete the graphical presentation introduced above, it is assumed that rents (R) vary in proportion to the level of output. The tendency to think of profits as a per cent of advances to labor suggests that the

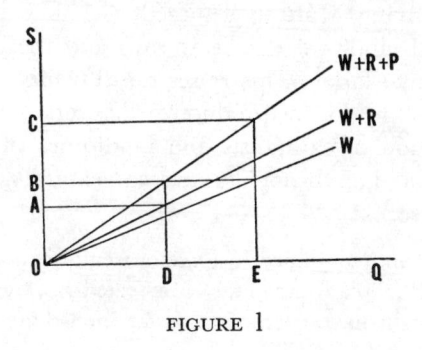

FIGURE 1

profits (P) required by capitalists, if they are to continue any level of output, be expressed simply as a per cent of the labor costs. Combining these assumptions gives total necessary costs $(W + R + P)$ dependent upon the level of aggregate output.

The demand side of the problem is considerably more difficult and most of the analysis will be concerned with Malthus' somewhat confused treatment of this subject. Malthus, when he was not concerned with changes in the value of money, defined effectual demand as a sum of money. To specify the level of effectual demand was to determine the level of national output. Thus if effectual demand in Figure 1 is OB, then required profits are earned at output OD. Any smaller output is impossible because of competition, while any larger output, so long as effectual demand remains at the OB level, gives less than the required level of profits (AB).

Demand is connected with the incomes of each class. In the case of laborers this connection is quite clear: laborers spend all of their incomes. Landlords and capitalists must then, if output OD is to be maintained, spend at least enough to cover the necessary rents and profits. Such spending need not be directly on product, but if spent on unproductive labor the result is the same, since presumably unproductive labor will spend all the income received upon product.

To show the importance of demand and the dangers involved in excessive saving Malthus assumed a change in which both capitalists and landlords decide to save and thereby to employ more productive labor. This raises no difficulty to begin with, since the consumption of productive laborers is substituted for the consumption of capitalists and landlords. In fact, only by such a diversion, i.e., through saving, can capital accumulate and wealth increase:

No permanent and continued increase of wealth can take place without a continued increase of capital . . . effected . . . by saving from the stock which might have been destined for immediate consumption.[26]

This was a perfectly orthodox proposition.

An extreme case may make the subsequent argument clearer. Suppose that capitalists and landlords decide to reduce their consumption to zero. Then they pay out OB in wages to productive labor. The product OD can still be sold profitably since productive laborers can now purchase the whole of the product OD. The capitalists and landlords, having acted on the assumption that OD of product would bring OB of receipts, find that their expectations have been realized. The difficulty arises only when we see that the product of the following period will be OE, having increased in the same proportion as the increase in productive labor. Note that there is no change in the money wage, an assumption that is in accord with Malthus' view that wages tend to be sticky, a fairly reasonable assumption under conditions of unemployment.

Malthus does not deny that output OE may be profitable; this would require a demand OC. It is also clear that labor income will be inadequate to create a demand OC: for the income of labor is only OB. If capitalists and landlords were to abandon attempts to save there would be no difficulty. They could maintain the wage bill intact at level OB, and demand for their use a sufficient amount of OE to raise the total demand above OB to OC. Then output OE would be profitable. But to Malthus this only emphasized the importance of demand.

Malthus preferred to examine the case where capitalists and landlords continue to save. He argues that in such cases demand must be inadequate:

> With regard to the capitalists themselves, together with the landlords and other rich persons, they have, by supposition, agreed to be parsimonious, and by depriving themselves of their usual conveniences and luxuries to save from their revenue and add to their capital. Under these circumstances, it is impossible that the increased quantity of commodities, obtained by the increased number of productive labourers, should find purchasers, without such a fall of price as would probably sink their value below that of outlay, or, at least, so reduce profits as very greatly to diminish both the power and the will to save.[27]

This is the crucial point in Malthus' argument. He seems to mean that effectual demand is unchanged at OB, so that output OE cannot earn the required profits and therefore will not be maintained. Capitalists and landlords as a matter of assumption are saving, that is to say, not consuming, so that the only demand arises from labor, and this demand is inadequate.

One way of examining this argument is to look at Ricardo's comments. He wrote:

> I am a farmer possessed of a thousand quarters of corn, and my object is to accumulate a fortune for my family. With this corn I can employ a certain number of men on the land, which I rent, and after paying my rent the first year, realize 1300 qrs. or 300 qrs. profits. The next year if there be plenty of labour in the market, I can employ a greater number than before, and my 1300 quarters will become 1700, and so from year to year I go on increasing the quantity till I have made it ten thousand quarters, and if labour be at the same price can command ten times the quantity of it that I could when I commenced my operations. Have I not then accumulated a fortune for my family? Have I

not given them the power of employing labour in any way they please and of enjoying the fruits of it? And what is to prevent me doing so but an increase in the price of labour, or a diminution of the productive powers of the land?[28]

The assumptions mentioned by Ricardo parallel the assumptions used above in interpreting Malthus: plenty of labor, constant returns, and a fixed price of labor. In effect Ricardo said that there was no reason why profits should fall no matter what the extent of the accumulation. Ricardo was reiterating the proposition that what is saved is consumed and will not impede profitable expansion of production. In this sense, he was claiming that what is lost to the capitalist is gained by the laborer, a proposition which Malthus denied. But whereas Malthus seemed to have interpreted the "loss" as implying the elimination of profits, Ricardo merely meant that what is not consumed by the capitalist is consumed by the laborer; this did not necessarily mean a fall in profits. Suppose we start off with a wages fund of 1000 quarters of corn, these quarters being consumed by laborers. If these laborers produce 1100 quarters (abstracting from rent), the rate of profits is 10 per cent. If all 1100 quarters are used to hire labor, then with fixed real wages and constant returns, consumption will be 1100 during a period in which 1210 quarters are produced; the rate of profit is again 10 per cent. As long as the assumptions are maintained, there is no limit to the expansion that can take place. Ricardo's proposition that what the capitalist loses, the laborer gains therefore appears to be valid.

The Ricardian argument appears to be equally valid if translated from real to money terms. Using the same basic illustration, suppose that the 1000 units of output that capitalists had on hand at the start of period I were the result of employing 910 laborers at a cost of £910. If during period I capitalists hire 1000 laborers at a total cost of £1000, the spending of this income by laborers will result in a price per unit of output of £1 and a profit rate of about 10 per cent. In period I, however, the increased labor force will result in an output of 1100 units, and, assuming no capitalist consumption, £1100 must be paid out as wages in period II if a 10 per cent profit is to be realized on the output of period I. If such wage payments are made, no glut arises, and the Ricardian conclusions stand. Alternatively, however, the capitalists might pay out less than £1100 in period II. If, for example, they paid out only £1000, profits on period I production would turn out to be zero. This outcome appears to be in accord with Malthus' conclusions, not Ricardo's.

The monetary "veil," however, makes it unclear whether or not the Ricardian assumption, never denied by Malthus, that all savings are invested automatically in productive labor has been maintained intact. If the inventory of 1100 units on hand at the end of period I is valued at market prices, that is at £1 per unit, then capitalist (unrealized) profits from period I production are £100. The capitalists, if they then spend only £1000 on labor in period II, say by implication that they wish to use £100, not for saving, but for consumption. Yet this £100 was not taken into account as expenditure on output, since capitalist consumption was assumed to be zero. But if this assumption is maintained, £100 more than £1000 (£1100) must have been spent in the hire of productive labor. This would leave the profit rate at 10 per cent. Thus, maintenance of the assumption that all savings are spent on productive labor leads to Ricardian, not Malthusian, conclusions.

Malthus was in fact unable to advance a convincing logical refutation of Ricardo because he never rejected the assumption that savings pass automatically into spending on productive labor. On the contrary, his arguments suggest again and again that he accepted this crucial assumption. To use modern terminology, Malthus failed to argue explicitly that savings did not necessarily pass into investment.

It is, of course, possible to argue back from the conclusions that Malthus reached to the assumption required, and state that this assumption was intended by Malthus, even though the assumption was not explicit. This would imply acceptance of the glut example just presented. In terms of the diagram this type of argument would deduce from the failure of profits beyond *OD* the assumption that effectual demand did not increase to an extent adequate to maintain profits. The demand schedule would no longer be identical with the cost (including required profits) schedule; beyond OD the demand would fall below costs. This implies that beyond OD, capitalist incomes are not entirely spent, that the capitalists do not consume all of their income and that their saving fails to flow completely into investment in labor.

In another terminology, the capitalists demand money, so that beyond OD the excess demand for money becomes positive. Oscar Lange suggests that Malthus probably had some such idea in mind and cites a footnote:[29]

Theoretical writers in Political Economy, from the fear of appearing to attach too much importance to money, have perhaps been too apt to throw it out of their consideration in their reasonings. It is an abstract truth that we want commodities, not money. But, in reality, no commodity for which it is possible to sell our goods at once, can be an adequate substitute for a circulating medium, and enable us in the same manner to provide for children, to purchase an estate, or to command labour and provisions a year or two hence. A circulating medium is absolutely necessary to any considerable saving; and even the manufacturer would get on but slowly, if he were obliged to accumulate in kind all the wages of his workmen. We cannot therefore be surprised at his wanting money rather than other goods; and in civilized countries, we may be quite sure that if the farmer or manufacturer cannot sell his products so as to give him a profit estimated in money, his industry will immediately slacken.[30]

This is the only reference to money in the section that Malthus devoted to saving and accumulation. It does nothing to justify a conclusion that Malthus understood clearly what he was talking about.

The above discussion has proceeded in terms of money costs and money demand, which was rarely Malthus' practice. Instead, as already pointed out, he deflated money values by the money wage of standard labor. This actually adds very little. It does mean, however, that when so expressed, a rise in effectual demand, in its effects upon profits, cannot be wiped out by a change in costs arising from a change in money wages.

Having reached the point where the Malthusian system more or less breaks down, it is necessary in order to go on with the analysis to accept the proposition, which seems so unreasonable in the light of Malthus' own assumption, that for some reason savings do not involve expenditure. If this is done the emphasis upon effectual demand becomes intelligible.

4. EFFECTUAL DEMAND

From the analysis of accumulation Malthus concluded that

the value of the whole produce cannot be maintained in the case of a rapid accumulation of capital occasioned by an actual and continued diminution in the expenditure and consumption of the higher classes of society in the form of revenue.[31]

As already indicated, this conclusion involves no difficulty in the case of full employment, but in the case of unemployment it was either logically incorrect, or dependent upon a failure of savings to find their way into investment in productive labor. The latter assumption is accepted in this and the following sections.

The general thesis on the role of effectual demand was clearly stated in Malthus' section on the means of distribution:

General wealth, like particular portions of it, will always follow effectual demand. Whenever there is a great demand for commodities, that is, whenever the whole mass will command a greater quantity of standard labour than before, without any greater value of capital having been required to produce them, there is the same kind of reason for expecting a general increase of commodities, as there is for expecting an increase of particular commodities when their market-prices rise; without a corresponding rise in their money-cost of production. And on the other hand, whenever the produce of a country estimated in the labour which it will command falls in value, while the same value of advances is continued, the power and will to set labourers to work will be diminished and the increase of produce must, for a time, be checked.[32]

As in the case of the related thesis concerning oversaving, Malthus applied this proposition indiscriminately to situations of both full employment and unemployment.

It is necessary to distinguish the kinds of changes that Malthus *may* have had in mind when he spoke of the effects of increases in effectual demand. If labor is the only factor of production, if the productivity of labor is given, and if the size of the labor force is given, then there are three ways in which wealth can increase. First, with a given flow of labor services, there will be the alternatives of producing personal services or wealth. Presumably under these conditions an increase in the demand for wealth will imply reallocation of labor with reduced output of personal services and increased output of wealth. Such a change can come about with no change in leisure, voluntary or involuntary.

Second, with a given flow of personal services, there will be the alternatives of leisure or production of wealth. Presumably under such conditions an increase in the demand for wealth will imply reduced leisure and increased output of wealth. Such a change in wealth is perfectly consistent with the absence, both before and after the change, of involuntary leisure (involuntary unemployment). A change in voluntary leisure is implied.

Third, there is the possibility, that with a given flow of personal services and a given level of voluntary leisure, wealth may be increased if a change in demand acts to eliminate such involuntary leisure as may exist. Although it is hard to distinguish this case from the second case in which there is a change in voluntary leisure, to this case only will the term unemployment be applied.

Malthus did not make these distinctions, but it is clear that at various times he used all three of these concepts of wealth increase, always stating that an increase of demand (for wealth) would lead to an increase of wealth. By examining his discussion of "means of distribution," a catch-all category that included such diverse topics as income distribution, commerce, and unproductive consumption, it is possible to cast considerable light on some of Malthus' more obscure propositions.

Under the heading "income distribution" Malthus discusses the influence of the distribution of landed property upon effectual demand. A contrast is made between the level of demand when property is concentrated in a few hands and that which will result when property is widely distributed.

The possessor of numerous estates, after he had furnished his mansion or castle splendidly, and provided himself with handsome clothes and handsome carriages, would not change them all every two months, merely because he had the power of doing it. Instead of indulging in such useless and troublesome changes, he would be more likely to keep a number of servants and idle dependents.[33]

On the other hand:

Thirty or forty proprietors, with incomes answering to between one thousand and five thousand a year, would create a much more effectual demand for the necessaries, conveniences, and luxuries of life than a single proprietor possessing a hundred thousand a year.[34]

This argument may apply either to full employment or to unemployment situations, but Malthus is apparently more interested in its application to full employment situations. As stated, it places emphasis upon diversion of demand from personal services to material objects, this diversion implying an increase in wealth. It is exactly the opposite of the more lengthy and more important argument used to defend unproductive labor (discussed below).[35]

In the same connection Malthus introduces a choice between leisure and wealth. A wealthy proprietor is likely

perhaps to sacrifice a considerable portion of his land in order to encourage more game, and to indulge, with more effect and less interruption, in the pleasures of the chase.[36]

Presumably a redistribution of property would lead to an increase in productive activity and hence to an increase in wealth, for the small proprietor would prefer material objects to the inactivity or leisure implied in the chase. Once again the argument seems to apply to full employment rather than to unemployment situations.

The arguments concerning commerce are somewhat more ambiguous. Trade, both domestic and foreign, and the transportation systems on which trade depends, would be unimportant if, in a given area,

> the inhabitants could be persuaded to estimate their confined productions just as highly, to be just as eager to obtain and consume them, and as willing to work hard for them, and to make great sacrifices for them, as for the commodities which they obtain from a distance. . . . Could we but so alter the wants and tastes of the people of Glasgow as to make them estimate as highly the profusion of cotton goods which they produce, as any articles which they could receive in return for them under a prosperous trade, we should hear no more of their distresses.[37]

Thus to Malthus the great virtue of trade, a virtue often attached to new commodities generally, derives from the fact that wants and demand are stimulated. The argument may imply a substitution of wealth for leisure in a full employment situation, with absence of any change in involuntary unemployment. Or it may be applied to an unemployment situation, implying that attractive goods will raise demand and increase employment. There is no reason why both arguments should not be used simultaneously, with new goods leading to both a substitution of goods for money and a substitution of goods for leisure. It is not clear, however, exactly what Malthus had in mind.

In so far as applications to involuntary unemployment situations are ignored, both the argument on distribution and the argument on commerce come down to a very simple proposition: any event that leads to demand for material objects instead of demand for personal services or leisure stimulates wealth. Malthus was, however, not interested in policy proposals based upon these arguments. Division of property would require the abolition of the law of primogeniture and would, he felt, injure the landed aristocracy which was the foundation of the British Constitution.[38] Nor did he draw any policy conclusions from the discussion of commerce.

Instead he turned to the third "means of distribution," the effectual demand that would result from the employment of unproductive labor. His argument seems to have been specifically designed for conditions of involuntary unemployment, such as those which existed in the wake of the Napoleonic Wars, and was closely related to the analysis of the dangers of saving. At this point, however, Malthus became somewhat more explicit about the spending habits of the main classes of society.

As already indicated, Malthus assumed that laborers spent all that they earned, thus implying that the demand of productive labor for output would be identical with the schedule representing the labor costs of producing output as shown in Figure 1. [39] Capitalists could, if they wished, supply an adequate demand for any level of output, but they were more likely to save than to spend:

> The great object of their lives is to save a fortune, both because it is their duty to their families, and because they cannot spend an income with so much comfort to themselves, while they are obliged perhaps to attend a counting-house for seven or eight hours a day.[40]

Clearly Malthus was again assuming that saving does not give rise either directly or indirectly to a demand for output, and he was suggesting, albeit vaguely, that capitalist consumption was relatively unresponsive to upward movements in capitalist income. Figure 2A, which abstracts from rent, landlord expenditures, and unproductive labor, may be a not unfair interpretation of Malthus, with output (OD) being determined by the equality of necessary profits (NP) and capitalist demand (CD). However, the drawing of the capitalist demand schedule as a horizontal line is not explicit in Malthus, although it is at least certain that, beyond some output, capitalist demand falls short of required profits. It should be noted that so far the model is unrealistic since it implies a zero level of saving by capitalists.

At this point Malthus introduces the landlord class and the stimulus to landlord consumption that arises from the possibility of employing unproductive labor. First, however, he notes that the direct demand for produce by landlords is limited, being dependent upon the expenditures that they have undertaken in the past: the larger the expenditures already made on durable goods, the smaller the current expenditures. Fortunately, however, landlords also spend on the services of unproductive labor, and this stimulates the demand for produce in two ways. Unproductive laborers purchase output, spending all of their in-

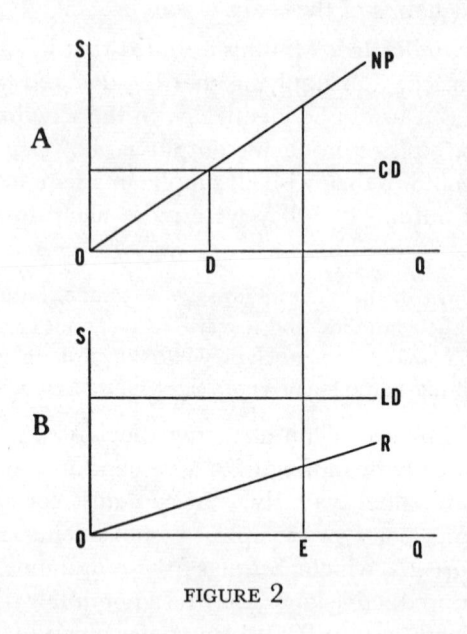

FIGURE 2

comes as in the case of productive labor. At the same time the existence of unproductive labor raises the direct landlord demand for produce, since certain types of produce are desirable only when personal services are available. In consequence, landlord expenditures, spurred by the attractions of employing unproductive labor, make possible capitalist saving:

There must therefore be a considerable class of persons who have both the will and the power to consume more material wealth than they produce, or the mercantile classes could not continue profitably to produce so much more than they consume. In this class the landlords no doubt stand pre-eminent; but if they were not assisted by the great mass of individuals engaged in personal services, whom they maintain, their own consumption would be of itself insufficient to keep up and increase the value of the produce.[41]

Figure 2B, in conjunction with Figure 2A, spells this out more explicitly, with output OE being determined by the equality of the landlord deficit (the excess of landlord demand, LD, for output both direct and indirect over rent, R) and capitalist saving (the excess of necessary profits over capitalist demand for output). It should be noted that there is no specific discussion in Malthus of the relationship between output, or rent, and landlord demand, except for the fact that a landlord deficit is usual: thus the drawing of the landlord demand schedule as horizontal is rather arbitrary.

The desirability of expenditures upon unproductive labor as a means of raising the level of output is clear from the analysis. It is notable, however, that Malthus' attitude toward personal services is the exact opposite of the critical view which he took in his discussion of distribution. The contrast tends to suggest that the latter discussion presupposed full employment, as against the conditions of unemployment that underlie the case for higher output through increased outlays on personal services.

5. PROSPERITY AND DEPRESSION

Aside from a tantalizing paragraph at the very end of the *Principles*, Malthus gave no indication that he recognized any regularly recurring fluctuations in general activity. Instead he was mainly concerned with analysis of changing levels of wealth.

When he did concern himself with the occurrences of the recent past he confined his remarks to two periods. The first of these was the period of war prosperity, which Malthus treated as a unit, with no more than passing reference to the shorter fluctuations that took place between 1793 and 1815. The second was the postwar depression. This collapse was undoubtedly the chief reason for his concern with the level of wealth.

The discussion of wartime prosperity in the *Principles* shows some changes in emphasis from the earlier treatment accorded the same subject in 1811. In 1811 Malthus was concerned with the effects of increased paper money issues upon capital. Usually, he says, the merchant and manufacturer are told that such issues have no effect upon capital. This is an error:

If such a distribution of the circulating medium were to take place, as to throw the command of the produce of the country chiefly into the hands of the productive classes,—that is, if considerable portions of the currency were taken from the idle, and those who live upon fixed incomes, and transferred to farmers, manufacturers and merchants,—the proportion between capital and revenue would be greatly altered to the advantage of capital; and in a short time, the produce of the country would be greatly augmented.[42]

This same redistribution had taken place in wartime England through the creation of new paper money.

The new notes go into the market, as so much additional capital to purchase what is necessary for the conduct of the concern. But before the produce of the country has been increased, it is impossible for one person to have more of it, without diminishing the shares of some others. This diminution is effected by the rise of prices occasioned by the competition of the new notes, which puts it out of the power of those who are only buyers, and not sellers, to purchase as much of the annual product as before: While all the industrious classes,—all those that sell as well as buy, are, during the progressive rise of prices, making unusual profits; and, even when this progression stops, are left with the command of a greater portion of the annual produce than they possessed previous to the new issues.[43]

Such note issues are desirable in so far as they result in increased production, but are unjust in that they lead to transfers of property. Malthus approves them only if they are held within limits compatible with a gold standard. However,

it frequently happens, we conceive, that the beneficial employment of the coin set free, and the increased command of the produce transferred to the industrious classes by the increase of prices, gives such a stimulus to the productive powers of the country, that, in a short time, the balance between commodities and currency is restored, by the multiplication of the former,—and prices return to their former level.[44]

It is notable that in this early article Malthus presents no theory of demand, says nothing in explanation of the willingness to increase production, and appears completely oblivious to any failure of demand.

Twelve years later, in 1823, Malthus, in reviewing Tooke, reexamined the war period. The war years were seen as a period of generally rising prices, interrupted by difficulties in export trades arising from the anticommercial decrees. Malthus felt that Tooke's survey proved the following proposition:

> That when the supply of commodities is in some degree deficient compared with the demand, whether this arises from the increase of demand, or the diminution of supply, the state of trade is brisk, profits are high, and mercantile speculations are greatly encouraged; and on the other hand, when the supply is abundant compared with the demand, there is a period of comparative stagnation with low profits, and very little encouragement to mercantile speculation.[45]

Tooke had argued that the war had not operated to raise general prices through the medium of increased demand, "the quantity of money, and its rate of circulation continuing the same."[46] To Malthus this was a strange assumption that led to barren discussion. It was acceptable to start with the diminution of the supply of commodities, but one must also take account of the rise in demand that was the result of decreased supply. "It is," wrote Malthus,

> of the very nature of war, and of the obstructions which it occasions to supply, to influence the quantity of money in a country, and the rate of its circulation. And surely the proper inquiry for us, on the present occasion, is, *the fact*, whether the circumstances of the late war did really create an increase of demand as well as an obstruction to the supply without precluding the natural means by which such a result would be effected.[47]

Malthus saw events as follows: deficiency of supply relative to demand gave rise to high profits, speculation, increased circulation of private paper and credit in the form of acceptances, and increased issues by the Bank of England. All this meant that demand had risen absolutely, at least in money terms. Malthus saw the effects in the sustained (and therefore profitable) increase in production and consumption, and also in the

> increase of draining and inclosures, roads and bridges, canals and harbors, paving and other local improvements, machinery, shipping, and exciseable commodities.[48]

It is notable that the emphasis shifts between 1811 and 1823 from the effects of price inflation in transferring property from revenue to capital, to the opposite kind of consideration. Instead of discussing the forced saving mechanism, Malthus now turned his attention to the reasons why the new money was created, and found them in the war shortages that led to high profits and in the conversion of capital to revenue that was the necessary concomitant of government war expenditures.

The role of government war expenditures received more attention in the *Principles* than in either of the articles cited. The exposition is somewhat fragmentary and makes little distinction between government expenditures financed by taxes and those financed by borrowing, and no distinction between borrowing from the public and from the Bank of England. Malthus wrote:

> The loans to government convert capital into revenue, and increase the demand [for commodities] at the same time that they at first diminish the means of supply. The necessary consequence must be an increase of profits. This naturally increases both the power and the reward of accumulation; and if only the same habits of saving prevail among the capitalists as before, the recovery of the lost stock must be rapid.[49]

A more cautious exposition of the virtues of tax-financed expenditures was presented. Government, in this case, is merely a channel through which unproductive consumption is undertaken. Taxation eliminates some of the power of saving, but the tax receipts are paid out to unproductive laborers by government, so that on the balance the demand for output increases. Malthus is aware that taxation, apparently visualized as falling on profits, may have adverse effects upon incentives and the ability to save and to extend production. But he argues that as long as the tax is not too large, no impediment to the will to extend production will appear. The argument seems to turn upon the differences in the spending habits of those taxed and of the unproductive laborers hired with the tax receipts. Malthus writes:

> With regard to . . . statesmen, soldiers, sailors, and those who live upon the interest of the national debt, it cannot be denied that they contribute powerfully to distribution and demand; they frequently occasion a division of property more favorable to the progress of wealth than would otherwise have taken place; they ensure that effective consumption which is necessary to give the proper stimulus to production; and the desire to pay a tax, and yet enjoy the same means of gratification, must often operate to excite the exertions of industry quite as effectively as the desire to pay a lawyer or physician.[50]

Malthus dated the postwar slump from 1813 or 1815, and again there seems to have been little recognition that there were shorter fluctuations. Judging by his review of Tooke, Malthus treated the whole period from the end of the war to 1822 or 1823 as a unit, marked by contraction and then by stagnation. The problem of explaining the onset of the contraction attracted him, though, as usual, he was not systematic in dealing with the question.

Malthus admitted that the transition from war to peace necessarily involved economic dislocation resulting from the redirection of capital from war industries to those that catered to peacetime demand: this was Ricardo's explanation, but it seemed inadequate to account for a depression that was still present in 1820. If the hypothesis were valid, then there should be profitable outlets for capital. But, Malthus asked,

> where are the under-stocked employments, which, according to this theory, ought to be numerous, and fully capable of absorbing all the redundant capital, which is confessedly glutting the markets of Europe in so many different branches of trade?[51]

The only alternative factor which seemed worthy of mention was the cessation of government demand.

> The returned taxes, and the excess of individual gains above expenditure, which were so largely used as revenue during the war, are now in

part, and probably no inconsiderable part, saved. . . . If some of the principal governments concerned spent the taxes which they raised in a manner to create a greater and more certain demand for labour and commodities, particularly the former, than the present owners of them, and if this difference be of a nature to last for some time, we cannot be surprised at the duration and the effects arising from the transition from war to peace.[52]

Thus the duration of depression seemed to be partly attributed to a reduction of taxes and expenditures, the reversal of factors that had earlier been instrumental in the creation of the war prosperity.

Of the process of contraction he wrote:

It commenced certainly with the extraordinary fall in the value of the raw produce of the land, to the amount, it has been supposed, of nearly one third. When this fall had diminished the capitals of the farmers, and still more the revenues both of landlords and farmers, and of all those who were otherwise connected with the land, their power of purchasing manufactures and foreign products was of necessity greatly diminished. The failure of home demand filled the warehouses of the manufacturers with unsold goods, which urged them to export more largely at all risks. But this excessive exportation glutted all the foreign markets, and prevented the merchants from receiving adequate returns; while, from the diminution of the home revenues, aggravated by a sudden and extraordinary contraction of the currency, even the comparatively scanty returns obtained from abroad found a very insufficient domestic demand, and the profits and consequent expenditure of merchants and manufacturers were proportionately lowered.[53]

At the same time, population continued to grow in delayed response to the great wartime demand for labor, and the increase in labor supply was further swelled by disbanded soldiers and sailors. The falling prices of farm and manufactured produce made it impossible to employ even a constant number of laborers without a proportionate fall in the price of labor, which did not take place. Malthus saw command over goods transferred in the deflation from manufacturers and producers to those who have fixed money incomes. But fixed income receivers have not the "will" to extend their demand. Malthus concluded that even the abundance of necessaries cannot ensure employment when the necessaries are controlled by inactive classes. Such changes in the distribution of produce were always the result of changes in the value of money.

These discussions of current fluctuations are all rather brief. They do not, moreover, cast much light upon Malthus' theory of fluctuations in the level of wealth. Rather they served to bolster his case for emphasis upon demand and to introduce the more interesting topic of remedies for the stagnation of the postwar period.

6. POLICY

Malthus was not radical in the policies he recommended for the cure of the economic stagnation from which England had suffered "since 1815."[54] The policies he rejected are perhaps as interesting as the rather mild positive suggestions that he made.

Both labor and capital were unemployed. The idleness of capital led to the rejection of remedies that looked to saving as a means to prosperity. Malthus asked: If wages were too low would one recommend an increase in population? So with capital: to save when profits are too low to warrant the employment of such capital as already exists would only mean lower profits and a further deterioration of economic conditions. Malthus did not deny the desirability of saving if economic progress is to take place, but he did argue that "something else is wanted before we can accumulate with effect."[55]

Low profits and unemployment were, he argued, the result of a situation in which prices had fallen but in which costs, particularly labor costs, had not fallen in proportion. Malthus probably believed that a reduction in wages would lead to renewed profits and reemployment of capital and labor. But over short periods Malthus viewed wages as sticky. Speaking of a fall in commodity prices, he argued that,

if the fall be gradual, and partly made up in exchangeable value by increase of quantity, the money wages of labour will not necessarily sink;

and the result will be merely a slack demand for labour, not sufficient perhaps to throw the actual labourers out of work, but such as to prevent or diminish task-work, to check the employment of women and children, and to give but little encouragement to the rising generation of labourers.[56]

He again referred to the failure of wages to fall in proportion to commodity prices in describing the events after 1815 and saw unemployment as a result. All this was in direct conflict with Ricardo, who wrote in a letter to Malthus:

You say "we know from repeated experience that the money price of labour never falls till many workmen have been for some time out of work." I know no such thing; and, if wages, were previously high, I can see no reason whatever why they should not fall before many labourers are thrown out of work. All general reasoning, I apprehend, is in favor of my view of this question, for why should some agree to go without any wages while others were most liberally rewarded? Once more I must say that a sudden and diminished demand for labour in this case must mean a diminished reward to the labourer, and not a diminished employment of him.[57]

Malthus appealed to experience rather than to general reasoning.

The stickiness of wages did not, however, imply absolute inflexibility according to Malthus, so that no unemployment equilibrium was envisaged. A slump in demand brought about unemployment,

a most painful but almost unavoidable preliminary to a fall in the money wages of labour, which it is obvious could alone enable the general income of the country to employ the same number of labourers as before, and, after a period of severe check to the increase of wealth, to recommence a progressive movement.[58]

This is the only passage implying that wage cuts would bring about a return to prosperity, and it is preceded by a passage which suggests the existence of some kind of a difficulty in this remedy for stagnation:

If, after labour has adjusted itself to the new level of prices, the permanent distribution of the produce and the permanent tastes and habits of the people should not be favourable to an adequate degree of effectual consumption, the clearest principles of political economy shew that the profits of stock might be lower for any length of time than the state of the land rendered necessary; and that the rate of production might be as permanent as the faulty distribution of the produce and the unfavourable tastes and habits which had occasioned it.[59]

It is probably best to interpret this earlier passage, not as a discussion of "involuntary" unemployment, but as a discussion of the voluntary unemployment implied in the choice in favor of leisure as against work and commodities resulting from such work. If so, Malthus is on record as suggesting that wage reductions would eventually solve problems of (involuntary) unemployment. He did not, however, press for wage reductions as a remedy for depression.

Another policy was, according to Malthus, much recommended by merchants. These recommendations (most closely associated in the public mind with the Birmingham School) favored an increased issue of paper money as a cure for depression.[60] Following his analysis of 1811, Malthus admitted that the immediate effects might be favorable. The issues of paper would transfer property from those with fixed money incomes to those who were producers. The power to produce and even production itself would increase.

Perhaps a sudden increase of currency and a new facility of borrowing might under any circumstances, give a temporary stimulus to trade, but it would only be temporary. Without a large expenditure on the part of the government, and frequent conversion of capital into revenue, the great powers of production acquired by the capitalists, operating upon the diminished power of purchasing possessed by the owners of fixed income, could not fail to occasion a still greater glut of commodities than is felt at present.[61]

In the war, when demand was high, additional currency stimulated production, but in a depression with inadequate demand, paper would do nothing to stimulate production permanently. Back of this condemnation of inflationary schemes lay Malthus' whole conception of saving and demand. New paper issues could lead temporarily to increased employment and production.

But profitable sale of this new production required more than the demand of laborers, for their demand would only cover labor costs, not required profits. Such an expansion of production was bound to be abortive, unless some extra demand were created.

Tied in with these doubts was Malthus' general view that money, though important, was a passive factor as far as turning points in activity were concerned:

In the history of our paper transactions, it will be found that the abundance or scantiness of currency has generally followed and aggravated high and low prices, but seldom or never led them; and it is of the utmost importance to recollect that, at the end of the war, the prices failed before the contraction of the currency began. It was, in fact, the failure of the prices of agricultural produce, which destroyed the country banks, and shewed us the frail foundations on which the excess of our paper-currency rested. This sudden contraction no doubt aggravated very greatly the distresses of the merchants and of the country.[62]

This view casts some doubt on the efficacy of paper issues even in creation of temporary expansions of production. It was, however, consistent with the emphasis on demand changes, which at bottom were probably changes in the velocity rather than in the quantity of money.

Thus Malthus rejected the monetary policies of the Birmingham School. Attempts to change price levels and employment through the issue of currency were vain, defying both "the laws of justice and the great principles of supply and demand."[63]

The positive proposals for curing economic stagnation involved changes in demand. Malthus was not too sanguine about exhortations directed at private citizens, though he did indulge in them. Rather he turned to the government as a means by which demand could be stimulated, profits increased, and the progress of wealth resumed. The arguments ran in terms of unproductive expenditure by the government, and were only variations on the themes already discussed. Tax-financed government expenditures were the means to the end. Expenditures were to be made in "unproductive" ways, on roads and public works.[64]

It is also of importance to know that, in our endeavours to assist the working classes in a period like the present, it is desirable to employ them in those kinds of labour, the results of which do not come for sale into the market, such as roads and public works. The objection to employing a large sum in this way, raised by taxes, would not be its tendency to diminish the capital employed in productive labour; because this, to a certain extent, is exactly what is wanted; but it might, perhaps, have the effect of concealing too much the failure of the national demand for labour, and prevent the population from gradually accommodating itself to a reduced demand. This however might be, in a considerable degree, corrected by the wages given.[65]

Malthus of course said nothing of stimulating investment (in the modern sense), for investment for him was not distinct from consumption: both were part of demand.[66] In so far as capitalists demanded goods they created the profits justifying higher production of wealth, but the demand could be either demand for consumption goods or for investment goods. Unproductive expenditure, however, played the same role as investment. Malthus in effect broadened his concept of unproductive to include not only the immaterial services of servants and statesmen, but also the kind of production that would not be sold, roads and public works. These projects were "unproductive" in the narrow sense in which Malthus used the term at this point. He chose to deal with a time period sufficiently short, so that those unproductive expenditures on public works created income that would be spent on output, but no increase in the output of goods to be sold in the market. Thus Malthus worked here on an assumption diametrically opposed to that which he utilized in his discussion of saving and capital accumulation. In such discussions savings actually spent on labor almost immediately gave rise to new output.

Malthus finally concluded

that the employment of the poor in roads and public works, and a tendency among landlords and persons of property to build, to improve and beautify their grounds, and to employ workmen and menial servants, are the means most in our power and most directly calculated to remedy the evils arising from that disturbance in the balance of produce and consumption, which has been occasioned by the sudden conversion of soldiers, sailors, and various other classes which the war employed, into productive labourers.[67]

7. CONCLUSION

Most modern interpreters, prior to Keynes, took the position that Malthus was simply confused. Hollander, for instance, in his introduction to Ricardo's *Notes on Malthus*, found Ricardo generally correct, Malthus obscure and often incorrect.[68] In sharp contrast writers since 1936 have tended to echo Keynes' view that Malthus had something important to say and that Ricardo, whatever his merits in certain respects, had led economics astray.

Thus recent interpreters have examined Malthus with a view to discovering both the merits of his arguments and foreshadowings of Keynesian doctrine. The pitfall lies in the fact that, while terminology and even some of the methods of Keynes can be found in the *Principles*, there can be no certainty that words meant the same thing to the two authors.

There is no basis, except in the conclusions reached, for the belief that Malthusian saving had much in common with Keynesian saving. An increase in Keynesian saving (in the schedule sense) implies a reduction in consumption. An increase in Malthusian saving appears, time and again, as an event which reduces capitalist consumption, but which also increases consumption undertaken by productive workers. If the increase in Keynesian saving is not to result in a fall in output and employment, an increase in investment is required. No such requirement appears explicitly in Malthus.

The difference is less striking only because Malthus made a logical jump and wrote as if an increase in saving involved a reduction in spending. Only in this way did the dangers of oversaving and the importance of effectual demand become the center of his doctrine. The failure to make this assumption explicit accounts for the failure of Malthus' *Principles* as a logical structure, though it does not destroy the importance of the work.

If the implicit and necessary assumption is introduced, thereby bringing Malthus into line with Keynes, the similarities become quite marked, though differences still remain. The great similarity lies in the discussion of aggregate demand, with the description of the way in which the level of demand is connected with the distribution of property, and with the incomes of the main classes of society. We can, however, discover nothing that looks very much like the consumption function as it was formulated by Keynes. Laborers consume all their income. Landlords consume more than their incomes, though there is little to suggest a stable relation between their incomes and their consumption, or to indicate that both income and consumption for this class move together. Capitalist behavior is even more obscure. The Malthusian proposition that saving and income increase together casts no light on the whole question, for Malthus always maintained that saving, by which he meant spending on productive labor, was a necessary, though not a sufficient, condition for the growth of income (wealth).

Adequate levels of income seem, however, to have required deficit spending, since capitalists fail to spend all of their income. Thus, for Malthus, as long as he excluded government from consideration, the landlords played a role similar to that played in Keynesian theory by the entrepreneurial class, considered both as consumers and as investors. But the deficit of the landlords does not necessarily, as does the deficit of Keynesian entrepreneurs, lead to an increase in the stock of capital. In fact, except for the final discussion, in which public works are considered, the only output of the Malthusian economy appears to be some type of consumption good. Thus maintenance of a given level of output necessarily depended upon consumption, not upon investment, which either did not deserve explicit mention, or else was subsumed under consumption.

The chief references to fixed capital formation in relation to effectual demand appear when Malthus turns to his policy recommendations. Here he emphasizes the desirability of public works, and doubting the possibility of influencing the private sector of the economy, suggests tax-financed projects. But he stresses the desirability of projects that do not involve the production of consumer goods. Production of consumer goods can only come about after demand has increased: the projects are a means to this end. No emphasis is placed upon deficit expenditures by government, so that apparently the argument that demand for produce will increase depends upon some difference in the spending habits of those who pay taxes and those that receive taxes as incomes earned in the course of working on roads and other public works. But this is not spelled out. Malthus, in preferring unproductive public works, is clearly worried about the productivity effects of investment, as distinguished from the desirable expenditure effects.

The other elements of the Keynesian system receive little consideration in Malthus. The quantity of money played a negligible role. Interest rates are neglected. Instead changes in spending arising out of changes in velocity induce changes in money supply. In this respect Malthus differs from many of his contemporaries. There is of course no consideration of an investment demand schedule, while the treatment of wage changes is too sketchy to be the basis for any firm generalization.

In Attwood's writings the short fluctuations in business activity receive much attention. In Malthus the emphasis is rather upon prosperity and depression; business cycles are barely discernible. This difference is partly the result of the fact that Malthus was not commenting on year-to-year changes in economic activity. Partly also this may be due to the fact that in 1820, there had been only brief experience with peacetime fluctuations, while after 1820 Malthus wrote little.

The reasons for Malthus' failure on an intellectual level are clear. By neglecting to make explicit the premises that were required for a logical statement of his argument, he left himself open to quite justified charges of obscurity. It is difficult to believe that the issues were clear in his own mind.

Thomas Joplin

THOMAS JOPLIN, like Attwood, was a banker. Connected for some years with the Provincial Bank of Ireland, he later resigned and devoted himself exclusively to the promotion of joint stock banks and to the writing of pamphlets and books on political economy.[1]

Joplin's writings were closely connected with his professional activities. He was interested in the reform of banking through the establishment of joint stock banks and in the reform of the currency with a view to the mitigation of fluctuations in economic activity. But he also wrote on other subjects, on the theory of value and on the corn laws. These were, however, subordinated to his primary concern, the currency.

Joplin's views have certain similarities to those of both Attwood and Malthus. He was primarily a monetary theorist, but whereas Attwood's doctrines were in a sense merely an application of the quantity theory of money to depression situations, Joplin tried to tie together the quantity theory and relationships between savings and "expenditure." In this latter respect, there is some similarity to the approach that Malthus had used in his *Principles*. More logical than Malthus, Joplin was in his policy proposals less extreme and considerably less consistent than Attwood.

Joplin seems to have envisaged two important reasons for changes in the level of economic activity. Section one below deals primarily with the first of these reasons, changes in savings and expenditures. This is the theoretical foundation of all of Joplin's writings on fluctuations. In section two a second basis for disturbances is isolated, international flows of gold. The third and fourth sections are concerned respectively with the use to which Joplin put his theories in interpreting the fluctuations of the period 1814-44, and in devising plans for reform of the currency.

1. SAVINGS AND EXPENDITURE

The savings-expenditure theory arose out of Joplin's dissatisfaction with the doctrines advanced by Tooke and Matthias Attwood. Each of these writers sought an explanation for the fall of prices that occurred between 1818 and 1822. Tooke had argued that the fall was essentially the result of increased production. Against this view Joplin advanced the argument used by Matthias and Thomas Attwood: a general decline in prices cannot be attributed to forces that are peculiar to each commodity.[2] But Joplin also disagreed with the explanation of the Attwoods: the Bank of England, they argued, had reduced its note issue and had forced a reduction in prices. Joplin found in this only a repetition of the error of the Bullion Committee. The received doctrine, he wrote,

not only implied, but it was distinctly expressed, that the issues of the Bank of England had an immediate effect on those of the Country Banks.[3]

Ultimately such an effect seemed reasonable, but for the relevant short period that argument was incorrect. Joplin supported this criticism with an appeal to statistics of country bank circulation, Bank of England circulation, and wheat prices; prices were related to country notes, not to Bank of England notes. The fact that country notes did not fluctuate with Bank of England notes required some explanation, and led Joplin into an extended analysis of the factors determining country circulation.

The real income of society consists, Joplin pointed out, not of money, but of the commodities that are purchased with money income. Money income consists of the income of individuals; this income can be divided into wages, profits, interest, and rent.

Each individual can use his money income in three ways: "He must either hoard it, lend it at interest to others, or expend it himself."[4] Joplin analyzed the effects of each choice upon prices and on business activity.

Hoarding depresses prices, but leaves real consumption unchanged. If an income recipient hoards,

> he takes money out of circulation, contracts the currency, reduces the price of commodities generally, and increases the power of consumption by those who possess the money left in circulation.[5]

When the money that has been hoarded is brought into circulation again, precisely the opposite effects are produced. Hoarding money, therefore, does not diminish the ultimate demand for commodities, it only alters the channel of their consumption.[6]

Joplin, however, was prepared to ignore hoarding altogether except under conditions of panic. Individuals require a stock of money to facilitate trade and to bridge the gap between income and outlay:

> No person can carry on his trade, at least with comfort and convenience, who does not possess a supply of cash, both for his current and for his occasional demands. The same observation will apply to individuals with stated incomes. Their incomes are paid them, say, twice a year, whereas their expenditure takes place daily, and they must, for the most part have money by them, from which to draw the expenditure as it occurs.... The amount of this stock varies with different individuals, but probably would not, in the natural order of things, be subject to any great and sudden variations in the aggregate.[7]

Thus, while the demand to hold money may vary for different individuals, in aggregate these variations could be neglected.

Joplin distinguished two ways in which money income might be spent. Expenditure involved either "actual consumption," in which commodities passed into the hands of ultimate consumers, or "commercial consumption," merely another form of "final consumption," in which commodities pass into the hands of merchants. Joplin illustrated "commercial consumption" and showed that its effects were similar to the effects of "actual consumption" by use of an example involving inventory accumulation. Merchants

> purchase the particular commodities in which they deal, with their profits or income, instead of purchasing commodities for their own consumption. By this, production is equally promoted, though consumption does not actually take place.[8]

For Joplin it was the possibility of lending money income that was most interesting and most relevant for an understanding of economic fluctuations. A decision to save usually involves the deposit of such savings in a bank. The bank would then lend such savings and the borrowers would make an expenditure just offsetting the original savings. Ideally the equality between the supply and demand for savings would come about through variations in the rate of interest charged to borrowers.

This proposition led Joplin into an analysis of the effect of interest rate changes upon the demand and supply of saving. The demand for savings arises from four sources: from those who live beyond their incomes, from those who have suffered losses in trade, from the government, and from those who wish to make expenditures on buildings, machinery, and commodities (commercial consumption). In his early writings Joplin minimized the importance of commercial consumption as a source of demand, but later he seems to have changed his mind.[9] A low interest rate stimulates both the demand for funds to finance inventory accumulation and also, taken in conjunction with the greater facility of obtaining money,

> leads to the embarking of capital in great public undertakings, which would otherwise not have been ventured upon.[10]

A high interest rate, on the other hand, restricts demand for savings.

The supply of savings is also responsive to changes in the rate of interest. Joplin distinguished three economic classes in analyzing the sources of savings. The laboring classes have as a rule such low incomes that saving is impossible. The rentier class have the incomes that would permit saving, but little inclination to save, said Joplin in 1823; by 1832 he had changed his view of rentier savings habits, arguing that rentiers would save if interest rates were sufficiently high. "Saving," he wrote,

is made by a sacrifice of present enjoyment, for a future good in the shape of an increase in annual income. But as the annual income to be derived from saving diminishes [as the interest rate falls], the temptation to save is reduced.[11]

But the most important class of savers consists of men who engage in trade:

The economists of society principally consist of the mercantile classes. ... It is necessary for every tradesman who means to do well, to save money, in order to provide against a future evil day, which the uncertainty of trade often produces. Thus necessity, the desire of independence, and the ambition to be rich, which the pursuits of trade usually generate, render this class, in general, economists, and the savings of society are principally made by them.[12]

These men have an alternative to present consumption that does not exist for rentiers. They can, if the rate of interest is too low, use their savings in their own trade. There is another reason that leads indirectly to reduced savings when the interest rate is low. Since low interest rates imply great activity in trade and hence low profits,

less income is obtained than before and though there is more capital in trade, less profit, upon the aggregate, is derived from it. Thus the trading part of the community are unable to save money as heretofore.[13]

To the general propositions that the supply of savings falls with lower interest rates, and that the demand for savings rises with lower interest rates, Joplin implicitly added the assumption that at some interest rate the demand could be brought into equilibrium with the supply.

With this background of analysis, Joplin turned to an explanation of the factors that led to the variation in country bank circulation and hence to variation in business activity. The stability of money incomes depends upon the easy passage of all savings into deposits, and out again in the form of loans, which are in turn spent. Joplin wrote that,

if the monied income of society is not spent as well as the real income, nothing but a derangement of the Currency is the consequence.

Now, in order to prevent this consequence, and secure the regular consumption, not only of the real, but of the monied income of society, the supply and demand for the savings of income, or money in the money market, must correspond.[14]

A particular rate of interest, which Joplin called "the natural rate," "the true rate," or "the real value of capital," would accomplish this end. In practice, however, the country banks do not adjust the interest rate, but hold it constant. Suppose an initial situation in which the natural rate exists, so that demand and supply are equal. Now suppose a sudden increase in savings. Deposits increase, but the banks, since they keep the rate of interest unchanged, do not increase their lending. As a result, savings are greater than "expenditure." The same situation is revealed by the circulation of the country banks; when they receive the savings in the form of deposited notes, and then fail to lend these notes to somebody who will spend, the note circulation contracts. Thus a decline in spending can be attributed either to an excess of savings over expenditures, or to a decrease in bank notes in circulation.

A decline in spending, reflected in a decrease in note circulation, has effects upon business activity, upon employment, and upon prices. Any decrease in note circulation affects business adversely, so that

traders are compelled to reduce their stocks of goods and order no more, enterprize is suspended, labour thrown out of employment, and distress rendered permanent by the destruction of income consequent thereupon.[15]

Joplin noted that the effects tended to be cumulative, so that reduced incomes or employment in one sector of the economy led to reduced incomes and employment elsewhere.

The reduced means of one person would curtail his expenditure in articles supplied by another; this would reduce his expenditure in those supplied by a third, and so it would run through all the ramifications of society.[16]

The contraction of income also involved a lower level of savings. Thus in describing the contraction from 1818 to 1822 Joplin saw the process as

the result of the effort of nature to restore the savings of the nation to a level with the reduced demand for them.[17]

He pointed out that the contraction would end when, once more, savings or "economy" were in balance with expenditures:

The economy of the country had previously exceeded its expenditures; and when the productive classes had been half ruined, its expenditure began to exceed its economy, the circulation to re-extend itself in consequence and prices to rise again.[18]

Joplin also described the expansion process as it arose from an excess of lending over saving. The excess might arise from a decision by country banks to increase their note issues by lowering interest rates: this would result in enlarged expenditures and hence in higher income. Or it might arise, if country banks kept interest rates fixed, when an increase in "enterprise" or in the government's need for funds led to increased lending. Thus expansion was simply contraction in reverse. Joplin notes:

No harm, of course, results from an abundance of money. When it can be obtained at a cheap rate, it encourages speculation, speculation gives rise to expenditure, expenditure to income, and income spent reproduces income; and thus a general promotion of industry and a creation of prosperity and wealth take place throughout the land.[19]

The expansion is not without a limit: higher incomes involve higher levels of savings, and the process seems to end when savings rise to equality with expenditures.[20]

Although the above discussion suggests that Joplin was advancing a theory of income determination bearing a marked similarity to modern savings and investment theory, there are some passages that cannot be reconciled with this interpretation. Thus in the course of describing the process by which savings are reduced to the level of expenditures, he writes:

The savings, for which there did not exist the usual demand, would have to be lent at less interest, or be employed in trade, where capital was already as great as was necessary, and where, by competition, the scale of profits would be reduced. By this means, the commercial classes would be deprived of the power of saving, until the economy of the nation were reduced to a level with its expenditure.[21]

The entire problem of the passage of savings into expenditure here disappears, and, as a result, the rationale for arguing that an excess of savings over expenditure will lead to a general decline in incomes is destroyed. It is also worth noting that some degree of interest rate flexibility is introduced at a point where, according to the preceding argument, such flexibility is ruled out.

Waiving the difficulty just described, it does not take much interpretation to present Joplin's analysis in a form that may serve both to clarify his thought and to show its relation to modern theory. First, Joplin generally assumed that the income velocity of money was constant; this is implied by his treatment of hoarding and by his references to the determination of the demand for money. Second, he assumed that "expenditures," playing a part similar to that played by investment in modern theory, depended upon the rate of interest, but that "expenditures" demand may shift as the result of changes in "enterprise" or because of government needs. Third, he generally assumed that savings depended upon the level of income, increasing with higher income, and falling with lower income; he also argued that savings depended, in part, on interest rate. Thus Joplin seems to have formulated a theory of the demand to hold money, a theory of "expenditures" (investment), and a theory of savings (or consumption).

With these fundamental relations, he then proceeded to formulate two general cases. In the first case, money income was determined by the money supply, or more narrowly currency in circulation (excluding London), and the interest rate was adjusted so as to keep savings and expenditures equal at that income level. This implied that money saved and deposited in banks was lent by the banks and spent by the borrowers, so that savings in no way interfered with the maintenance of a constant level of total spending and income. In such a system, changes in savings and "expenditures" had no influence on the quantity of currency in circulation.

Figures 3 and 4 illustrate the main relations of this case in graphical form—a method of presentation that was of course alien to Joplin. In each figure, the northeast quadrant shows the relation between "expenditures," E, and the interest rate, i; the southeast quadrant, the relation between savings, S, and income, Y; and the southwest quadrant, the relation between the money supply, M, and income. The original equilibrium is indicated by

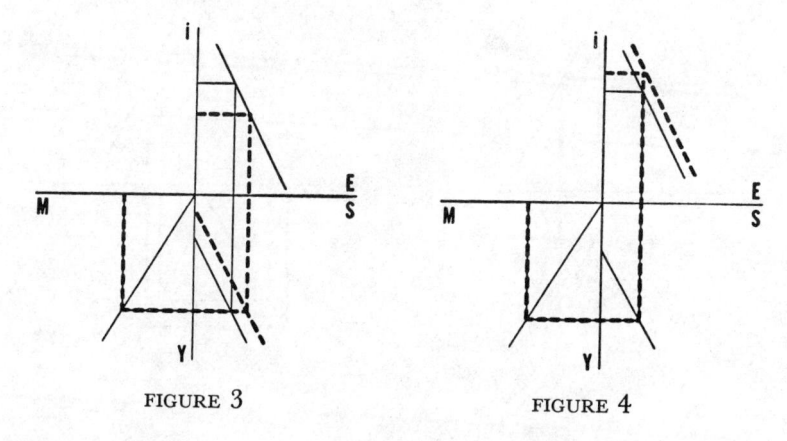

FIGURE 3

FIGURE 4

the solid-line schedules, verticals, and horizontals; the new situation, by the dashed-line verticals and horizontals, derived from the new dashed-line schedule and unchanged solid-line schedules.[22] Both figures presuppose that no changes occur in the money supply and that the market rate of interest adjusts to the natural, or true, rate. To simplify the treatment, shifts in the savings schedule which might result from changes in the market rate of interest are neglected.

In the general case illustrated by these two figures, changes in savings out of a given income can have no influence on income itself. Thus an increase in savings, represented in Figure 3 by a right shift in the savings schedule, leads to a lower interest rate and to a resulting increase in "expenditures" which just offsets the implied decrease in consumption. Income itself does not change.

Nor can changes in "enterprise" or in government needs have any effect on income. If increases in these variables—which would be represented by the right shift in the "expenditures" schedule in Figure 4—occur, the interest rate will rise. As a result "expenditures" are actually unchanged, so that income remains constant.

In the second general case, the one that Joplin considered more realistic, the interest rate is unresponsive to changes in savings

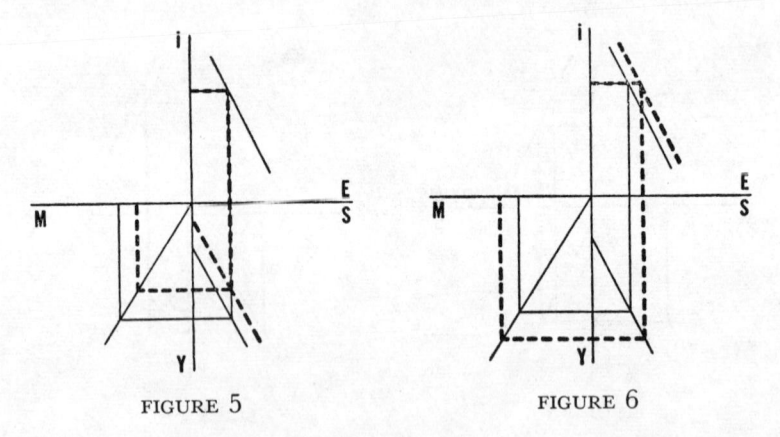

FIGURE 5

FIGURE 6

and "expenditures." If all of the relations are satisfied in the initial situation, then changes in savings or in "enterprise" will have quite different effects from those in the first general case. Thus a rise in savings out of a given income will involve an initial reduction in consumption, but will not result in a lower interest rate and an equal rise in "expenditures." At the fixed interest rate, savings is in excess of "expenditures," the money supply declines, and income falls. The contraction ends when income has fallen sufficiently to reduce savings to the old level, as illustrated in Figure 5. This case can also be formulated in terms of an inequality between the market and natural rates of interest: the original fall in savings implies a natural rate that is below the (fixed) market rate.

The response of such a system to changes in the "expenditures" schedule also differs from that described earlier. If this schedule shifts to the right, "expenditures" are in excess of savings at the old income level; or, in other words, the natural interest rate is above the market rate. This leads to expansion of income, which continues to rise until income has risen sufficiently to make savings equal to the higher level of "expenditures." Figure 6 illustrates this case.

All of the above analysis runs in terms of money, not "real," measures. However, for Joplin, changes in money spending and changes in money income involve movements in the same direction in real output, employment, and prices. Thus the analysis of money income determination is at least in part an analysis of the determination of real output and employment.

2. INTERNATIONAL GOLD FLOWS

Joplin saw another source of disturbance in the reaction of the banking system to international gold flows arising out of a favorable or unfavorable balance of payments.

The first point concerned the independence, at least for short periods, of country circulation and Bank of England circulation. When the balance of payments is favorable, the Bank's stock of gold is increased and its note issue extended. This is desirable since the favorable balance indicates that prices are too low, below the "national" level that would eliminate gold flows. But since prices and activity depend mainly upon country issues, and since country issues are more dependent on the relation between saving and expenditure than upon Bank of England decisions as to its note circulation, there is no reason for the correct adjustment to take place immediately. Increased Bank issues can have no immediate effect upon prices since,

until this additional issue shall have produced an increase of circulation by the Country Banks, which it may eventually do, it cannot affect prices generally, the increased issues of the bank [of England] being confined to the tills of the London bankers.[23]

The abundance of money in London will affect the rate of interest in the London market, for this is a flexible rate, but only gradually will this affect the country at large. Thus Joplin is not surprised to find that

the exchanges have so little effect upon our circulation, if the economy or expenditure of the Nation at the time should affect the currency in the opposite direction.[24]

At other times Joplin took a somewhat different approach. He then argued that economic disturbances may arise out of the violent fluctuations in money supply that result from gold flows. Thus in the conclusion of his book on *Currency Reform*, he writes that

derangements are originally produced by pressures or scarcities of money in the London Money Market, caused by the exchanges, or influx and reflux of the precious metals: the influx causing an abundance of money, which is lent at a low rate of interest and expended by the parties borrowing it; and the reflux causing a demand for the money thus spent, which can only be supplied by a suspension of the national industry, settling down into permanent distress.[25]

This conclusion was based on an analysis of the way in which gold flows affected London banks and country banks.

In London, bank deposits have all the functions that fall to notes in the country. Normally London banks keep on hand a 20 per cent reserve in Bank of England notes or in gold. This means that, acting as a group, London banks will expand deposits by £50,000 in response to a £10,000 gold inflow. Thus an inflow of gold leads to easier credit, lower interest rates, and increased expenditures on goods and labor. Loss of gold leads to the opposite course of events: loans and deposits are reduced fivefold (or more), expenditures fall off, and labor is thrown out of work. Eventually the entire country is affected since

the abundance or scarcity of capital in the Money Market of London, has always the effect, in time, of producing an abundance or scarcity of money in the country.[26]

In practice, Joplin admitted, the effect of gold flows upon economic activity was mitigated by the operations of the Bank of England. Both inflows and outflows of gold are "always, in a certain degree, neutralized by the operations of the Bank of England."[27] When gold is flowing out, the Bank may reissue the notes used to purchase the gold, by purchasing exchequer bills. In practice a drain of £8-10 million of gold has been associated with a £3-4 million contraction of Bank of England notes, so that the multiple contraction effects of gold drains are less violent.

The same analysis also applied to country banks. If a local citizen receives gold in return for exports, he receives country bank notes from the country banker, who, in turn, receives the gold. This gold becomes the basis for loans by the country banker in London. Saying nothing, in this case, about normal reserves, Joplin left the impression that the expansion of money was twofold. Again, however, neutralization by the Bank of England might mitigate the resulting changes in the money supply.[28]

Thus, although uncertain about short-period effects, Joplin had no doubt that over longer periods an influx of gold would raise incomes and an efflux reduce incomes. Interestingly, Joplin made almost no use of the savings-expenditure analysis in his treatment of gold flows. This neglect probably stemmed from the fact that, for such purposes, a modified quantity theory approach gave identical results, and was, at the same time, easier to understand.

3. APPLICATION

Joplin's books and pamphlets were published between 1823 and 1844. In the course of writing he commented on some of the swings in economic activity that are recognized today. But there are notable exceptions, in which Joplin either ignored or failed to recognize turning points, contractions, and expansions. A comparison between the reference dates of the National Bureau of Economic Research[29] and those which can be gleaned from Joplin's works shows some discrepancies:

JOPLIN'S TURNING POINTS		NBER TURNING POINTS	
Trough	*Peak*	*Trough*	*Peak*
	1814		1815
1816	1818-19	1816	1818
1822-23	1825	1819	1825
—	—	1826	1828
—	—	1829	1831
—	1836	1832	1836
1837	1838	1837	1839
1844(?)		1842	

The most noticeable disagreement appears in the period 1826-35, on which Joplin, for the most part, fails to comment. There is, moreover, a certain vagueness about the dating of the troughs that contrasts sharply with the exactness of his references to upper turning points.

In describing these fluctuations Joplin had provided himself with an analysis of the cumulative process that worked well enough once an upward or downward movement in activity had gotten underway. Turning points were the real problem. Like most writers of the period Joplin was more interested in upper turning points, in crises, than in the means by which contraction turned into expansion. For the most part the upper turning points, as he saw them, were the result of events that did not grow automatically out of the preceding expansion.

Joplin saw the war years as a period in which the rate of interest was kept high as the result of government borrowing to finance the war. The demands of the government for funds and the spending of these funds ensured that no difficulties involving an excess of savings over expenditure would arise. But, as a result,

a scale of profits and power of saving, from a corresponding anti-pressure of capital, must have become accommodated to this demand.[30]

By 1814, however, the special demand for savings arising out of the war diminished, and the increased supply of savings became excessive in relation to demand at the existing rate of interest.

The "economy of the nation," or money savings, outstripped the "expenditure" of the nation.[31] In part this was offset by the opening of new channels of trade, but nonetheless, country bank circulation contracted. Excessive savings, involving contraction of the note circulation, led to reduced business activity. In part the note contraction was the result of a loss of confidence in banks, with bank failures the result. Joplin denied that either harvests or the loss of gold had a bearing on the contraction of activity in 1814-16.[32]

He argued, however, that the upswing in 1816 was the result of a bad crop. Using a theory of harvest influences that he later abandoned, Joplin maintained that the poor crop led to increased country bank issues so that prices rose.

> This went on until 1818. Trade was brisk, profits good, and speculation considerable; by which latter, the circulation would be still further enlarged. The extra profits of 1817 and 1819 were, it is probable, sufficient to make up for the loss of capital by the failing crop of 1816; and in 1819 a pressure of capital, with its effects upon the currency, again commenced.[33]

The slump in 1819, like that in 1814-16, was essentially the result of excessive savings. The contraction was merely a continuation of the adjustment process after the war that had been temporarily interrupted in the expansion of 1816-18. Since country banks maintained fixed interest rates, the adjustment could only come about through the destruction of the "power" to save, that is through a reduction of incomes, particularly a reduction of profits which were the chief source of savings.[34] The balance of payments and the harvest situation were again unimportant for this downswing. Little stress was placed upon unemployment during this contraction.

Joplin was rather vague about the process leading to the subsequent expansion. He apparently dated the upturn from price series, for the dates implied are 1822-23, rather than 1819. The explanation suggests that this time the turn is the outcome of a self-correcting process:

The economy of the country had previously exceeded its expenditures; and when the productive classes had been half ruined, its expenditure began to exceed its economy, the circulation to re-extend itself in consequence and prices to rise again.[35]

Thus the lower turning point is dismissed in a sentence. The expansion itself received no better treatment, for his next comment relates to the crisis of 1825.

From 1825 on, Joplin's explanations ran largely in terms of international gold flows. Invariably crisis and contraction result from a loss of gold, and, usually, the reasons for the loss of gold remain in the background. Presumably, though seldom explicitly, expansion led to excessively high prices, excessive imports, and low exports, so that in this sense the expansion process brought about its own end. Thus, in writing about the 1836 crisis, Joplin quoted with approval a memorial sent from Birmingham, probably written by Thomas Attwood, to the government:

When the masses of the people were lately fully employed, and received in some degree reasonable wages, *with six days' work per week*, they required more sovereigns than the Bank of England could supply; the Bank of England became nearly exhausted, and was compelled, *in its own defense*, to adopt measures to force back the gold into its coffers out of foreign countries, and out of the uses of industry at home, in defiance of all the misery and distress which such a terrible operation produces in the country. It is only by placing the industrious workmen *upon reduced wages, and upon three days' work per week*, and by *crushing and ruining a large proportion of their employers*, that the Bank of England has now been enabled to force back gold into her coffers, and save herself from ruin by scattering ruin, misery, and desolation among thousands and hundreds of thousands of families.[36]

The idea of an external drain thus seems to have been in the back of Joplin's mind as a mechanism by which expansion turned into depression.

In describing the panic of 1825, Joplin placed the blame for the disaster upon the Bank of England. Admitting that the drain of gold required some contraction of credit, he argued that the

Bank had acted too suddenly. The contraction of Bank notes led to a scarcity of money in London. As a result banks failed, and panic spread to the rest of the country. The panic started on December 12 and became increasingly severe until, on the 14th, the Bank reversed its previous policy, increased its discounts, lent on government securities, and purchased government securities. This continued until the extraordinary demand for money had abated.

The delay of two days between the start of the panic and measures that were taken on the 14th is attributed to the erroneous theory under which the Bank was operating. The Bank accepted the common view that any relief through increased issues would lead to adverse exchanges and stoppage of gold payments. Joplin disagreed:

> The balance of payments can only be affected through the prices generally; by which the demand of foreigners for our commodities, and our demand for foreign commodities is altered. While, on the other hand, the price of commodities can only be affected through the Country Bank circulation, over which the Bank of England has a very imperfect, if any command.
>
> Now, the contraction of issues by the Bank had had no effect upon the issues of the Country Banks; and, therefore, had had no effect in altering the exchanges in our favour. Neither, on the other hand, would an increase of issues, made to relieve the then existing embarrassment, have the effect of turning the exchanges against us.[37]

Another error arose from the peculiar nature of the demand for money. Bank notes only affect prices if they are spent upon goods and labor. But during a panic the demand for money arises, not from a desire to spend, but from a desire to hold money. Once confidence is restored, such money can be withdrawn without difficulty. This distinction between money issued for hoarding and money issued for spending had been recognized, Joplin argued, by Henry Thornton and the Bullion Committee, but had been forgotten in 1825. A third difficulty in the way of immediate adoption of proper policy lay in the fact that lack of confidence was so widespread that money could not be issued upon bills of exchange but required lending upon government securities, which was not customary and was therefore resisted.

In vain does one search for any discussion of the period between 1825 and 1836. Aside from a passing reference to financial strain in 1831 and 1834, these years are a blank as far as Joplin is concerned.

The year 1836 is the occasion for another outburst of theorizing and description. Here again stress is laid upon the loss of gold, the pressure in the London money market, and resulting depression. By implication the drain of gold was a result of high prices induced by increased note issues, but Joplin was more concerned with the events that followed the gold drain:

In 1836, England was in a state of great prosperity. There was no undue speculation, but every trade was flourishing, and the labouring population of the country was well employed, and in comfortable circumstances, and the agriculture of the country was rapidly recovering from a state of previous depression, when a pressure suddenly occurred in the Money Market of London, which suspended the industry of our manufacturing districts: that is, Capital became suddenly scarce, the bankers were compelled to withdraw the accommodation that they had previously afforded to the mercantile and manufacturing classes, they were, in consequence, compelled to restrict or to suspend their operations, and such restriction or suspension threw a large portion of the industrial community out of employment, or produced a serious diminution of their wages.[38]

Joplin also noted that this distress was temporarily relieved in 1838 and then renewed in 1839 when the nation plunged into a period of distress. The end was visible, Joplin thought, in early 1844:

The recent rise in Railroad shares, and the number of Acts for new Railroads, which, it appears, have been applied for since the opening of Parliament, indicate the return to a better state of things.[39]

Joplin denied that "over-trading" was responsible for the crisis of the late 1830s.

In every extensive trade there is always an *oscillation* between over-trading and under-trading. It cannot be otherwise in the nature of things, when numerous persons in different parts of the country are engaged in the same business, whether of production, manufacture, or export, they can never know so much of each other's operations as to very nicely calculate what their own ought to be.[40]

There is nothing dishonest or evil about the "speculation" that must be involved in preparing goods for an imperfectly known market. Over-trading can only lead to general difficulty extending over the whole nation, if over-trading takes place in importing, and as a result the currency is contracted. If currency contraction were eliminated, over-trading would never produce the "violent shocks" that are at present experienced, "even if it should generally pervade all trades at the same time."[41] In theory then Joplin admitted that economic fluctuations might occur even without the aggravating effects due to currency contraction and expansion. In practice, however, the severity of the shocks could be attributed to the behavior of money, particularly its response to international gold flows.

Joplin explained the depression after 1838 in familiar terms. The contraction of the country circulation was the result of "the economy of the country having exceeded its expenditure."[42] The outcome is a grinding process by which through contraction of income, particularly profit incomes, "economy" is reduced to a level with "expenditure." But the question arises: why is the "economy" excessive? Joplin answered in terms of enterprise.

Now this economy may proceed, in a great degree, from the absence of enterprise, resulting from the want of confidence, which the late embarrassments have produced.[43]

In the passage that followed Joplin pointed out the advantages of both spending and "adventures," even when unsuccessful:

Individuals may save money by parsimony, but a Nation must save money by spending it. The savings of a Nation consist in its income not being solely spent in personal enjoyment, but in those enterprises and improvements by which the future amounts of its annual enjoyments are increased. And the progress and advancement of a Nation in wealth, much depends upon the quantity of its income which may be thus expended.... The luxury of adventure is not more injurious than the luxury of fox-hunting, they both contribute to maintain the national income, by consuming it, and in that respect they are not only not injurious but beneficial. The luxury of adventure, however, has frequently the advantage of leaving behind it experience, which could not otherwise be obtained, and which may point out other modes of proceeding by which any contemplated improvement may be realized. And if even several failures occur before the improvement is completed, and though when completed it may not return a remunerating profit to any party for the labor and capital expended upon it, yet, if it cheapens any commodity, or adds in any way to the public comfort, or convenience, it is a national advantage, and is a gain to the Nation, however much it may have been a loss to individuals.[44]

Such "adventures" were the natural outcome of abundant capital, but might be hindered by lack of confidence resulting from frequent panics of the type that England had experienced.

4. POLICY AND REFORM

Joplin was primarily concerned with structural changes in the English currency system that would eliminate or at least mitigate economic fluctuations. His suggestions for antidepression measures were scattered and uncoordinated.

Antidepression Policy. In general Joplin was sympathetic with any measures designed to increase the quantity of money during depression. He criticized the Bank of England for neutralizing the gold inflows of 1819-23 at a time when the depressed state of activity and the gold inflow itself indicated a need for easier credit and increased spending. Increased issues were also the solution for the depression that followed 1839:

We are suffering at present, not from any natural deficiency of capital, or any deficiency that would have been experienced had these pressures not occurred, but, from a deficiency which is susceptible of an immediate remedy.[45]

England was suffering from the high interest rates and the lack of confidence that made bankers keep larger reserves. Neither a good harvest nor increased savings were a solution. Only increased issues by the Bank of England could ease credit conditions and stimulate the enterprise that was necessary if activity was to revive.[46]

Recognition of the fact that the severity of contractions was related to gold drains led Joplin into an ambivalent attitude toward the maintenance of specie payments. In his earlier works on currency he had pointed out that a balance of international payments could be achieved either through price changes or through changes in exchange rates. Later he suggested that crop failures, with accompanying imports of corn and exports of gold, would have unfavorable effects upon the domestic economy. Such effects could be avoided by suspension of specie payments, a course which Joplin felt was desirable on such occasions. He praised the instructions issued by the lieutenant-governor of Canada, when Canadian banks faced a drain of gold:

"Pay in gold as long as you can, and when it is exhausted, we will authorize you to do what you would be compelled to do, namely, to stop payments until the gold returns."[47]

This led Joplin to remark that the experiment might establish a good principle, the avoidance of

a real panic by the artificial one, which the idea of losing our gold has hitherto had the effect of creating.[48]

Joplin's recommendations are generally similar to those of Attwood, though the language is milder. But these *ad hoc* measures seemed less important to him than the more fundamental changes which he proposed for the currency and banking system.

Currency Reform. Joplin's earliest proposal for reform of the currency appeared in 1823, and except for slight variations remained unchanged throughout his writings.

The plan was based on the proposition that stability of income and expenditure, and hence of prices and employment, depended upon the balance of savings and expenditure. Fluctuations arise from the fact that banks have the power of issuing and withdrawing notes at pleasure. As a result expenditures may first outrun savings, leading to rising prices and employment, or on other occasions, may fall below savings when banks fail to pass on deposited funds to borrowers (spenders). The quantity of notes in circulation should depend upon the balance of payments and should adjust so as to maintain a national level of prices that would eliminate gold flows.

In the existing currency system, prices may vary because of the autonomous acts of country bankers in varying their note issues, i.e., in varying the relationship between expenditure and savings. If for some reason issues expand and prices rise, the balance of payments becomes unfavorable. But the gold drain which takes place as a result, while it may affect the London market, only ultimately affects country bank issues and prices.

As a result of the independent decisions of the country banks, tied neither to the savings decisions of the public, nor to gold flows, the nation experienced fluctuations in prices and economic activity. Joplin sometimes visualized these fluctuations as rather mechanical alternations of high and low prices, the result of delays in reaction to gold flows:

Thus every low state of prices will be as necessarily followed by a state of prices proportionately high. Prices will rise as much above the national level as they were previously below it, until the metallic money which has come into the country has again disappeared, and the circulation of London is brought to its proper level.[49]

The adoption of a currency that cannot be issued at pleasure is the remedy for this state of affairs. This in turn necessitates that all savings deposited in banks be lent and expended, and that variations in the balance of payments resulting in international gold flows have an immediate and not a lagged effect upon the domestic money supply. More specifically, measures must be adopted to ensure (1) the adjustment of interest rates so that borrowing and expenditures will always equal savings and (2) a currency that varies with the stock of gold.[50]

The plan of 1823 envisaged the establishment in various parts of the country of public banks, that is, joint stock banks.[51] Each public bank would be assigned a certain amount of currency. The currency would be backed both by the capital of the bank and by a government guarantee. Each bank would pay the government a certain percentage for this currency, say 3 percent; in this way the government would receive the profits on the currency. Joplin wrote:

> The currency belongs to no individual, and is therefore the property of the state. Government ought to receive the profits derived from that which is so properly its own.[52]

The charge must be low enough to leave the banks a profit on lending.

Joplin considered the problems of adjustable interest rates solved at this point. While allowing the banks to lend or not to lend at their own discretion, he felt that the plan would ensure lending:

> If they paid interest to government for the circulation, they would not let it lie idle, for their own sakes. If they could not lend it at one rate of interest, they would take another, and would lend it upon any description of sufficient securities that [were] offered, rather than suffer the loss of keeping it unemployed.[53]

The problems involved in coordinating the domestic circulation with international gold flows were to be solved through the operations of a Board of Commissioners. All imported gold would be sold to the Commissioners at the mint price; perhaps, in order to ensure sale to the Commissioners, at a little above the mint price. The gold would be purchased with Bullion Receipts, which could be turned into currency at any bank at the discretion of the holder. The bank receiving such Bullion Receipts would be authorized to increase its circulation of currency by the same amount, the additional currency being obtained by presenting the Bullion Receipts to the Commissioners, who would then issue the additional currency to the bank. In this way the currency would vary with gold flows, and the additional currency would appear in the district of England responsible for the favorable balance of payments, instead of at first being confined to London.

Bullion Receipts would provide a convenient method by which unnatural price levels in any part of England would be eliminated. If prices in a particular district were too high, this would lead to an unfavorable balance of payments between this and other districts. The deficit would show up in a demand for London bills exceeding the supply of such bills. The local bank would purchase Bullion Receipts, contract its local circulation, the Bullion Receipts providing the means by which the excess demand for bills on London could be satisfied. Presented in London, or in any other district, the Bullion Receipts would expand currency to an equal extent. In this way prices within England would be kept at the national level, just as the use of Bullion Receipts for purchase and sale of gold for international purposes would keep England's prices at such a level as to achieve a balance of payments with the rest of the world.[54]

The Commissioners would have control of the public banks in the sense that they would determine the necessary capital and the boundaries within which each bank would operate. But as far as the currency was concerned, the Commissioners would have no discretion. On the principles outlined above, they would act mechanically, making no decisions:

Let the currency on these principles regulate itself, and the Commissioners have no power over it, without the authority of Parliament.[55]

Joplin's plan for currency reform was related to his proposals for banking reform. When he surveyed his writings in 1832, he emphasized that reform of the banking system through the establishment of joint stock banks was an essential prerequisite to currency reform.[56] There were two reasons why currency reform would be disastrous if the existing system of private banks were retained. First,

to talk only of taking the currency from them [the existing private banks], would be to lead to such a preparation for it, and a contraction of their issues, as might cause the most serious consequences.[57]

These consequences would include falling prices and unemployment. Second, since private banks were extremely susceptible to panics, the present system required a flexible currency to meet the demand for money in such periods; but with the plan for currency reform in operation, such emergency issues would be impossible, so that panics could easily lead to national disaster. The establishment of joint stock banks would avoid both these difficulties.[58] The complete reform of both banking and currency would, Joplin added, have three desirable effects:

1st. We should get rid of fluctuations in the prices of commodities generally, and agricultural produce in particular, from which such indescribable miseries have arisen. 2nd. We should get rid of those fluctuations in the money market of London, from which so much evil continually flows. 3d. We should, in a great degree, prevent those variations in the demand for our manufactures, which are the constant source of misery and distress.[59]

By 1839 Joplin was satisfied with the changes in the banking system: joint stock banks had become important,[60] and private banks seemed to be more secure. Joplin modified his original plan in two minor ways: all existing banks would be substituted for the public banks of the 1823 plan, and the Bank of England would perform the actual operations of purchasing and selling gold. As in the original plan, a Board of Commissioners would be established to settle and conduct the details of the plan.[61]

Some doubts, however, seem to have arisen in Joplin's mind on the issue of purely mechanical, nondiscretionary operation of the reformed currency system. In view of the deranged state of the currency, Joplin suggested that perhaps, for a time, the Commissioners should have discretionary power

to modify the effect of the influx and reflux of the precious metals upon the circulation, should it appear to them desirable, until the working of our system is brought into a more healthy condition.[62]

The other doubt involved a question that was not transitory but permanent: perhaps, said Joplin, the Commissioners should have the power to suspend cash payments, or to prevent the contraction of the currency, in case of a bad harvest and the resulting drain of gold. On neither the temporary nor the permanent cases where discretionary power was suggested did Joplin lay down any positive program.[63]

Two years later the plan appeared in identical form, but reading between the lines, it seemed that the desirability of a discretionary policy had increased. Joplin recognized that prices and employment might be affected by changes in bank deposits and bills of exchange as well as by changes in note circulation, and that gold flows with a fractional banking system were likely to lead to exaggerated effects upon these forms of money. Since deposit banking was mainly a London phenomenon, the currency plan would, by spreading the diminution in currency over the whole nation, reduce the effects of gold drains upon deposit creation. But discretionary action by the monetary authorities might still be necessary. Contraction of deposit money, Joplin noted, is

caused by a drain of money from the tills of the London bankers, by which bank money to the extent of five or ten times the amount of the drain is destroyed. The only remedy for this is to restore this money to the tills of the London bankers again.[64]

If these drains were serious, then the monetary authority would make extra issues to the banks, though only temporarily. To make such temporary issues intelligently, statistics should be collected every week or every month showing the amount of bank money in circulation. Any sudden deficiency would be a sign for increased issues by the Commissioners.

In 1844 Joplin published a pamphlet on *Currency Reform*, in which the weaknesses of the plan in so far as it failed to regulate or stabilize near-currency were considered. Joplin was doubtful about the propriety of regulating deposits:

Deposits are local money, created by the public rather than by the bankers, with which it is probable the Government will never be able to interfere, so far, at least, as to put down the system.[65]

Hopefully he suggested that elimination of the exaggerated effects of gold flows in the London market would mitigate the importance of fluctuations arising from this source. At the same time the possible effects of bills of exchange that circulate as money were recognized more explicitly than in his earlier works. He wrote that

> anything is money that the public will receive as such. And if, after the power of issuing notes were taken from the bankers, they were to agree amongst themselves to receive each others draughts upon London as cash, in all payments, they would immediately become the same description of money as bank notes. And whether any regulation to prevent such new creations of money would be desirable or not, must be for the government to determine.[66]

Thus the original plan of an automatic currency was modified by the suggestions that discretionary power might be granted to the Commissioners in a period of transition, in cases of crop failures, and possibly in cases where deposits fluctuate. But direct control of either deposits or bills of exchange used as money was an issue on which Joplin refused to take a stand, saying that this was "for the government to determine."

Two considerations appear to have been the main factors in Joplin's opposition to the Bank Act of 1844, despite its similarity to his original reform proposal. First, he felt that not enough attention had been paid to the catastrophic effects that would result when gold drains led to a fivefold, or more likely a seven to tenfold, contraction of London deposits. Second, he believed that the act was somewhat deflationary in effect, while, in contrast, the immediate need of the country was an enlarged circulation.[68]

5. CONCLUSION

The difficulties in associating Malthus with any of the modern saving and investment theories arose out of the fact that saving, from all explicit statements, implied spending. In the case of Joplin, however, savings and "expenditures" are usually distinguished, so that an increase in savings does not necessarily mean an equivalent increase in expenditures.

If the interest rate was flexible, then no difficulty arose, for then the deposited currency would be lent and the borrowers would spend. In this way the stream of income would be unaffected by changes in savings, or for that matter by changes in expenditures resulting from changes in enterprise or government demand for funds. The stability of total income could also be expressed in terms of equality between the natural rate of interest and the market rate. Moreover, since Joplin associated levels of money income, in short periods, with particular levels of output (and employment) and prices, the constancy of money income implied a constancy of real variables as well as monetary variables. There was, however, no reason for this state of affairs to be associated with any particular level of activity. In this flexible interest rate model, Joplin's argument was essentially classical, despite the parallel movements of prices and output, since savings and expenditures could have no effect upon money incomes.

Joplin's alternative and allegedly more realistic assumption of institutionally fixed interest rates yielded results that were Keynesian rather than classical. An increase in expenditures led, through a multiplier process, to a rise in income; moreover, a new and apparently stable level of income was reached when the induced rise in income generated a level of savings equal to "expenditures." The same process could also arise from a decline in savings, and by similar reasoning contractions in economic activity could be analyzed. In either expansion or contraction the conditions giving rise to the change in income could be expressed in terms of a relationship between the natural rate and the market rate of interest. It is worth noting that the quantity of money generally moved with changes in income in Joplin's analysis, since, except in periods of panic, the velocity of money was assumed to be roughly constant.

In the context of a closed economy, Joplin was strongly in favor of two policies, which were not altogether consistent. On the one hand he advocated a policy that would keep the natural rate equal to the market rate. This presupposed that stability of income and prices was desirable, increases in income and hence prices being associated with the injustices arising from the forced saving entailed by rising prices. On the other hand, the analysis apparently suggested that income might settle at a level that was unbearably low. Joplin therefore advocated increased note issues in times of depression, for as long as he considered prices and output as moving together, there was no obvious way, other than by an increase in money, by which activity could be raised. Increased money supply covered both the flexible interest rate case and the inflexible interest rate case. Only in the case of inflexible interest rates was it relevant to speak of the desirability of spending, either through reduced saving or increased enterprise, as a means of raising income, and this necessarily also involved an increase in money supply.

In discussing an open economy, Joplin paid little attention to the savings-expenditure analysis and confined his argument for the most part to a relatively simple quantity theory approach. With respect to policy he ran into the same difficulty as that which arose in the closed economy case. If fixed exchange rates were to be maintained, the domestic level of prices had to be held at a "national" level, with deviations from this level being corrected through inflows or outflows of gold. As a result, the domestic income level was tied to the balance of payments. From this point of view, Joplin was very much interested in making sure that the domestic money supply did react to gold flows: hence his criticism of country banks when they held interest rates stable. At the same time, he felt that if reactions to gold flows were too violent, as seemed likely under the deposit creation process in London, then a series of oscillations might be set up in which prices would fluctuate violently around the correct "national" level. Therefore, he proposed a currency reform that would make the domestic money supply fluctuate in the same way as would gold coin if gold coin were the only currency. Even then the difficulties created by deposits and other near-currencies led to some doubts, particularly in his later pamphlets, concerning the desirability of a completely nondiscretionary policy.

In other moods, Joplin was strongly inclined to sacrifice exchange rate stability to price level stability, or to the avoidance or correction of severe depressions; hence the proposals that, at their mildest, give to the monetary authorities considerable discretion in their response to gold flows, and, at their most extreme, advise suspension of specie payments. In this respect, as in respect to the closed economy case, Joplin was far less sure of his own position than was Attwood.

James Wilson

JAMES WILSON was a prominent and respected figure in Victorian England. In 1843 he founded the (London) *Economist* as a free trade journal and became its first editor, after a career as a hat manufacturer and as an unsuccessful speculator in indigo. Later he was elected to Parliament, where he remained from 1847 to 1859. He also served as Vice President of the Board of Trade, as Financial Secretary of the Treasury, and as Financial Member of the Council of India.[1]

Wilson formulated two theories concerning economic fluctuations. His earliest effort, examined in section one, sought to explain recurring fluctuations in the price of corn in terms of variations in supply, variations which were in turn a reaction to earlier prices and expectations of future prices. This doctrine was later extended to provide the nonmonetary theory of industrial fluctuations which is discussed in section two. Wilson adopted a somewhat different approach in explaining the railroad boom and crisis of the 1840s, and, in doing so, compared saving and capital formation, advancing an early version of the overinvestment theory of crises; this is considered in section three. In the later sections, Wilson's comments on the international aspects of fluctuations and his remedies, particularly for the depression after 1847, are examined.

1. FLUCTUATIONS IN THE PRICE OF CORN

Wilson's first book, *Influence of the Corn Laws as Affecting All Classes of the Community and Particularly the Landed Interests*, was designed as an attack on the corn laws. These laws were said to be responsible for the fluctuations in the price and production of corn, which were, in turn, the cause of misery and hardship.

Wilson presented a table which showed the annual price averages of wheat and the "quantity of home-grown wheat which has arrived at *Mark Lane*, the chief market in the kingdom."[2] This table led to a rejection of two theories designed to explain price fluctuations: the theory of demand fluctuations due to variations in the quantity of money, and the theory of supply fluctuations due to weather. The first theory was thrown out since in both 1825 and 1835 general prices were high, while the price of wheat was low; this indicated that the demand for wheat was only slightly affected by money variations, or (in modern terms) the demand for wheat was unresponsive to changes in money income. If fluctuations originated on the supply side, variations in weather might have been the explanation. But this theory was rejected on the ground that the "uniform cycles"[3] in prices and supply at Mark Lane suggested some regular cause that could not be attributed to the weather.

Wilson's own explanation turned out to be a sort of cobweb theory combined with an emphasis upon changes in the corn laws. Thus wheat prices fell in 1812 and the low prices of 1814-15 discouraged production. By 1817 reduced cultivation, aggravated by bad seasons, so reduced the supply of wheat that prices were again high. Such prices in themselves stimulated cultivation, but an added stimulus was provided by the corn law of 1815 which seemed to guarantee continued high prices. As a result

a larger breadth of land in cultivation was diverted to wheat, new lands were called into cultivation, moors and morasses were reclaimed, and capital was in every way most lavishly expended to secure the glittering advantages of such high prices.[4]

The supply of wheat increased in succeeding years so that prices fell, reaching a low in 1822.

Low prices led to a repetition of the previous cycle. Cultivation was restricted, inferior soils were abandoned, and the supply of wheat was reduced so that prices were again high in 1829.[5] This time the stimulus of high prices was reinforced by the corn law of 1828. While the 1815 law had permitted imports only when the price of wheat reached 80 shillings per quarter (eight bushels), the new law laid down a fluctuating scale of duties, the duty falling as the price of wheat rose. The law of 1828, like the law of 1815, gave rise to sanguine expectations with regard to wheat prices. Believing that the high prices of 1829 were permanent, farmers extended cultivation to such a degree that prices fell until 1835. Low prices gradually reduced cultivation so that prices rose after 1835; writing in 1838, Wilson noted that the price rise was still continuing.

Thus the process involved a constantly recurring cycle of production and prices, partly endogenous but partly the product of false expectations created by the corn laws. Cultivation, Wilson argued, was extended

by the farmer, stimulated by the natural hope of securing the high prices which the legislature in effect promised should be permanent; a natural competition arose for farms, and the rents accordingly advanced:—the farmer went on year after year improving and cultivating, but he found that year after year prices were lowering. With a view of paying his enhanced rent and his increased expenses, he pressed his production further and further to make up in quantity what he lost in price.[6]

Eventually the excessive supply broke the market, and huge losses deprived the farmer "of the means and inducement to go on producing at the same rate."[7] As a result production declined and "the old surplus stocks become gradually, and silently, and unwittingly consumed as the prices advance."[8] When prices again rose, the farmer

as recklessly as ever enters the arena of competition to produce: the high prices of two or three years furnishing him with more capital, he is again tempted to a similar operation as that which before brought him to the brink of ruin.[9]

Wilson also dealt, though somewhat sketchily, with the influence of this corn cycle upon manufacturing and mercantile prosperity. Since a low wheat price reduces landed incomes, expenditures on manufacturing and mercantile products decline, and these sectors suffer along with agriculture.[10] At the same time fluctuations lead to hardships for both agricultural and manufacturing labor. Reduced cultivation, the result of low wheat prices, leads to agricultural unemployment and hence to misery, arson, highway robbery, and increased poor rates; the latter in turn are a further charge upon rents and farm income. Moreover, manufacturing labor suffers when wheat prices are high and as a result there are "riotous and often murderous scenes."[11]

The remedy for corn law fluctuations Wilson found in the repeal of the corn laws, since the false expectations created by these laws were the basis for the fluctuations. The sliding scale principle of the 1828 law, while designed to maintain more stable prices, actually was ineffective:

If such a principle were applied to regulate the supply of an article which could be produced instantly, when required, and the production of which could, without loss, be instantly abandoned, then it might have a tendency to keep a very uniform supply and price: but when it is considered that the arrangements for the production of wheat require two or three years to come into full operation, either in extending or in diminishing the cultivation, it is quite clear that any influence . . . would not come into effect until the whole face of affairs might be changed.[12]

In contrast Wilson argued that under free trade

a confidence can be felt by the parties interested [in wheat] . . . that any slight fluctuations which momentary or temporary causes might create, would soon pass away, and thus confidence would become general to maintain an equality of price by fair and legitimate support, and speculative purchases by the regular dealers, of which, in the present uncertain state, the trade is entirely deprived.[13]

While advocating free trade in corn as a matter of principle, Wilson made two qualifications. Outright repeal would be dangerous when the supply of wheat was especially low, as in 1837 and 1838: repeal would then lead to expectations of huge imports and would discourage cultivation when production was most needed. The ideal time for repeal would be a period in which prices were falling and yet were near to their proper average. For the existing situation Wilson recommended the imposition of a flat 10 shilling duty with gradual reductions specified in advance.

The other qualification was more important. In combining an endogenous cycle with the corn law theory of price fluctuations, Wilson had proved a little too much: the analysis suggested that, even with repeal,

fluctuations to a small extent, comparatively, would ever continue to be experienced, as long as the landed interest remains in its present state of ignorance and uncertainty from time to time as to the real extent of cultivation which is going forward, of the comparative result of different harvests, or of the stocks remaining on hand.[14]

Such information, collected and published by a "Board of Internal Industry," would mitigate fluctuations even under the corn laws. Wilson went further and suggested that information of this type would also alleviate the "extreme changes—to depression and the reverse" to which products such as iron, lead, and coal had been subject.[15]

2. GENERAL FLUCTUATIONS

In 1840 Wilson extended his earlier analysis in *Fluctuations of Currency, Commerce, and Manufactures; Referable to the Corn Laws*. Wilson assumed that the corn cycle and its causes were an established fact and went on to explore the repercussions of agricultural cycles on other sectors of the economy. The theme and its importance were set forth in the opening sentence:

The frequent recurrence of periods of excitement and depression in the monetarial and commercial interest of the country, and the serious evils which have thereby been inflicted on all classes of society, have become matters of the gravest interest.[16]

To his earlier argument that the demand for corn or wheat was only slightly responsive to changes in money in circulation, Wilson now added the familiar assumption that the demand for wheat was not very responsive to changes in price, i.e., inelastic demand. As a result bad crops would lead to a rise in price that would more than offset the diminution in quantity sold, so that the total money expenditures upon wheat would increase.[17]

Wilson set up a hypothetical equilibrium situation in order to show how a reduced supply of wheat would affect the economy in general. Suppose, he said,

there was a given distribution of the entire capital of the country; so much in mercantile operations, so much in manufacturing establishments—so much in government securities—so much in agricultural property and industry, etc., etc., and, for the sake of illustration, let us suppose that the capital thus sunk in these various ways bore the exactly proper proportion to each other to supply the wants of the community.[18]

What, asked Wilson, would be the results if a shortage of wheat occurred leading to high prices and increased aggregate expenditures upon wheat?

Such a change in expenditures would work a hardship on mercantile and manufacturing interests in two ways: first, through reduced demand, and second, through increased costs of borrowing. Apparently using the terms "circulation" and "money" where greater clarity would have required some such term as "loanable funds," Wilson expressed his conclusion as follows:

The increased absorption of national income in agricultural produce has two obvious tendencies; first, to reduce the demand for the produce of all other capital and industry, and consequently the profits; and, secondly, to diminish the amount of the circulation, or money, by increasing the amount of fixed capital stock, and thus to cause a rise in the rate of interest at the moment of the greatest depression of commerce.[19]

These two effects, both tending to reduce profits in the nonagricultural sector of the economy, are the crucial points in Wilson's exposition, and yet the most obscure.

The first tendency apparently presupposed, not only an inelastic demand for corn, but also a constant level of aggregate money expenditures. From these assumptions it followed that an increase in outlays on corn, resulting from a short supply, would be accompanied by reduced expenditures upon manufacturing products. Wilson then deduced a decline in manufacturing production and employment. It should be noticed that the constancy of aggregate money expenditures played an important role in the argument, though the assumption is implicit; if a rise in such expenditures were coincident with a rise in corn prices, expenditures on manufactures might be stable or increase so that depression in the nonagricultural sector would then be avoided.

While the first tendency supposedly showed that the low level of wheat output, through its effect upon the demand for manufactured commodities, tended to reduce manufacturing activity, the second tendency purported to show that a low level of corn output raised the interest rate and thereby had adverse effects upon manufacturing from the cost side. The reasoning is difficult to reconstruct, but is connected with the rise in the "amount of the fixed capital stock,"[20] and apparently with increased investment in agriculture resulting from the higher price of wheat.[21] The following passage may be relevant:

The floating capital, or currency, of the whole country must, under such circumstances [a fall in corn production], have very materially diminished; or in other words, at this period our means must have become very much contracted for commercial enterprise.[22]

But it is hard to tell whether this passage shows a connection by way of the interest rate between the low level of wheat output and reduced manufacturing activity, or whether it merely states the conclusions that result from the operation of both tendencies.

Wilson seems, however, to be arguing that the increased demand for loanable funds ("floating capital"), arising from the agricultural sector, tends to reduce the supply of such funds left over for "commercial enterprise," so that, as a result, the interest rate rises and manufacturing activity is restricted. He may also be arguing that real national output is necessarily reduced when wheat output is reduced, so that the total supply of loanable funds declines.

Wilson pointed out that the higher rate of interest and the lower profits in manufacturing would tend to reduce the value of fixed capital goods that were used only in this sector. In time lower profits would lead to the "abstraction" of some capital from manufacturing.

> But such abstraction is only practicable to a certain extent, while in many of the chief objects of investment it is quite impracticable; for example, in the capital represented by manufactories, machines, mines, ships, etc.[23]

High profits in agriculture and low profits in manufacturing had adverse effects on the laboring classes for a similar reason: immobility. Manufacturing labor is not drawn into agriculture, even when depression and unemployment occur in manufacturing. The fact that 61 per cent of the laboring families in England were, in 1831, engaged in manufacturing, and only 31 per cent in agriculture, explained why depression in manufacturing had such serious effects on the condition of the laboring classes, while depression in agriculture was of lesser importance. Hence the coincidence of crime, bloodshed, and rioting with high wheat prices and manufacturing depression.[24]

Such a combination of agricultural prosperity and manufacturing depression characterized the years 1828-31, but increased cultivation also led to increased supplies of wheat and lower prices in 1832. As a result expenditures upon wheat were reduced:

> Such an amount of national income . . . becoming available for all other purposes, could not fail to give a fuller currency, part of which

would remain available as currency [for lending?], and part of which would be absorbed in the products of other industrial pursuits, which, in their turn, would give a stimulus to industry and credit, and ultimately to a further extension of the currency.[25]

Thus the two factors that operated in 1829 to create depression in manufacturing and mercantile pursuits now operated in reverse: the demand for manufacturing produce increased and, at the same time, interest rates dropped since loanable funds were more plentiful.

Wilson contrasted the effects of high and low wheat prices:

When capital is flowing into the agricultural interest in greater than average proportion, it is owing to great scarcity, and an absorption immediately takes place to stimulate a larger production, and the currency is thereby contracted: whereas, when capital is again flowing back by a redundant supply of that article [wheat], and not by a too limited supply of the results of other industrial pursuits: they only ultimately become stimulated by the expanded currency which is thus effected, and consequent greater ability to consume their products on the part of the community; but the first influence is to enlarge the currency or available capital of the country.[26]

An abundant "currency" acted slowly in stimulating manufacturing activity. In 1833, for instance, a further reduction of expenditures upon wheat took place, and

towards the close of that year we consequently find that the currency became very full—money very abundant; for as yet commerce had not shown sufficient symptoms of recovery to induce an extension of operations equal to the disengaged capital.[27]

In time activity did respond so that the period from 1832 to mid-1836 was marked by speculations of all types. Some, such as the establishment of joint stock banks, served to increase the currency even more. Not only did investment take place in usual channels, but new internal improvements, particularly railroads, were undertaken, and speculators in foreign countries were led into the "wildest undertakings" under the stimulus of the low interest rate.[28]

Along with the high profits, resulting from great demand and low interest rates, went the prosperity of the laboring classes. The great mass of consumers represented by the laboring class actually received higher wages as a result of the demand for labor resulting from the internal improvements. Unemployment in agriculture was reduced by a movement of agricultural labor into manufacturing. As a result the period of expansion and manufacturing prosperity meant "full employment, high wages, and a low price of provisions."[29]

The limit to expansion, the end of prosperity in manufacturing, might come about in one of two ways, both of which were illustrated in the 1830s. The first break occurred in 1836 and had no immediate connection with the corn cycle. The second, and more serious, break came in 1838 as a result of diminished corn production.

The derangement of 1836 was marked by an unfavorable turn in the foreign exchanges, a loss of bullion, and a growing scarcity of money; it was a "mere reaction" to the previous abundance of money. Its effects were mainly in the monetary sector, among those who had engaged in extensive speculations in foreign loans and domestic improvements. The shortage of "money," loanable funds, was, in part at least, the result of these speculations. Wilson described the crisis in terms that were later elaborated in his discussion of the railroad boom of 1845:

At this period it was evident that a great part of the rapidly accumulating surplus capital of the few previous years had been absorbed by the extension of private enterprise, by the huge number of public undertakings at home, and by investments in foreign securities; and that thus the actual available currency of the country had become much contracted.[30]

By the autumn of 1837 confidence was restored; there was a "sufficient abundance of money" and neither speculation nor depression. This healthy condition continued until the fall of 1838.

At that time the effects of the corn cycle created a serious collapse in nonagricultural activity. A long period of low prices had reduced cultivation, finally affecting the supply coming to the market. The rise in corn prices was precipitous in 1838. The effects on nonagricultural prosperity were those Wilson had already described: demand for manufactures fell off and the rate of interest rose.

By the spring of 1839 the failure of demand became apparent: the anticipations of dealers were disappointed. As a result, dealers did not replenish

> stock to the ordinary extent, the deficiency falls back upon the manufacturer, and ultimately upon the merchant, for the raw material, and the suffering artisan for his labour.[31]

> Mills were, therefore, by common consent, put on short work, and production checked in every possible way: but there arose two new evils; it soon became apparent, first, that in proportion as production is checked, its cost is enhanced in all mechanical operations by a given amount of capital invested with its whole management, producing so much less than before; and, second, that a number of working men must be thrown either altogether or partially out of employment, and the whole ability of consumption being thus lessened, was soon felt to re-act again on the demand for production.[32]

Depression spread and became general in the nonagricultural sector.

Wilson emphasized the interdependence of the economy and that the initial contraction had repercussions that worked into a cumulative contraction of incomes, production, and prices. Later, writing in the preliminary number of the *Economist* in 1843, he went one step further and suggested that even the agricultural prosperity that was the cause of manufacturing depression would ultimately be destroyed by this cumulative process. The bad harvest of 1838 led, he argued, first to industrial depression and then to agricultural depression through "increased charges, diminished demand, and lower prices."[33] But in 1840 he confined the cumulative contraction to the industrial sphere of the economy.

Wilson felt that this theory, though applied particularly to 1829-39, would also account for earlier fluctuations in economic activity. Thus the contraction of 1817-20 was attributed to the high price of corn and the absorption of the currency into agriculture. With increased supplies of corn and low prices in the period 1821-25, expenditures on food were reduced. The result was

> so great an accumulation of wealth, such an expansion of the currency, such a depreciation of the value of money [interest rate?] and so much difficulty of finding profitable employment for it, that a spirit of daring enterprise and speculation was engendered.[34]

Such speculations occurred in mines both at home and abroad, and in loans to foreign governments as well as to industry. This period, like the period 1832-36, was marked by investment in new productive facilities, in industry, and in transportation; in this case, too, investment was undertaken to an extent that was excessive in relation to the real wealth of the country. The outcome was the crisis of 1825 which, like that of 1836, was not the result of a poor harvest. The harvest-induced contraction arose later, in 1828, and thus corresponded to the similar contraction that started in 1838.

3. RAILROAD OVERINVESTMENT

In 1845 Wilson wrote the first of a series of articles in the *Economist* which were collected in 1847 under the title *Capital, Currency, and Banking*.[35] The first article estimated annual savings and argued that the planned expenditures on railroad construction were excessive in relation to savings. Later, in 1847, when the crisis of that period was an acknowledged fact, Wilson returned again to the essay of 1845 and sought to clarify his terminology while demonstrating that the crisis was the direct result of excessive investment in railroads.

The more theoretical of the essays written in 1847 are really a prerequisite to an understanding of the 1845 article, and may therefore be treated first. Wilson's terminology and analysis were traditional, being for the most part merely a restatement of Ricardo's chapter "On Machinery."[36] Capital is defined as the stock of produce existing at a point of time which will facilitate future production.[37] The annual excess of production over consumption is "saving" or "accumulation"; this is the annual increment to "capital."[38] "Floating capital" is that part of capital which can be consumed (eaten, for example), and so can be used to pay labor. "Fixed capital" is that portion of capital that cannot be so used.[39]

Capitalists, Wilson argued, have a certain stock of floating capital available at a point in time. If these goods are used during the year to hire labor which produces similar goods, then the stock of floating capital is unimpaired and usually augmented. In the following year the same (or a greater) quantity of floating capital is therefore available for payment of wages. If, on the other hand, the floating capital available at the beginning of the first year is used to hire labor which produces fixed capital, then the stock of floating capital in the second year may be diminished and wages and consumption may not remain as high in the second year as in the first.[40]

However, to the extent to which the community is willing to abstain from consumption, or save, it is possible to devote floating capital and the labor that it will purchase to the production of fixed capital goods. But even then, if floating capital is turned into fixed capital at an annual rate that is greater than the annual rate of saving, there must be a reduction in available floating capital, and so in consumption goods available; such a reduction in floating capital will cause hardship.

It is . . . quite clear that no community can, without the greatest inconvenience and derangement, increase its fixed capital faster than it is able to spare labour from the production of those commodities on which the community relies for its daily subsistence. Under all circumstances it can only be the amount of labour which the savings of the country can command and sustain, that can be applied to the increase of its fixed capital.[41]

Wilson's attempt to deal with the same situation in terms of money flows is less successful. Money is only a device for making exchanges more easily.[42] Thus the deposit of money is only a transfer of command over commodities, and when the banker lends, a second transfer of this command takes place. Wilson believed that money and banks were acted upon by real causes, rather than the other way round.[43]

The interest rate can apparently be viewed either as the outcome of the demand and supply of floating capital in real terms, or as the outcome of the demand and supply of floating capital expressed in money terms. If money, and so floating capital (real goods), is used to produce fixed capital in excess of saving, the money passes into the hands of nonsavers, and no new floating capital is produced. The capitalist only gets back interest on his investment, so that the flow of money savings offered for loan is reduced;[44] if the demand remains unchanged, the interest rate must rise. This merely reflects the underlying fact that the quantity of floating capital in real terms has been reduced.

During the period in which floating capital is being converted into fixed capital, there will be a "momentary appearance of great prosperity."

the production of commodities required for daily use being unequal to the consumption, they would continue to rise in price.[45]

Ultimately a reaction will take place, harmful to the nation,

and especially to those of the labouring classes who will have been exhausting the food on which their future employment depended without producing more. The ultimate effect of such a disturbance or misdirection of the *floating* capital of the country must be to create a great scarcity of it, which will be evinced by the high rate of interest, and ultimately a great diminution in the demand for labour, in consequence of the exhaustion of the fund on which it depends for continuous support.[46]

This theory was implicit in the article that Wilson wrote, in 1845, on the railroad boom. Wilson asked the question: was investment in railroads outrunning the savings available for that purpose? An answer required a quantitative estimate of both the magnitudes involved. Plans for railroad construction called for an expenditure of £74 million. Past experience suggested that it would take fifteen years to complete these projects, but other factors indicated that construction would take place more rapidly. Thus the railroads themselves had increased annual production, thereby increasing the possibility of saving. Initially the railroads had had to struggle against prejudice, but their value to the nation and their profitability had been proved; as a result there was greater willingness to venture capital in railroad construction. Since there were fewer impediments to construction, Wilson concluded that annual expenditures were likely to run £15 million per year on the average for the next four years, with larger expenditures at first and smaller outlays later on.[47]

Wilson then estimated annual savings at £60 million. In effect this part of annual production could be spared from current consumption; any greater sum would lead to an (involuntary) restriction of consumption. Despite the fact that past savings, and presumably future savings, were far in excess of the estimated expenditures on railroads, Wilson was doubtful about the outcome:

Even admitting [that] the annual accumulation of the country be equal to *sixty* or *seventy* millions sterling, when it is considered that they are divided over a population of more than twenty-seven millions of people, that the bulk of accumulators have purposes of their own to which they can more profitably than in any other way apply their savings, it is a most exaggerated view to suppose that such accumulations are wholly, or even in a great part, applicable to the construction of railways or any other public work.[48]

If investment in railroads did prove to be excessive, the immediate results would be similar to those experienced in the years 1802-16. That period of government expenditure had seen the diversion of capital, to uses unproductive of floating capital, and, as a result, a rise in the rate of interest, an appearance of prosperity, and eventually a severe reaction. Excessive railroad construction has the same effect. More money is paid out to workers and as a result expenditures on consumption goods increase. At the same time production of consumption goods is reduced since resources are diverted to railroad construction. Prices of consumption goods therefore rise.[49] Ultimately, of course, the effects of railroad construction would be different from the effect of government war expenditures, since railroads add to national wealth, but this was not Wilson's immediate concern.

The crisis of 1847 enabled Wilson to point with pride to the 1845 article. In 1845, he wrote,

> we endeavoured to show that any attempt to make railways to an extraordinary extent must . . . have the tendency of leading to the absorption of capital in other ways more rapidly than usual, by stimulating the demand for all commodities of general consumption . . . . More commodities must be supplied—more must be imported and manufactured—more ships and more factories would be required to effect those objects, and more dwellings, and in new localities, would be necessary for the accommodation of those whose means were thus added to by an extraordinary expenditure; and, moreover, more iron-works must be erected—more means used to supply timber—all involving an investment of fixed capital to facilitate increased production.[50]

If an unusual expenditure takes place on railroads, stockholders in effect transfer their command over goods to railroad companies and, as a result, "a new consumption . . . is called suddenly into existence."[51] This reduces the capital available for other uses and so raises the rate of interest. Higher wages are paid, labor is diverted to railroad construction, and production of other goods is restricted.[52] Prices rise.

The crisis that results from this process is described in terms of a struggle between the railroad construction companies and the consumption goods industries.

> The first operation . . . would be to withdraw capital from other sources, and so materially to increase the rate of interest, until those other sources held out a stronger inducement than railways or the railway companies could offer . . . . The next effect would be, by rendering commodities of consumption scarce, to increase their demand, and to afford, thus, a stronger inducement to continue capital in its existing channel, than to divert it into a new one. . . . The next operation would be a struggle between various interests for the use of capital;

and the last and inevitable result of that struggle, it was plain, would be that a very great majority of the railway schemes must be abandoned or indefinitely postponed.[53]

The visible result of railroad overinvestment Wilson found in the adverse foreign exchange situation, in the high interest rates, and in the small stocks of consumable goods. The poor harvest was only an aggravating factor that accentuated the international difficulties.

Wilson did not predict a violent crisis of credit, or a violent drop in prices. High demand, the low level of debt, and the low stocks of goods, combined with an absence of speculation in commodities, would prevent any spectacular events. But the impossibility of continuing railroad construction[54] and other projects led to the prediction that a severe depression of uncertain duration would ensue.

The great amount of employment which has been promoted during the last two years, by the expenditure of the *capital* in place of the *income* of the country, has led to a greatly increased demand, especially for those articles which constitute the chief consumption of the working classes. This increased demand has necessarily led to the adoption of means and facilities for supplying it. The impossibility of obtaining money to continue these undertakings . . . must end in a general suspension of the works, such as took place in 1839-1842. A suspension of these works, which have so mainly contributed to the employment of the working classes, directly or indirectly, during the last six months particularly, while business in the manufacturing districts otherwise has been dull, will deprive great numbers, throughout the whole country, of employment, and which will be followed by a considerable reduction in the demand for all articles of general consumption.[55]

These difficulties arose fundamentally from a shortage of consumable goods and the resulting high rate of interest.

4. INTERNATIONAL ASPECTS

In Wilson's work we may distinguish several types of crisis: one based on bad harvests; a second based on overinvestment in railroads; and, less elaborately, a third, connected with commodity speculation and, in part, overinvestment.[56] None of these crises is dependent on the workings of the gold standard: a crisis is never simply the result of high prices, a deficit in the balance of payments, and an outflow of gold. In each instance the international effects merely reinforce the underlying difficulties which would exist even in a closed economy. Lower turning points, although not discussed in as much detail, appear to be similar in that gold flows play a negligible role.

In the *Fluctuations* Wilson repeatedly drew attention to the fact that the shortage of wheat resulting from years of low prices and reduced cultivation would in itself create difficulties for manufacturing and mercantile interests even aside from the international problems arising from the necessity of wheat imports paid for with bullion. Speaking of the "absorption of capital" into agriculture, Wilson wrote:

This cause, sufficient as it may appear to account for any derangement in the currency—the abstraction of 300,000 £ weekly from the channels in which, by all the existing arrangements of society and commerce, it was at this moment finding useful and convenient employment—was accompanied by the usual attendants on high prices, a large foreign importation.[57]

But the importation of wheat and the resulting outflow of gold are merely aggravating factors, as was revealed most strikingly in Wilson's discussion of an international cycle congruent with the English cycle.

Wilson argued that periods of high wheat prices in England had the same effect upon the economies of France, Denmark, and the Germanies as upon the internal English economy. Agricultural profits rose and money was diverted from purchase of manufacturing and mercantile products to the purchase of wheat; in France, for example, this meant manufacturing depression, and would account for political disturbances such as the Revolution of 1830.[58] Cycles of agriculture and cycles of manufacturing on the Continent were therefore similar in timing to the cycles in England. Yet of necessity large English imports in times of wheat shortage meant large Continental exports; so that England's loss of bullion was a gain to the Continent. The secondary importance of wheat imports and gold flows in creating turning points was thus clearly revealed.

For England, however, the loss of gold induced by wheat imports was an aggravating factor. Bullion

must always be abstracted in great measure, from that portion of the capital of the country constituting the currency, or convenient medium of exchange; or from the portion which constitutes the stock of what is termed the money market.[59]

At the same time, since the Bank of England acts to reduce its circulation in the same proportion as bullion is reduced, a further factor operates to lower the prices of manufactured articles.[60]

The treatment of the crises of 1825 and 1836,[61] while not very detailed, indicates that, as in the case of crises based on bad harvests, gold drains were not essential. Such drains did, however, aggravate the severity of these difficulties.[62]

The crisis of 1847 was in actual fact, Wilson thought, a mixed case involving a shortage in consumable goods as the result both of overinvestment in railroads and of the crop failure of 1845. But the railroad investment process alone would have been sufficient to create difficulties. From the first Wilson saw the railroad boom as an international phenomenon.[63] And the crisis, though it involved an outflow of gold, was international. Thus in discussing the possibility of increased exports to offset the imports of food and raw materials, Wilson wrote that, in addition to the high prices and low stocks of English goods, there was a further difficulty:

The depressed state in which, from exactly similar causes, our largest customers, consisting of the most populous countries in the west of Europe, France, Germany, Holland, Belgium, Spain, and Portugal, as well as the countries to the south of Europe bordering on the Mediterranean, except Russia [find themselves], will also materially tend to lessen our exports.[64]

5. POLICY

In 1840 Wilson had emphasized that the corn laws were the major cause of fluctuations and that the remedy was to be found in repeal.[65] But in 1846 the corn laws had been repealed and yet fluctuations continued. The warning against overinvestment in railroads had gone unheeded and the outlook in 1847 was depressing. The railroad boom, although exhausted, had reduced the stocks of goods that could be used for export, the bad harvest had impaired the food supply necessary for maintaining the population, and gold that could be used to finance imports of food was rapidly disappearing.

We look forward to the future condition of the commerce of the country, and that of the labouring population with much greater alarm than to the mere money market; for past experience has proved that the condition of capitalists may be rendered easy, and the exchanges corrected, while the trade of the country continues to suffer severely for a long period afterwards.[66]

Some remedy, at least for the immediate situation, was required.

Wilson dismissed the remedy of increased currency. There was no lack of currency, but there was a lack of capital (commodities). No action which did not increase the supply of commodities would be of any use.

Seeking a way in which to obtain more capital with which to support laborers and keep industry active, Wilson turned to that part of national wealth which was in the form of gold coin. This part of wealth was an expense that was desirable simply because a circulating medium facilitated trade. But if some other medium could be substituted, then the unproductive gold could be shipped abroad in exchange for badly needed commodities. Wilson proposed the substitution of £1 notes issued by the Bank of England or some other body for the gold coinage. In this way probably £20 millions of bullion could be obtained and could be shipped abroad as needs required while still maintaining convertibility.

Wilson argued that such a measure would not be inflationary, that increased imports would actually reduce prices. At the same time he saw no danger to convertibility in the scheme. Essentially the measure was the logical extension of the common proposal of the period that the bullion stock be used as a buffer that would permit England to ride out a temporary international deficit without recourse to the restriction of incomes and real consumption domestically.

6. CONCLUSION

Wilson's writings foreshadow several theories that reached greater prominence in later economic thought. In his first book, which was not concerned with general fluctuations, but rather with a commodity cycle in corn, the similarity between his reasoning and that used by writers on the cobweb theorem is quite striking. The modern argument, as presented for instance in Ezekiel's article,[67] turns upon the assumption that supply in any period depends upon price in earlier periods. Wilson was very explicit about the dependence of supply upon past prices: he pointed out that the whole argument rested upon the fact that output could not be adjusted quickly, the adjustment actually taking two or three years. Both writers assume that reality could be approximately represented by the assumption that price is determined by current output, though both mention qualifications. Both note that the individual producer acts as if price were given regardless of individual output.

The chief differences turn on the elaborate discussion of divergent, convergent, and continuous cases in the modern theory and upon the greater emphasis that Wilson placed upon exogenous factors. The role of exogenous factors, the corn laws, were after all the chief reason why his first book had been written. Yet, when forced by the logic of the argument to consider what would happen in the absence of the corn laws, Wilson was inclined to predict that there would still be a mild, apparently continuous, oscillation.

Later parallels to Wilson's theory of the relationship between harvests and industrial activity are not wanting.[68] W. S. Jevons, while he did not follow Wilson in explaining why harvest fluctuations took place, used almost exactly the same argument that had been employed in showing the connection between a poor harvest and industrial depression. Thus he referred favorably to Wilson's second book and then wrote:

The idea may have been a novel one forty years ago; but it is now well known to manufacturers that an active demand for their produce is to be expected only when food is cheap. By far the largest part of the population have but a small margin of income remaining when their necessary expenditure on food has been provided for. Thus arises the singular connection between the prosperity of Lancashire and the price of rice in India.[69]

The belief in some kind of connection of this sort has been quite persistent since Jevons' day, though less and less stress has been put on harvests as an explanation for changes in business activity. In this connection it is interesting to note that even in Wilson's work upper turning points need not arise exclusively from the effects of a poor harvest. Thus combined with the harvest theory, arguments based on speculation and overinvestment were applied to 1825 and 1836. The harvest theory undoubtedly had greater validity when Wilson wrote than today.[70]

Much more acceptable in recent times is the theory advanced in connection with the railroad boom of the 1840s. Before Wilson, writers had tended to stress aggregate spending, or, when references were made to investment in connection with fluctuations, the emphasis was upon inventory investment. Wilson, however, impressed by the influence of railroad construction, emphasized the role of fixed capital formation in the cycle, thereby applying the earlier speculations of Barton and Ricardo to a new problem.

Wilson was not altogether successful in making his assumptions clear. Thus the interesting discussion of saving and investment suggests in rudimentary form a concern with the "inflationary gap" and seems to imply full employment.[71] But Wilson also indicated that railroad investment had been the basis of an expansion of employment and production as well as of price increases.

The cumulative process of expansion was not original to Wilson: recognition of interactions between income and expenditures was far older. The change lay mainly in the use of fairly clear distinctions between consumption and investment. Railroad investment led to increased incomes, which resulted in increased consumption expenditures. These, in turn, gave rise to additional investment. Thus, as the result of the initial railroad outlays, a general expansion took place, accompanied by increases in both prices and employment. It is interesting to note that a part of the labor force for this expansion was recruited from the agricultural sector.

Crisis arose when, with rising demand for consumer goods, a struggle for resources took place between the new industries and the old industries, essentially between the demand for resources stemming directly from railroad investment, and the demand for resources originating in the attempt of the consumers goods industries to meet higher consumer demand. The conflict is marked by higher interest rates, which force the suspension of railroad projects. Suspension of these investment projects led to a contraction of incomes and to depression. The theory bears a striking resemblance to that advanced in Hayek's *Prices and Production*, a fact of which Hayek was aware.[72] There is no discussion of the mechanism by which contraction will end.

One further point must be made. The theory of crisis arising from reduced production of wheat and the theory of crisis arising from overinvestment have much in common. Not only did Wilson, in different circumstances, maintain the validity of both theories, but Jevons also mentioned overinvestment as well as harvest failure as a cause of crisis.[73] The following tabulation compares in oversimplified form the mechanisms that operate in the two theories, using the "second tendency" or interest rate version

HARVEST THEORY	OVERINVESTMENT THEORY
Reduced corn output	Increased railroad investment
Demand for corn greater than supply	Demand for consumers goods greater than supply
Rise in price of corn	Rise in prices of consumers goods
Rise in investment in agriculture	Rise in investment in consumers goods industry
Rise in interest rates	Rise in interest rates
Fall in investment in industry	Fall in investment in railroads
Depression in the industrial sector	Depression in the whole economy

of the harvest theory and contrasting it with the overinvestment theory. The chief difference is in the final item, where the harvest theory leads only to industrial depression while the overinvestment theory leads to depression in both railroad construction and consumers goods industries. This difference suggests why, sometime after his book on the harvest theory, Wilson indicated that depression in the industrial sector might react back on agriculture and lead to general depression. It also suggests, to look at the whole question from another point of view, one of the chief problems in the overinvestment theory: the need for a convincing exposition of the reasons why a fall in railroad investment, resulting from heavy consumer demand, must lead to depression in the consumers goods industry, and hence to general depression.

Thomas Tooke

THE FAME of Thomas Tooke, like that of Malthus and Mill, and unlike that of Attwood, Joplin, and Wilson, has not diminished with the passing of time.[1] His great work, the *History of Prices*,[2] remains a monument to his energy. In his own day also he was not without influence. This success occurred despite the fact that he was not really concerned, as were Malthus and Mill, with value theory. In fact his chief interest was in economic fluctuations, particularly fluctuations in prices, but also fluctuations relating to the currency, interest rates, trade, and, to a lesser degree, output and employment.

By profession Tooke was a businessman, actively engaged in the Russian trade. By avocation he was an economist actively concerned with all the larger questions of the day in so far as they related to money and prices, and very few questions could not be related to these two subjects in one way or another.

Unfortunately Tooke was far more expert as a chronicler than as an historian and theorist of price fluctuations. Though he early expressed a desire to avoid a history that would be merely business annals, and though he was constantly concerned with questions of policy and with the polemics of the day, he was nonetheless one of the most unsatisfactory theorists of the period. While most writers plunged in to generalize with scant recourse to empirical material, the collection of price statistics that formed the basis of his work seemed to make generalization difficult and almost impossible for him. At the same time this did not prevent

Tooke from taking very definite positions on issues, positions that would often be modified, if not denied, in the next chapter, edition, or book.

In this chapter, attention is focused on the first four volumes of the *History of Prices*. Published between 1838 and 1848, these volumes cover the period between 1792 and 1847. They are, particularly when taken in conjunction with the last two volumes done in collaboration with Newmarch (and others), the most elaborate contemporary attempt to record and analyze the fluctuations of the period. Much of the material used in Tooke's earlier publications was incorporated in the *History*. His other important work during the same period of his life was published in 1844 as *An Inquiry into the Currency Principle*.[3] Portions of this work appear in the *History*, accompanied by his replies to critics.

Section one below is concerned with the picture of economic fluctuations that is obtained from the *History*. Section two deals with Tooke's treatment of currency, money, and the interest rate, a treatment that has probably been more influential than any other portion of his work. In the third section Tooke's attitude toward mitigation of fluctuations is considered, particularly as it relates to the controversy over the Bank Act of 1844.

1. ECONOMIC FLUCTUATIONS

Tooke's *History of Prices* started out quite auspiciously with a statement of the way in which he would organize a vast work which would cover price history and related topics. He proposed to divide his history into time periods so that the exposition would be clear:

The most convenient mode that has suggested itself to me is that of a division into epochs of about five years each. Shorter intervals, annual periods, for instance, would, properly speaking, be of the nature of annals, and would weary and distract the attention by the inevitable minuteness of the details, besides that an interval so short would not admit of continuous observation of the whole, or even of the greater part of the phases, within which the changes and alternations between periods of confidence and discredit, of the spirit of enterprise and despondency, have revolved. . . . It so happens that intervals of about five years do afford resting places, at each of which an examination may conveniently take place of the rise and progress, and in many instances of the termination, of a series of events, all tending to throw light on each other.[4]

Both the implication of a regularly recurring fluctuation in prices and the suggestion that certain phases could be distinguished appear promising. Unfortunately when the scheme is carried into effect, the reader is quickly disillusioned. The "resting places" which divide the work appear to be the result of accidental decisions on the part of the author rather than the outcome of the facts which are the subject of study. The desire to avoid mere chronicle was not carried into practice. Although, as we shall see, many of the individual cycles recognized today can be identified in Tooke's history, and were even recognized by Tooke himself, his failure to organize the material on this basis makes for considerable confusion.

To this difficulty must be added another. Tooke is specifically concerned with prices, not with fluctuations in production, employment, or any of the other variables that would attract a modern writer. Moreover, in practice, a disproportionate amount of space is devoted to detailed descriptions of wheat prices. Beyond the price of wheat and related grains, attention is concentrated upon the prices of internationally traded commodities. There is a paucity of material on production, employment in general, and a shortage of material on prices of domestically produced goods consumed at home. The plethora of material on money hardly makes up for these deficiencies. To a great extent these gaps reflect the lack of readily available statistical material. But the gaps mean that identification of cycles, when cycles mean something more than cycles in prices, becomes difficult, and must finally depend upon the qualitative statements that Tooke makes on the state of business activity.

Another difficulty arises from Tooke's emphasis upon individual prices. Prices are never combined into price indices. Instead the data for each individual commodity are presented, sometimes in tabular form, sometimes in a literary interpretation with statistics relegated to an appendix. Tooke felt that each individual commodity price deserved a specific and separate analysis. Only the fact that he often violated this principle enables one to detect general cyclical movements in his history.

Although Tooke's history covers the years from 1792 to 1856, examination is here confined to the years between 1808 and 1848. It is possible to draw up a list of cycles involving what appear to be fluctuations in general business activity on the basis of Tooke's history. These dates can be compared with the reference dates determined by the National Bureau of Economic Research:[5]

TOOKE'S TURNING POINTS		NBER TURNING POINTS	
Trough	*Peak*	*Trough*	*Peak*
1807-8	1809-10	1808	1810
1811	1814-15	1811	1815
1816	1818	1816	1818
1819 (?)	1825	1819	1825
—	—	1826	1828
—	—	1829	1831
1833	1836	1832	1836
1837	1838-39	1837	1839
1842	1847	1842	1845

The comparison reveals both the effectiveness of Tooke's observations and the weaknesses that were implicit, from a cyclical point of view, in reliance upon price statistics. Tooke's though in 1819, for example, is somewhat indefinite, since he notes that by the end of that year "discredit" had disappeared, and then attributes the continued fall of prices up to 1822 or 1823 to higher production and lower costs. Even more striking is the fact that Tooke skips the cycles of 1826-29 and 1829-32. These omissions, like the doubts about 1819, arise from the emphasis upon price series. Modern price indices would also skip these cycles; thus export prices fall from 1825 to 1832, while import prices and wholesale prices show only one slight rise during the period from 1830 to 1831. In sharp contrast Hoffmann's index of industrial production shows both of the cycles that Tooke skipped.[6] It is interesting to note that the skipped cycles are, according to Rostow, the cycles showing the weakest prosperities during the period surveyed.[7]

Tooke repeatedly called upon exogenous factors to explain the origins of expansion. Thus the expansion starting in 1807-8 is attributed to the effects of Napoleon's Continental System. Another factor stimulating activity at the same time was discovered in South America:

> The transfer of the seat of government from Portugal to the Brazils, and the virtual emancipation of the colonies of Spain from the control of the mother country, opened the trade of a great part of South America in 1808.... So vast and comparatively untried a field was not held out in vain to the merchants and manufacturers of this country; and, accordingly, the spirit of speculation was on the alert to export every article, not only, that might probably, but that could possibly, come into demand.[8]

The expansion starting in 1811 was also attributed to a special event: the opening of north European ports and the expectation that French ports would soon be opened. The 1819 expansion was at least partly the result of the preparations for recognition of the South American states which, it was expected, would provide markets for British goods. Again in 1842, the peace with China following the Opium War was a factor tending to stimulate activity. Thus at least four of the seven revivals that Tooke recognized are related to some exogenous event, which was either the sole cause or an important cause of increased activity.

In some cases, however, endogenous events played a role. The revival in 1816 appears to be primarily an automatic result of the preceding contraction. Low prices stimulated consumption, imports were discouraged, and reduced exports eventually led to increased demand abroad and larger profits. Importers, dealers, and manufacturers found that stocks of goods on hand had been reduced to excessively low levels that justified increased activity:

Such a falling off of supply was naturally calculated to attract attention during the progress of the importations; and when these were ascertained to be deficient in so great a degree, a general disposition among dealers to lay in stocks became evident; such a state of things is usually the precursor of a spirit of speculation.[9]

But even in this case, Tooke mentions an exogenous event: crop failures in Europe. The endogenous type of explanation was also important in 1819, in 1833, and in 1842. His description of the state of affairs in 1833 is probably the most general statement that Tooke ever made on the subject.

But as a state of rising markets, and eventually a high range of them, in consequence of supplies having for some length of time fallen short of expectation, or of the estimated rate of consumption, is usually followed first by stagnation, and then by reverses; so a long course of falling markets is eventually followed by a reduction of stocks, while the consumption is extended; and this state of things is the precursor of improved markets, and of a period of prosperity in the branches of trade to which previous distress from low prices had applied.[10]

Thus Tooke did visualize some kind of an automatic mechanism by which depression turned into revival without the assistance of more or less fortuitous events.

When he considered upper turning points Tooke was far more willing to throw the burden of explanation upon forces that were implicit in the preceding course of business. If contraction sometimes turned into revival because supply contracted more rapidly than demand, it was only reasonable to suppose that the opposite chain of events could explain the turn from prosperity into recession. An endogenous explanation is advanced for the first five downturns identifiable in Tooke's writings, but no clear explanation is advanced for 1838-39 and 1847. There is only one reference to a clearly exogenous factor, this being the confiscation of exports to Germany in 1810. As in the case of lower turning points there is much emphasis upon foreign influences and upon international trade. In 1818 speculative imports of raw cotton receive special attention, the disappointment arising from excessive importation being one factor in the downturn.[11] In 1825 both imports and exports are referred to. During the expansion improved markets gave rise to orders for foreign products and to orders from abroad for English products. The disappointment of expectations, when markets became glutted and prices fell, was one factor in the 1825 downturn.[12] Tooke also indicated that in the 1840s railroad investment had been injurious in "absorbing an unusually large proportion of floating capital and converting it into fixed capital, and therefore diminishing the capital available for mercantile purposes."[13] This explanation of the downturn did not usually play an important role in his thinking.

The weakest feature of Tooke's exposition lies in the treatment of the process of expansion and contraction. Partly this was a product of the separation of the discussion of money from the discussion of prices, a procedure that is followed in much of the *History*. Partly it arose from Tooke's propensity to seek out a special explanation for the price of each individual commodity.

The typical treatment of repercussions arising from an initial revival in activity appears in the description of the course of events after 1807. Expectation of large overseas demand led,

as usual on such occasions, to hazardous adventure, . . . extending itself to new projects of various kinds, such as canals, bridges, fire offices, breweries, distilleries, and many other descriptions of joint stock companies.[14]

There is no mention of further effects arising from such undertakings. Again, with reference to 1811, Tooke pointed out:

The extraordinary demand arising out of that speculation for the manufactures of this country, occasioned such an extra employment of workmen in the manufacturing districts, as entitled and enabled them to command a considerable advance in wages.[15]

But no mention is made of the further effects of such wage increases, though on another occasion Tooke did recognize the influence that wage increases might have on demand and prices.

One of the most detailed descriptions of the expansion phase appears in the chronology of events prior to 1825. Scarcity having given rise to price increases, Tooke then described the speculation that followed:

> The impulse to a rise in prices being thus given, and every succeeding purchaser having realised, or appearing to have the power of realising, a profit, a fresh inducement appeared, at every step of the advance, to bring forward new speculative buyers.[16]

Speculation spread from articles in which shortages justified the price increases to articles in which speculation was not justified. As usual there is little or nothing to suggest that speculation in commodities, involving increased production, might, through the creation of larger money incomes, lead to greater demand and price increases generally.

At times, however, Tooke outlined the sequence of events in somewhat greater detail. He recognized that the export of capital through loans increased, at least sometimes, the demand for British manufactured goods. He also saw a connection between imports and exports:

> The reduced stocks of raw materials in this country, and the speculations thereupon, would, in most cases, be attended, in the first instance, with improved markets abroad for the manufactured goods into which those raw materials extend; and the improved markets abroad would give an impulse both to orders from thence, and to speculative shipments thither.[17]

And Tooke adds that these shipments abroad would soon prove excessive in relation to consumption at the advanced prices.

Tooke gave some attention to the role of fixed capital formation during the expansion of activity in 1833-36. The years 1833 and 1834 were marked by high demand:

> Among the greater number of manufacturers, the orders on hand exceeded what could be executed within the time prescribed. New mills were in the course of being constructed, but could not come into operation fast enough to meet the great and increasing demand for wrought goods.[18]

This state of affairs was particularly marked in the iron industry, where, Tooke believed, a considerable number of furnaces had been closed down between 1828 and 1833. The high demand for iron, in part the result of railroad construction in England and America, was accompanied by

restoration of furnaces that had been put out of blast, and by erection of new ones, with the application of improved machinery.[19]

Tooke did not attribute the expansion of economic activity to fixed capital formation, though he did argue that it played a part in increasing employment and in raising wages. Employment in rural areas had an especially close connection with railroad construction.

Railroads again played a part in the 1842-47 expansion. This boom began in manufacturing and trade. Tooke notes, in a rare statement, that this activity led to increased demands for food, clothing, and household furniture. Railroad construction appeared after expansion was underway, in 1844 and 1845, partly as the result of low interest rates and partly as the result of low prices of iron and other raw materials. Unemployment in agricultural areas was not alleviated until some time, roughly a year, after unemployment had been eliminated in manufacturing districts.

All this indicates that Tooke was better at recording the events of an expansion than at presenting a reasoned description of a cumulative process. Aside from the idea that price increases in one or two commodities create speculation in other commodities, there is but slight recognition of the ways in which various parts of an economy are interrelated. A connection between demand and income is barely mentioned.

The treatment of the contraction is hardly more illuminating, though there are some interesting observations. In describing the slump after 1809, Tooke notes that distress spread from the overextended merchant to the unpaid manufacturer, and from the manufacturer to those employed in the mills, but a connection between reduced incomes and reduced demand is unmentioned. Elsewhere he emphasized the role of inventory speculation, with purchases being postponed when prices are falling:

Manufacturers work up, and the dealers and shopkeepers run off, their previously accumulated stocks, before they buy afresh. . . . There is, in such cases, a postponement of demand, as, under opposite circumstances of apprehended scarcity and rising markets, an anticipation of demand.[20]

Whatever the process may be, depression itself is characterized by all the features that have since become familiar: prices, employment, production, interest rates, and consumption are all at lower levels than in the previous prosperity.

Taking the cycle as a whole, the key factor in changes in business activity would seem to be investment in inventories, with fixed capital formation playing a lesser role. Inventory investment is often undertaken because of specific events occurring in foreign countries, so that the resulting expansion is exogenously caused. The expansion process runs mainly in terms of prices, with little attention to income. Expenditures by consumers do not keep pace with rising prices, so that eventually inventories become excessive, and inventory investment ceases and turns into disinvestment, which sets off a downswing. Since changes in money income are not emphasized in the *History*, statements to the effect that rising prices limit demand apparently involve no difficulty as far as Tooke is concerned. The contraction phase is described so vaguely that it is hard to say that Tooke really has any conception of a cumulative process. The upturn occurs either because of exogenous factors, as already noted, or because of inventory reduction that is excessive in relation to demand, so that expectations improve and inventory accumulation starts once again.

2. CURRENCY, MONEY, AND INTEREST RATES

It is particularly striking that Tooke in writing his *History* was able to to treat money supply in sections that were separated from those in which he treated prices. Clearly this meant that money supply did not, on any definition, play an important role in the determination of the fluctuations which were the subject of his book.

The explanation for this view appeared most fully when Tooke undertook to expose the errors of the Currency School. The central proposition of this group of thinkers was, according to Tooke, the ascription

to the amount of Bank notes in circulation, to the exclusion of other forms of credit, an influence on prices, and through prices, on the state of trade and credit.[21]

Unfortunately, in devoting most of his efforts to an attack on this theory, some of the most interesting points were lost sight of. There were in fact three questions that were relevant: the relation between notes and prices, the relation between the whole of the circulating medium and prices, and lastly the relation between interest rates and prices.

The first question was actually of little interest except in the context of the controversies over the Bank Act. Tooke denied flatly that convertible notes had any influence over the price level. Bank notes and coin, he argued, are used primarily for exchanges between dealers and consumers, either when consumers purchase goods, or when dealers (broadly interpreted) hire consumers in their role as wage earners. Other forms of circulating media, bills of exchange and checks drawn on deposits, are used for dealer-to-dealer transactions. Thus the quantity of notes outstanding depends essentially upon the level of transactions between dealers and consumers, that is, upon the level of aggregate money income and expenditure. In one direction causation runs from income and expenditures to prices:

In a convertible state of the currency, given the actual and contingent supply of commodities, the great or less demand [for commodities] will depend, not upon the total quantity of money in circulation, but upon the quantity of money constituting the revenues, valued in gold, of the different orders of the state under the head of rents, profits, salaries, and wages, destined for current expenditures.[22]

And on the other hand it runs from prices, which apparently vary with expenditures, to the quantity of notes:

The prices of commodities do not depend upon the quantity of money indicated by the amount of bank notes, nor upon the amount of the whole of the circulating medium; but that, on the contrary, the amount of the circulating medium is the consequence of prices.[23]

Tooke's position was obscured considerably by an attempt to contrast the passive role of convertible notes with the active role of inconvertible notes. He argued:

When a government issues paper money, inconvertible and compulsorily current, it is usually in payment for—
  1. The personal expenditure of the Sovereign or the governing power.
  2. Public Works and Building.
  3. Salaries of Civil Servant.
  4. Maintenance of Military and Naval Establishments.

It is quite clear that paper created and so paid away by the Government, not being returnable to the issuer, will constitute a fresh source of demand, and must be forced into and permeate all the channels of circulation. Accordingly, every fresh issue beyond the point at which former issues had settled in a certain rise of prices and of wages, and a fall of the exchanges, is soon followed by a further rise of commodities and wages, and a fall of the exchanges.[24]

It turned out that this passage was extremely misleading. Thus Tooke admitted that the difference between convertible and inconvertible notes had nothing to do with the fact that the government was assumed to spend, rather than lend. He further admitted that the fact that the money created took the form of notes rather than deposits was irrelevant. Thus there was essentially no basis for the distinction that he was trying to make. Notes were passive because the public could never be made to hold more notes than it wanted, could always in fact exchange notes for some other type of asset, bank deposits for example. In debate Tooke suffered from his attempt to contrast convertible and inconvertible notes.[25]

The second question, that concerning the relation between the whole of the circulating medium and prices, is of far greater interest. In the first edition of the *Inquiry* Tooke had stated unambiguously that "the whole of the circulating medium" was dependent upon prices; thus deposits and bills of exchange, like notes, were passive.[26] This passage remained unchanged in the second edition, but Tooke added a footnote that flatly contradicted the view he expressed in the text:

> Now, I beg leave most emphatically to deny that I ever denied the power of banks of issue to add to the circulating medium, including in that term deposits and bills of exchange. . . . It never entered into my head to imagine, much less to state distinctly, that banks, whether issuing or non-issuing, had not the power of adding by bills of exchange and deposits to the circulating medium. Indeed nobody can have been more alive than I have been to the fact . . . that the banks, both issuing and non-issuing, were instrumental by an undue extension of credit in 1835, 1836, to an excessive circulation of bills of exchange.[27]

However, though he did not deny this power, he tended to argue that the importance of the circulating medium had been exaggerated. Bank creation of additional circulating media could facilitate an expansion, but such creation could not take place unless there was something in the state of markets to begin with that made demand for such credits active.

This point of view came out rather more clearly in connection with the third issue, that concerning the influence of interest rates. Here he argued strongly that low interest rates and great availability of credit could not create a rise in prices. There were, Tooke stated, always idle funds available that could be used when profitable opportunities existed:

> The power of purchase by persons having capital and credit is much beyond any thing that those who are unacquainted practically with speculative markets have any idea of. The error is in supposing the *disposition* or *will* to be co-extensive with the power. The limit to the motive for the exercise of the power is in the prospect of resale with a profit.[28]

Not only was availability of bank credit relatively unimportant, but the interest rate would not influence, Tooke sometimes argued, decisions to make purchases:

> To suppose that persons entitled to credit are likely to be induced . . . by the mere circumstance of a low rate of interest to enter into specula-

tion in commodities ... argues a want of knowledge of the motives which lead to such speculations. These are seldom if ever entered into with borrowed capital, except with a view to so great an advance of price, and to be realized in so moderate a space of time, as to render the rate of interest or discount a matter of comparatively trifling consideration.[29]

But these views were not consistently held and can be interpreted as applying to depression situations.

Thus he also argued that price fluctuations were phenomena

of credit, too easily and extensively given in the first instance, and withdrawn of necessity in the end with more or less violence, according to the previous greater or less undue extension.[30]

And this opinion was not limited to credit advanced by merchants but included also bank credit. Again he emphasized the importance of low interest rates and abundance of bank accommodation in connection with the expansion of 1842-47:

There can, I imagine, be no question but that this low rate of interest, and the consequent abundance of banking accommodation, tended to facilitate and promote the railway speculations which were then in progress, and which reached their culminating point in the summer of 1845. And it is no less clear that the same low rate of interest and abundance of banking accommodations tended to promote the spirit of adventure which was then abroad for other undertakings involving the outlay of borrowed capital.[31]

In another passage he referred to the "undue extension of credit" in both 1825 and 1847 as "preceded, and probably caused, and most certainly favored ... and promoted" by a low rate of interest.[32] These cases suggest that interest rate and bank credit, while not capable of creating an expansion, did facilitate an expansion once expectations were such as to bring about a revival in activity.

A similar refusal to take an extreme position appears when the effectiveness of interest rates in cutting off a boom is under discussion. The most clearly recognized effect of high interest rates lay in their power to attract foreign capital to England and thus mitigate or eliminate the necessity for exports of gold. But the domestic effects could not be stated in such a precise and simple way. Tooke writes:

> A forcible operation by the Bank on its securities, in either direction will not, of necessity . . . be attended with an immediate and direct effect on the prices of commodities. The effect, if any, can only be indirect, through the medium of credit, and dependent on the previous state of the market.[33]

Later he argues that if a rise in the rate of interest is to be effective in cutting off a boom, then the rise in interest must be

> so great, or the circumstances from previous overtrading such as to affect credit and entail failures. Now, commercial discredit, involving extensive failures, is calculated to depress prices, and thus, with an advanced rate of interest, to stop a drain and to force an influx of bullion.[34]

Tooke's position on currency, money, and interest rates can thus, with some simplification, be summarized as follows. Currency is entirely passive, at least when convertible, depending upon income and expenditures, or on prices, which in turn were related to income and expenditure. Other forms of the circulating medium, credit given by merchants and banks, cannot create speculation, but can facilitate the continuation of a speculation that is underway. In some circumstances a reduction in the availability of bank credit and increases in interest rates can do little to cut off a boom, but if the speculation has gone so far that it is on the verge of collapsing of its own accord, then a rise in interest rates would speed the onset of contraction; or if the rise in interest rates were sufficiently violent to create "discredit," then the boom might be cut off at any time during its process.

One further point should be made. Despite the interest that has since been aroused by Tooke's use of income and expenditures as the determinant of prices, this played a very minor role in his discussion of money. He used it essentially for only one purpose, to explain why currency was passive. He made no attempt to explain the way in which income was determined; and in his

History of Prices, the concepts of income and expenditures play almost no part.

3. MITIGATION OF ECONOMIC FLUCTUATIONS

Tooke advanced no grandiose schemes for the control of economic activity. Instead he concerned himself with the less ambitious goal of mitigating economic fluctuations.

The proposals of Thomas Attwood and the Birmingham School were naturally rejected. Even aside from Tooke's devotion to a convertible currency, he felt, for much the same reasons as had earlier been advanced by Malthus, that the forced creation of currency could only lead to overproduction.

If, indeed, 5 millions of bank notes were by some magical operation to be so issued by the Bank of England, that . . . 5 millions of persons of the working classes depending for the means of their expenditure on their weekly wages, should each, on rising in the morning, find himself richer than when he had laid down, by discovering a 1 £ note in his pocket, the effect would be great and sudden upon prices. Each probably of these 5 millions of persons would immediately lay it out in purchases of articles constituting the necessaries and luxuries of those classes. . . . All the markets for these articles would exhibit great briskness of demand. And as the consumption would thus outrun the ordinary supply, there would be a disposition among the producers and importers to anticipate a continuance or increased ratio of such demand.[35]

But resulting speculation would not be lasting:

The cause of increased consumption being by supposition not permanent, the increased supplies would prove to be beyond the demand, and losses, and failures, and discredit, would follow.[36]

The possibility, if necessary, of a continuous injection of new notes was not considered.

Tooke was not particularly sanguine even about the possibilities of mitigating fluctuations:

I am wholly unable to suggest any scheme of regulation by which the occasional recurrence of periods of commercial discredit and distress can be prevented.[37]

This view was apparently grounded on several characteristics of economic fluctuations. First, since exogenous events beyond the control of any national agency were a fundamental basis for speculative expansions, control was in this respect impossible. Within fairly wide limits, the existence of merchant credit that involved neither note issues nor bank credit permitted such events to induce speculative price increases. Second, since note issues were passive, nothing could be accomplished through regulation or control of notes in any form. On the other hand, control over other types of credit seemed an undesirable form of government intervention. The one method of control which might have some influence was action via the rate of interest.

The major subject of controversy was the Bank Act of 1844. Advocates of the act had stated that the proposed reforms would mitigate the cycle. Samuel Jones Loyd had written as early as 1837 that separation of the banking and issue departments would limit the possibilities of overtrading, and that, as a result,

> the crisis which must follow would probably be limited in its extent and intensity by an earlier and more steady application of the restrictive power.[38]

Later Loyd stated that the act was not intended primarily as a measure to combat "commercial revulsions," but still left the impression that "oscillations of commercial excitement" would be restrained.[39]

Tooke argued against this view before passage and, after passage, cited the severity of the 1847 crisis as an indication that the act had been an aggravating factor. He concerned himself with two doctrines on which the act was based, the first implying automatic action to contract the currency whenever gold drains took place, and the second, which argued that through earlier action the excesses of speculative excitement would be avoided, with a resulting mitigation of the extent of collapse. In contradiction to some of his other pronouncements Tooke agreed that the availability and cost of funds did influence activity, and that therefore, excepting the convertibility of the paper and the solvency of banks, which are and ought to be within the province of the legislature most carefully to preserve, the main difference between one system of banking and another, is the greater or less liability to abrupt changes in the rate of interest, and in the state of commercial credit incidental to one as compared with the other.[40]

The act, Tooke predicted before passage, would lead to more abrupt and violent changes in both interest rates and commercial credit.

First, there could be situations in which gold drains occurred and in which no action should be taken by the Bank. Such drains had occurred in 1828-29 and 1831-32, when gold was lost and then regained without sale of securities by the Bank or change in the bank rate. But under the separation, the demand for gold would probably fall on the banking department and the directors would be forced to act immediately in order to maintain their reserves.

They must sell securities, or allow the existing ones, if short-dated, to run off, and they must inexorably shut their doors to all applications for advances and discounts. This would . . . operate as a limitation of the power to overtrade in discount and loans. Most effectual, indeed, would it be, and under certain circumstances of the trade, it would operate with a [high] degree of violence on the state of credit.[41]

Thus Tooke felt that the automatic nature of the mechanism set up in the act was such as to create violent fluctuations when actually a hands-off policy might lead to a painless correction of the difficulty.

Second, Tooke predicted that action under the act might easily result in a situation where the banking department would be forced to suspend payments, even though the issue department still had adequate reserves of bullion. This kind of result would be a product of separation, and would have no desirable effects.[42]

Tooke did agree that, when drains of gold were large and continuous, Bank action was essential. But he felt that many drains were temporary in nature and required no such action. The solution for large drains was, first, the building up of gold reserves so as to provide a larger buffer, and second, Bank measures to restrict credit. But the key difference lay in Tooke's opinion that Bank action should properly depend upon circumstances; it was essential to permit discretionary action, instead of following precise rules that could lead to disaster.

4. CONCLUSION

It is difficult to obtain a clear picture of business cycles from Tooke's writings. Despite his desire to avoid a mere chronicle, he often fell into this useful but relatively uninteresting trap. In so far as cycles can be distinguished in Tooke, he used elements of both an exogenous and an endogenous explanation.

Revivals are often explained exogenously. Disturbances arise as the result of events which cannot be controlled and which take place, as a rule, overseas. Short supplies of imported raw materials, the opening of South American markets, disturbances connected with the Napoleonic Wars play a large role in explaining the onset of speculation. Little support is given to theories that attach importance to low interest rates or abundance of money as a cause of speculation, for something must always exist in the demand and supply of commodities before advantage will be taken of easy money conditions. Endogenous explanations of revival are sometimes suggested: thus in several cases Tooke pointed to contractions in supply that exceeded those in demand and led to a rise in prices and a general upswing.

The expansion process shows Tooke at his poorest. While other writers of the period generally had no difficulty in describing an expansion in terms of income and expenditures, Tooke is almost oblivious to such interactions. Even when he advanced the idea that income and expenditures were related to prices, he left income and expenditures themselves hanging in the air, unexplained and mysterious. It is hard to understand this gap in his thought, since he was one of the few writers so handicapped; and particularly since the idea of inventory speculation could have fitted so nicely into his conception of income and expenditures. Instead of the usual explanation, Tooke speaks of the process by which legitimate price rises in one commodity spread by some psychological mechanism to other commodities.

There are enough references to the association between price increases and employment and output increases to warrant the belief that periods of speculation involved more than simply price increases. During such expansions interest rates and the availability of credit may play a part. Low interest rates may even stimulate speculation that would not otherwise occur. It is also implied that a sufficiently violent tightening of interest rates and restriction of bank credit could stop such an expansion, the violence required apparently depending upon the extent to which the speculation had run its course.

Although expansion may end because of high interest rates and restricted bank credit, more stress is placed upon other factors. These factors may be exogenous, but more often they are the outcome of the previous expansion. Increases in prices eventually reduce demand, and, as a result, the speculative boom breaks; or speculative shipments overseas may glut froreign markets, leading to a cessation of exports. Howeve, Tooke generally skipped lightly over the reasons why demand becomes inadequate. The subsequent contraction is treated in considerably less detail than the expansion, though there is evidence that the process involved reduced employment and reduced output as well as falling prices.

At no point does investment in fixed capital play a prominent role in the argument, though in the 1830s and the 1840s it received more attention than earlier. Tooke, on the contrary, seems to be arguing in terms of inventory cycles, as had Attwood, rather than in terms of fixed capital formation. The speculative booms are essentially based on inventory investment, while downswings represent, on the other hand, a process of disinvestment in inventories.

While Tooke's attitude toward money and interest rates was ambiguous, certainly the whole tendency of his writings was to suggest that these factors had been overemphasized. In his more extreme statements, the usual reasoning of the day, the argument from money to prices, seems to have been exactly reversed. In this respect Tooke is one of the earliest of those writers who de-emphasize the role of money supply and interest rates. This is, of course, to make Tooke much more extreme and much more consistent than he actually was. Money supply and interest rates were not so important as other writers, particularly his Currency School opponents, thought, but they did apparently play a part. Thus the fluctuations that he observed could take place, within limits, without any variations in money supply and interest rates, but low rates and abundance of bank accommodation aggravated expansions. It followed also that monetary policy was not powerless to prevent speculation, though it was powerless or nearly powerless to create speculation, when demand and supply conditions were adverse.

Tooke attached enough importance to interest rates so that his criticism of the Bank Act of 1844 could be based almost exclusively upon the proposition that the act would increase the amplitude of interest rate fluctuations. Essentially he was fearful that any automatic system of managing money would create unnecessary fluctuations in business activity in response to gold flows that would, without interference, have been self-correcting. Thus he advocated larger reserves of gold, reserves that would in some measure insulate the domestic economy from international developments. If such reserves proved inadequate, then he was prepared to utilize the traditional measures of credit restraint both to attract foreign capital and to depress the domestic economy, and so to correct the balance of payments.

John Stuart Mill

JOHN STUART MILL differs from the writers that we have considered in that he wrote a treatise that seemed to summarize and consolidate the political economy of his day.[1] His major work, the *Principles of Political Economy*,[2] was, in its main outline, Ricardian, but was not oblivious to the controversies and developments that had taken place in the thirty-odd years since Ricardo had published his *Principles*. Actually, Mill seems to have been more highly conscious of the literature on economic fluctuations than were his contemporaries, despite the fact that they, and not Mill, were specifically concerned with the subject. Thus the old controversy over general gluts, the debates with Attwood, and the indebtedness to Tooke all appeared in the *Principles*, and had appeared earlier in the essays and reviews that Mill wrote.

As a Ricardian, moreover, Mill added considerations that had, for the most part, been neglected in the earlier discussions of economic fluctuations. Thus fixed capital formation, generally ignored, except for James Wilson, was introduced as a characteristic feature of the expansion phase and also as a factor explaining the revulsion; this feature stemmed, directly or indirectly, from Ricardo. At the same time the cycle was related to the Ricardian argument concerning the secular tendency for profits to decline. The cycle in fact became one of the forces which permitted continued economic growth despite this tendency. Thus economic growth and the cycle were closely related in Mill's presentation.

At the same time economic fluctuations came in Mill to have a more clearly cyclical character than in earlier writers. The idea of an endogenous cycle, with distinct phases, one merging into another in semiautomatic fashion, was not entirely new, but the concept seems to be more developed in Mill than in the case of any earlier writer. Even Wilson's agricultural cycle depended to a great extent upon the exogenous disturbances created by changes in the corn laws.

In section one, below, the observations concerning consumption, production, and superabundance that appeared in Mill's *Essays* are considered.[3] While somewhat peripheral to the main subject, the ideas here presented are helpful in interpreting some passages in the *Principles* and at the same time show clearly the role that Say's Law played in Mill's thinking. In section two Mill's treatment of commodity speculation, a treatment that owed much to Tooke, is examined. The third section turns to the role of fixed capital formation in the cycle and the relation of the cycle to economic growth. In the fourth section Mill's attitude toward mitigation of general economic fluctuations is considered.

1. CONSUMPTION AND PRODUCTION

Mill's most detailed treatment of the relation between consumption and production appeared in his *Essays*. Here he examined the proposition that "a great and rapid consumption was what the producers, of all classes and denominations, wanted to enrich themselves and the country."[4] Alternative formulations of this proposition might speak of "brisk demand" or "rapid circulation," but these differences were merely verbal. Mill was, in fact, taking issue with Attwood, Malthus, and other writers who accepted the high consumption view.

The proposition gains an appearance of credibility, according to Mill, since it is valid as far as an individual producer is concerned. This point is laboriously analyzed. Mill argues that normally a dealer keeps a stock of goods on hand to be ready for a sudden demand; this implies a delay between production and sale. During this delay capital is idle. Any increase in demand, by cutting down on the delay, will tend to bring capital into full employment, thus stimulating profits and production of the article in question.

In the same way, national production will increase if there is a brisk demand in all or most industries.

> The annual produce of a country is never anything approaching in magnitude to what it might be if all the resources devoted to reproduction, if all the capital, in short, of the country were in full employment.[5]

> There is a brisk demand and a rapid circulation when goods, generally speaking, are sold as fast as they can be produced. There is slackness, on the contrary, and stagnation, when goods, which have been produced, remain for a long time unsold.[6]

Thus Mill is prepared to agree with the proposition concerning high consumption in so far as it merely argues that a brisk demand will raise national production.

He does not agree, however, that such an increase in production is desirable. Periods of brisk demand extending to all commodities must involve "some general delusion."

> For, the calculations of producers and traders being of necessity imperfect, there are always some commodities which are more or less in excess, as there are always some which are in deficiency. If, therefore, the whole truth were known, there would always be some classes of producers contracting, not extending their operations. If *all* are endeavouring to extend them, it is a certain proof that some general delusion is afloat.[7]

The cause and explanation of this delusion is then stated:

> The commonest cause of such delusion is some general, or very extensive rise of prices (whether caused by speculation or by the currency) which persuades all dealers that they are growing rich. And hence, an increase of production really takes place during the progress of depreciation, as long as the existence of depreciation is not suspected.[8]

Essentially the rise in production results from the fact that there is a temporary money illusion in the supply of effort, presumably shared by all classes of society. Thus higher money returns, associated with higher prices, give rise to increased effort and increased production. If it were not for the illusion, that is to say, if the "whole truth were known," some producers would be contracting, but as a result of the illusion, all producers are extending production. But since it is merely a delusion, the increased effort and production are actually undesirable, since people are not behaving the way they really (with no money illusion) want to behave.[9]

The delusion eventually vanishes and it is found that effort is too great in relation to real returns:

> Those whose commodities are relatively in excess must diminish their production or be ruined; and if during the high prices they have built mills and erected machinery, they will be likely to repent at leisure.[10]

There is no more than a suggestion that a similar general delusion, leading to excessively low production, may exist when prices are falling. Mill does, however, see an alternation between periods of "unreasonable hopes and unreasonable fears":

> General eagerness to buy and general reluctance to buy, succeed one another in a manner more or less marked, at brief intervals. Except during short periods of transition, there is almost always either great briskness of business or great stagnation; either the principal producers of almost all the leading articles of industry have as many orders as they can possibly execute, or the dealers in almost all commodities have their warehouses full of unsold goods.[11]

This conception of a delusion arising out of changing prices played some part in Mill's view of the business cycle in the *Principles*. In the *Essays* he turned at this point to a consideration of "general superabundance."

For Mill "great stagnation" suggested that there was "general superabundance," a state of affairs whose possibility, he notes, has been contested by many economists. As far as the short run is concerned, Mill argues that the issue is "merely a question of naming," though an important question:

> As those economists who have contested the possibility of general superabundance, would none of them deny the possibility or even the fre-

quent occurrence of the phenomenon which we have just noticed, it would seem incumbent on them to show, that the expression to which they object [general superabundance] is not applicable to a state of things in which all or most commodities remain unsold, in the same sense in which there is said to be a superabundance of any one commodity when it remains in the warehouses of dealers for want of a market.[12]

The usual argument by which general superabundance is denied —inadequate demand is impossible since whoever offers a commodity for sale desires to obtain a commodity, so that a seller is automatically a buyer—is only true under certain conditions:

The sellers and the buyers, for all commodities taken together, must, by the metaphysical necessity of the case, be an exact equipoise to each other; and if there be more sellers than buyers of one thing, there must be more buyers than sellers for another.[13]

This presupposes, says Mill, a state of barter, and is correct under such circumstances, but as soon as we introduce money the proposition ceases to be "exactly true."

Now the effect of the employment of money, and even the utility of it, is, that it enables this one act of interchange to be divided into two separate acts or operations; one of which may be performed now, and the other a year hence, or whenever it shall be most convenient. . . . The buying and selling being now separated, it may very well occur, that there may be, at some given time, a very general inclination to sell with as little delay as possible, accompanied with an equally general inclination to defer all purchases as long as possible.[14]

Such periods can legitimately be described as periods of superabundance or "general excess."

These periods are transitory: they mean only a temporary fall in the value of commodities relative to money, "since those who have sold without buying will certainly buy at last, and there will then be more buyers than sellers." Thus Mill, for the short run, accepts the phrase "general superabundance" and rejects Say's Law, though the law is not mentioned by name.[15]

For long periods, "permanently" as Mill puts it, there is no possibility of general superabundance. For then

nothing is more true than that it is produce which constitutes the market for produce, and that every increase of production, if distributed without miscalculation among all kinds of produce in the proportion which private interest would dictate, creates, or rather constitutes, its own demand.[16]

Thus Say's Law comes into its own, with Mill making an explicit distinction between what is possible temporarily and what is possible permanently.

In the *Principles* essentially the same position is taken, though with increased emphasis on the permanent in the chapter that is specifically devoted to "excess of supply." As far as short-run fluctuations are concerned Mill leaves the view of the *Essays* unchanged. Speaking of crises, Mill writes:

At such times there is really an excess of all commodities above the money demand: in other words, there is an under-supply of money. From the sudden annihilation of a great mass of credit, every one dislikes to part with ready money, and many are anxious to procure it at any sacrifice. Almost everybody therefore is a seller, and there are scarcely any buyers; so that there may really be, though only while the crisis lasts, an extreme depression of general prices, from what may be indiscriminately called a glut of commodities or a dearth of money.[17]

But Mill, while reasserting the facts that provided the justification for the use of the term "general superabundance" in a temporary stagnation, also reasserts his conclusions with respect to permanent stagnation:

The permanent decline in the circumstances of producers, for want of markets, which those writers contemplate, is a conception to which the nature of a commercial crisis gives no support.[18]

Clearly, there was nothing in Mill's acceptance of Say's Law that prevented him from analyzing short-run fluctuations. In fact, in all the discussions of Say's Law, Mill does at the same time recognize the existence of such fluctuations. Say's Law, as treated by Mill, excludes only permanent stagnation.

2. COMMODITY SPECULATION AND THE CYCLE

In the *Essays*, general economic fluctuations were discussed because they had relevance to the central subject, the influence of consumption on production. In the *Principles*, the same procedure, involving the subordination of the business cycle to discussion of other subjects, was followed.[19] There is, as a result, no organized treatment of the almost periodic fluctuations that Mill observed.

In fact it is possible to isolate two different conceptions of the cycle in the *Principles*. On the one hand, the cycle appeared to be primarily a question of commodity speculation, a view which followed from the remarks in the *Essays* and which leaned heavily upon Tooke's doctrines. The second conception placed more stress on the conversion of circulating capital into fixed capital, thus owing a debt to Ricardo, and perhaps to Wilson. Broadly speaking, the first conception concentrated upon inventory cycles, while the second concentrated on cycles in fixed capital formation. Mill appears to have believed, however, that in most historical cycles, both factors were involved. In this section inventory cycles, those involving speculation in commodities, are considered, discussion of fixed capital being postponed to section three.[20]

Mill distinguished explicitly between two "states of the markets."

The first is that in which there is nothing tending to engender in any considerable portion of the mercantile public a desire to extend their operations. The producers produce and dealers purchase only their usual stocks, having no expectation of a more than usually rapid vent for them. Each person transacts his ordinary amount of business, and no more; or increases it only in correspondence with the increase of his capital or connexion, or with the gradual growth of the demand for his commodity, occasioned by the public prosperity.[21]

This state of business Mill called "the quiescent state." There are good reasons for believing that the quiescent state was a phase in the cycle for Mill, though he is never explicit on the matter.[22]

The second state of markets, the one which normally succeeded the quiescent state, was the "expectant, or speculative, state."[23] This arises

when an impression prevails, whether well founded or groundless, that the supply of one or more of great articles of commerce is likely to run short of the ordinary consumption. In such circumstances all persons connected with those commodities desire to extend their operations. The producers or importers desire to produce or import a larger quantity, speculators desire to lay in a stock in order to profit by the expected rise of price, and holders of the commodity desire additional advances to enable them to continue holding.[24]

The sanguine expectations characteristic of the speculative state appear to be the result of various exogenous events, short crops, obstructions to importation, or the opening of new foreign markets; it is also argued that even without such events periods of quiescence would automatically give rise to speculation.[25] Mill stresses the importance of credit in permitting this speculation to get underway. There is no necessary reason why an increase in the quantity of transferable paper, that is, in bank notes, bills of exchange, and checks, should be involved. Particularly in the earlier stages of speculation, credit is likely to be extended through book credits granted by suppliers. It is emphasized, however, that the activation of potential credits depends upon profit expectations.

Given these expectations, there results "a disposition among dealers to increase their stocks, in order to profit by the expected rise," the expectations and the disposition being at first confined to one or a few commodities.[26] Mill notes that for a time at least expectations of rising prices are an active factor in raising prices.

This disposition tends in itself to produce the effect which it looks forward to, a rise in price: and if the rise is considerable and progressive, other speculators are attracted, who, so long as the price has not begun to fall, are willing to believe that it will continue rising.[27]

Though the speculation starts with a few commodities, it may extend to others. Holders of stocks "realize, or appear to have the power of realizing, great gains."

In certain states of the public mind, such examples of rapid increase of fortune call forth numerous imitators, and speculation not only goes much beyond what is justified by the original grounds for expecting a rise of price, but extends itself to articles in which there never was any such ground: these, however, rise like the rest as soon as speculation sets in. At periods of this kind a great extension of credit takes place. Not only do all whom the contagion reaches employ their credit much more freely than usual; but they really have more credit, because they seem to be making unusual gains, and because a generally reckless and adventurous feeling prevails, which disposes people to give as well as take credit more largely than at other times, and give it to persons not entitled to it.[28]

While speculation can, at the start, be based upon the book credits granted by suppliers, credit in the broadest sense of the term is vital to a general and prolonged speculation. Mill used "money" to mean gold and silver, while credit as a substitute for money included bank notes, bills of exchange, checks, as well as book credits by suppliers. Thus he argued that if the only means of purchase were money, speculation could not become general. Greater demand for one commodity would, in such circumstances, withdraw money from the purchase of other commodities, and price reductions would result. One qualification was noted:

The vacuum might, it is true, be partly filled up by increased rapidity of circulation; and in this manner the money of the community is virtually increased in a time of speculative activity, because people keep little of it by them, but hasten to lay it out in some tempting adventure as soon as possible after they receive it. This resource, however, is limited: on the whole, people cannot, while the quantity of money remains the same, lay out much more of it in some things, without laying out less in others.[29]

Thus it is the existence of credit which permits a general rise in demand and prices to take place.

In the *Essays*, periods of speculation involve an increase in aggregate output, though the impression is created that the increases are not large. In the *Principles* the matter is complicated by the fact that increases in output are normal even in the quiescent state, so that the relevant question is different. Is the increase of aggregate output more rapid during speculative periods? It is not easy to get a straight answer on this question. The neglect of this whole matter in the treatment of credit and prices suggests that a more rapid increase in aggregate output was not an important characteristic of the speculative period.[30] Elsewhere, however, Mill makes a distinction between two different types of commodity speculation and seems to imply that an accelerated rise of production is usually characteristic of speculative periods.

During the ascending period of speculation, and as long as it is confined to transactions between dealers, the issues of bank notes are seldom materially increased, nor contribute anything to the speculative rise in prices. It seems to me, however, that this can no longer be affirmed when speculation has proceeded so far as to reach the producers. Speculative orders given by merchants to manufacturers induce them to extend their operations, and to become applicants to bankers for increased advances, which, if made in notes, are not paid away to persons who return them to deposit, but are partially expended in paying wages, and pass into various channels of retail trade, where they become directly effective in producing a further rise in prices.[31]

Normally speculation does not stop short with dealers, but extends to producers. This suggests that there is some increase in the rate of growth of aggregate output during speculative periods.

Mill added little to Tooke's treatment of the process of speculative expansion, which was mainly or most strikingly a rise in prices. There is almost no analysis going beyond the process of "imitation" already sketched. There are a few suggestion of a connection between speculation, increased payments to wage earners, and hence increased expenditures on commodities which tend to generalize the price increases to all or many commodities.[32] But there is no emphasis on this mechanism in explaining how speculation spreads from one or a few commodities to many commodities.

The end of the speculative period, which is marked by the downturn in prices, arises essentially because of the cessation of demand for additions to inventories.

When, after such a rise [in prices], the reaction comes, and prices begin to fall, though at first perhaps only through the desire of the holders [of stocks] to realize, speculative purchases cease.[33]

This shift in attitudes toward inventory investment seems to arise because speculators have some notion of a normal price level, or range of prices. Deviations from this level or range, if great enough, create expectations of price reductions.

At the periods which Mr. Attwood mistook for times of prosperity, and which were simply (as all periods of high prices, under a convertible currency, must be) times of speculation, the speculators did not think they were growing rich because the high prices would last, but because they would not last, and because whoever contrived to realize while they did last, would find himself, after the recoil, in possession of a greater number of pounds sterling, without their having become of less value.[34]

There is also a vague suggestion that prices get out of line with the "state of the consumption and of the supply," but the meaning of this remark is obscure.[35]

The reference to convertibility does not imply that Mill agreed with the view that speculation ended because of external drains of gold. He notes that in fact the issue of notes

tends to prolong the duration of the speculations; that it enables the speculative prices to be kept up for some time after they would otherwise have collapsed; and therefore prolongs and increases the drain of precious metals for exportation, which is the leading feature of this stage in the progress of a commercial crisis.[36]

This finally forces banks to contract credit in order to maintain convertibility. These developments are

generally the proximate cause of the catastrophe. But these phenomena, though a conspicuous accompaniment, are no essential part of the collapse of credit called a commercial crisis; which . . . might happen to as great an extent, and is quite as likely to happen, in a country, if any such there were, altogether destitute of foreign trade.[37]

Thus the role of gold drains resulting from high prices was important in fact, but was not essential. Basically Mill depended for his explanation of the recoil of prices upon the rather vague notion that speculators decide that prices have reached a peak and so cease their purchases.

Apparently it is the downturn in prices which generally ushers in a "commercial crisis" or "commercial revulsion," two interchangeable terms. The crisis is defined and its origin indicated:

There is said to be a commercial crisis, when a great number of merchants and traders at once, either have, or apprehend that they shall have, a difficulty in meeting their engagements. The most usual cause of this general embarrassment is the recoil of prices after they have been raised by a spirit of speculation, intense in degree, and extending to many commodities.[38]

Such crises may also occur for other reasons, even when no prior period of widespread commodity speculation exists; discussion of such cases will be postponed to section three of this chapter.

The crisis or revulsion, as visualized by Mill, seems to be a period of time of some duration, though apparently shorter than either the quiescent period or the speculative period. To use more modern terms it corresponds roughly to a contraction or recession. Prices fall during the revulsion, and

were this all, prices would only fall to the level from which they rose, or to that which is justified by the state of the consumption and of the supply.[39]

But actually credit, which had been abundant during expansion, is now difficult to obtain:

When everybody seems to be losing, and many fail entirely, it is with difficulty that firms of known solidity can obtain even the credit to which they are accustomed, and which it is the greatest inconvenience to them to be without; because all dealers have engagements to fulfill, and nobody feeling sure that the portion of his means which he has entrusted to others will be available in time, no one likes to part with ready money, or to postpone his claim to it.[40]

Moreover, the rate of interest, low during the speculative period when sanguine expectations create a willingness to lend as well as a willingness to borrow, now in the crisis

rises inordinately, because, while there is a most pressing need on the part of many persons to borrow, there is a general disinclination to lend. This disinclination, when at its extreme point, is called a panic.[41]

Thus commercial revulsion involves falling prices, high interest rates, and sales of goods at any price. Mill concludes that

general prices, during a commercial revulsion, fall as much below the usual level as during the previous period of speculation they have risen above it.[42]

It is more difficult to be sure that a contraction of output and employment is involved, though this seems probable.[43] As usual, prices and credit are the phenomena emphasized, while interactions between incomes and expenditures are neglected. Moreover there is no discussion of revival.

The full cycle, as Mill probably saw it, is illustrated in Figure 7. The speculative state (SS) emerges out of the quiescent state (QS) and involves, probably, an increase in the rate of growth of

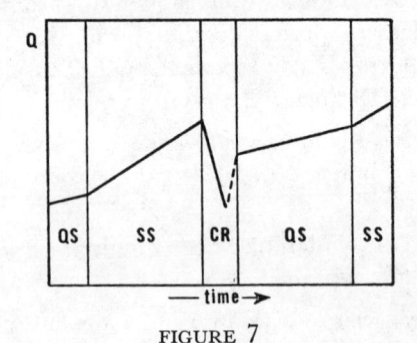

FIGURE 7

output (Q). This is followed by a period of commercial revulsion (CR) in which there is an absolute drop in output, involving temporary unemployment. The revival problem is ignored, for the next state that claims attention is again the period of quiescence, in which no industry is "unusually prosperous, and none particularly distressed."[44] One is strongly inclined to the hypothesis that the quiescent state is one of "full employment" in the sense that all factors of production, including labor, that wish employment at existing real returns are active.[45]

Fluctuations in inventory investment seem on balance to be the most important causal factor in this cycle. The explanation

JOHN STUART MILL 161

of the onset of speculation leans heavily upon exogenous events, with an endogenous explanation being added when Mill examined the secular tendency of profits. The explanation of commercial revulsion is vague, being essentially based on the expectation that prices have reached a limit, though external drains of gold resulting from high prices were usually a factor in actual cycles.

3. FIXED CAPITAL AND THE CYCLE

Mill's treatment of fixed capital in relation to the commercial cycle is closely connected with his discussion of secular change, or industrial progress. The argument on the approach of the stationary state is an elaborate version of Ricardian doctrine, but the role of fixed capital is new and the connection between fixed capital and the cycle did not appear explicitly in Ricardo's work.

Mill starts out by examining the conditions under which there would be a secular tendency for the rate of profits to fall. A number of conditions must be fulfilled: no exportation of capital, no loans for unproductive expenditure either by the government or by private persons, no waste of capital through miscalculation, and "no new channels opened by industrial inventions, or by a more extensive substitution of the best known processes for inferior ones."[46] The last condition rules out the conversion of circulating capital into fixed capital.

Suppose that capital increases. Then, says Mill, either population will also increase, or it will not. Suppose that population does not increase. The increase in capital then implies a larger wages fund and so

wages would rise, and greater capital would be distributed in wages among the same number of labourers. There being no more labour than before, and no improvements to render the labour more efficient, there would not be any increase of produce and as the capital, however largely increased, would only obtain the same gross return, the whole savings of each year would be exactly so much subtracted from the profits of the next and every following year.[47]

The rate of profit must fall.

The same outcome also holds when the connection between real wage level and population increase is introduced. Then the higher wages lead to growth of population. The growth of population could, but for diminishing returns in agriculture, ultimately result in a rate of profit equal to that which existed prior to the increase in capital. However, diminishing returns lead to an annual produce that increases at a less rapid rate than capital, and, since wages increase at the same rate as capital, profits are squeezed and the profit rate must fall.

Under either assumption with regard to population, accumulation leads to a fall in the rate of profit. Mill then argues:

There is at every time and place some particular rate of profit, which is the lowest that will induce the people of that country and time to accumulate savings, and to employ those savings productively.[48]

The level of this minimum rate depends upon the "effective desire of accumulation" and upon the "degree of security of capital engaged in industrial operations." The first of these factors influences the inclination to save and depends upon "the comparative estimate, made by people of that place and era, of future interests when weighed against present." The second, while it "no doubt affects also the disposition to save," is chiefly important for its effect on the willingness to employ savings productively. There is, Mill notes, a greater risk in such employment than in holding savings as a hoard. Mill is, however, not interested in applying these observations to cyclical problems, but only in noting the reasons for the observed fact that the minimum differs from place to place and from time to time. If, however, the minimum is reached, then capital accumulation ceases and the stationary state is attained.[49]

Mill felt that in the England of his time the rate of profit was "habitually within, as it were, a hand's breadth of the minimum."[50] The actual minimum would be reached very rapidly. Yet as a matter of fact the wealth, population, and capital of the country continued to grow, which indicated that there were forces serving to counteract the tendency that he had examined.

In other words, some of the assumptions had to be modified. This was the setting in which Mill introduced a discussion of the cycle, with particular emphasis upon the role of fixed capital.

Mill viewed fixed capital in essentially the same way as Ricardo. Assume a fixed population, an economy which initially produces corn, and in which land is a free good. Start out with a stationary state. This can be illustrated in the accompanying table, where initial gross produce can be used either for capitalist consumption, or as circulating capital. With the figures assumed in column 1, the profit rate on the circulating capital is 10/90ths, and this being the minimum rate, no saving takes place, so that the economy continues with unchanging magnitudes.

COLUMN

	1	2	3	4
Initial gross produce, in corn	100	100	80	120
Capitalist consumption, in corn	10	10	10	30
Circulating capital, in corn	90	90	70	90
Corn production	100	80	120	120
Machine production, value in corn	0	20	0	0
Final gross product, value in corn	100	100	120	120
Profits, value in corn	10	10	50	30
Rate of profit on circulating capital	10/90	10/90	50/70	30/90

Now suppose that for some reason circulating capital is diverted to fixed capital. This involves a diversion of resources, including labor, from the production of corn to the production of a machine: "The result is that so much food and clothing and tools have been consumed, and the country has got a railway instead."[51] This is illustrated in column 2, which differs from column 1 only in the different use of labor and the different nature of the product. There is no change in wages or in profits.

In the next phase occur the two changes that interest Mill. Since the corn output of column 2 is smaller than that of column 1, it follows that, with no change in capitalist consumption, the wages fund must be smaller in the succeeding period. (It may be smaller even if savings increase.) Suppose that circulating capital falls from 90 to 70. This would reduce wages and raise the rate of profit on circulating capital. For capital, in Mill's language, has been sunk: "It has been converted from circulating into fixed capital, and has ceased to have any influence on wages or profits."[52] But Mill usually assumed that the sunk capital is useful and productive, so that in column 3 we not only have a lower figure for circulating capital, but also a higher figure for corn output, reflecting the fact that fixed capital increases labor productivity. Thus, when both effects are considered, the rate of profit rises from 10/90ths to 50/70ths.

The final step is represented in column 4, in which, as the result of the higher profits of the previous period, accumulation takes place and circulating capital increases. In the illustrative figures, circulating capital is assumed to return to the original level of 90, so that wages are at their original level. The profit rate remains higher than originally; hence there is still an incentive for further accumulation. Mill says:

These transformations of capital are of the nature of improvements in production, which, instead of ultimately diminishing circulating capital, are the necessary conditions of its increase, since they alone enable a country to possess a constantly augmenting capital without reducing profits to the rate which would cause accumulation to stop. There is hardly any increase of fixed capital which does not enable the country to contain eventually a larger circulating capital than it otherwise could possess and employ within its own limits.[53]

This is the ultimate outcome of Mill's analysis of fixed capital. The rate of profit falls with every increase in circulating capital and rises with every increase of fixed capital.

With this set of ideas Mill approached the relations between the tendency of profits to fall, the cycle, and fixed capital formation. The above analysis was indeed implicit in Mill's discussion of the crisis of 1847. That crisis was related to railway speculation, involving conversion of circulating capital into fixed capital, but was not marked by extensive speculation in commodities as in the crisis of 1825. Apparently, however, Mill believed that fixed capital investment was characteristic of all speculative periods, so that the true difference between 1847 and 1825 lay not in the presence of fixed capital formation in the former, but rather in the absence of commodity speculation in 1847.

Mill's argument concerning 1847 was very similar to that which had been used by James Wilson. The railroad construction involved, said Mill,

continual demands on the circulating capital of the country by railway calls and loan transactions of railway companies, for the purpose of being converted into fixed capital and made unavailable for future lending.[54]

This conversion of circulating into fixed capital affects the rate of interest, which is determined by the demand and supply of real capital, monetary influences being of secondary importance.[55]

This combination of a fresh demand for loans, with a curtailment of the capital disposable for them, raised the rate of interest, and made it impossible to borrow except on the very best security. Some firms, therefore, which by an improvident and unmercantile mode of conducting business had allowed their capital to become either temporarily or permanently unavailable, became unable to command that perpetual renewal of credit which had previously enabled them to struggle on. These firms stopped payment: their failure involved more or less deeply many other firms which had trusted them; and, as usual in such cases, the general distrust, commonly called a panic, began to set in.[56]

The shortage of real capital and the rise of interest rates, both growing out of the conversion to fixed capital, set off the difficulties that gave rise to panic. This argument differs from the reasoning used elsewhere by Mill, in which high interest rates were attributed to heavy demands for money resulting from failure of confidence.[57]

Mill, when he considered the forces working against the tendency of profits to fall, treated an additional counterinfluence that was in part related to the cycle: waste of capital which was characteristic of both the speculative period and the period of revulsion.[58]

Mill gave two instances of the waste of capital that would occur during speculative periods. Waste might arise because of "hasty purchase of unusual quantitites of foreign goods at advanced prices." It might also arise from wasteful conversion of circulating capital into fixed capital, typical of speculative periods:

> Mines are opened, railways or bridges made and many other works of uncertain profit commenced, and in these enterprises much capital is sunk which yields either no return, or none adequate to the outlay. Factories are built and machinery erected beyond what the market requires, or can keep in employment.[59]

The inadequacy of the profits on such projects was not, however, relevant to the tendency of profits, for once the capital was sunk, it "ceased to have any influence on wages or profits." Instead Mill stressed the fact that any such conversion, whether "absolutely wasted" or not, reduced the size of the circulating capital and hence raised the rate of profit on circulating capital.[60] He also argued that conversion usually led to a rise in productivity of labor. Thus the rate of profit on circulating capital would rise, not only because of the reduction in circulating capital, but also because of the higher productivity of labor.[61]

The revulsion also made a contribution in raising the rate of profit on circulating capital.

> There is a great unproductive consumption of capital during the stagnation which follows a period of general over-trading. Establishments are shut up, or kept working without any profit, hands are discharged, and numbers of persons of all ranks, being deprived of income, and thrown for support on their savings, find themselves, after the crisis has passed away, in a condition of more or less impoverishment.[62]

Thus there was a period, following the crisis, that involved a number of recognized features of business contraction: reduced employment, low profits (apparently meaning profits on sunk capital, not profits on circulating capital), and reduced production. The low profits on sunk capital and the low level of employment both force consumers to live on accumulated savings, so that these savings are reduced. This seemed to be another way of saying that capital is consumed unproductively. As a result circulating capital shrinks and the rate of profit on circulating capital rises.

The revulsion and stagnation that follow the crisis appear, however, to be of rather brief duration. Mill seems to imply that a return to full employment takes place quite rapidly. Moreover, the effects of unproductive consumption in raising the rate of profit are quickly offset, perhaps because the higher profit rate itself stimulates accumulation. Mill writes that after

a few years have passed over without a crisis, so much additional capital has been accumulated, that it is no longer possible to invest it at the accustomed profit.[63]

Elsewhere he notes that

in the intervals between commercial crises, there is usually a tendency in the rate of interest to a progressive fall, from the gradual process of accumulation.[64]

This period of full employment, accumulation, and declining rates of profit and interest, which follows the revulsion, may be identified with the quiescent state, though Mill does not do so explicitly. The revival, or more accurately, the transition from the period of revulsion to the quiescent state does not receive any attention.

Mill is more interested in explaining the outburst of speculation that arises after accumulation has gone on for some time. The rate of profit and the rate of interest, as indicated above, fall during the quiescent state. Business goes on in a more or less routine way. The falling rate of profit applies, however, only to routine operations, for there are always riskier investments that could be undertaken, but are not as long as a reasonable return can be obtained in routine, nonspeculative activities. When the routine rate of profit is sufficiently low, then advantage is taken of the risky projects. Speculation, and the conversion of circulating into fixed capital, once again get underway.

Mill thus uses the cycle, with its characteristic feature of fixed capital formation during the speculative period, as an explanation of the continued growth of the economy. The tendency of profits to fall is in fact the basis of the cycle:

> Such are the effects of a commercial revulsion [in raising profits]: and that such revulsions are almost periodical, is a consequence of the very tendency of profits which we are considering.[65]

Mill even emphasizes that some kind of regular round is involved, with one phase leading into another. Thus, starting with the interval between crises, he writes:

> The diminished scale of all safe gains inclines persons to give a ready ear to any projects which hold out, though at the risk of loss, the hope of a higher rate of profit; and speculations ensue, which, with the subsequent revulsions, destroy, or transfer to foreigners, a considerable amount of capital, produce a temporary rise of interest and profit, make room for fresh accumulations, and the same round is recommenced.[66]

The close connection between secular change and cyclical change leads Mill into predictions as to the future course of the cycle. Given the secular tendency for profits to fall, there is little chance that the cycle will disappear. In fact, it is argued that these fluctuations have not become less frequent or less violent, but rather more frequent and more violent. This is the result of the dissatisfaction with the "ordinary course of safe mercantile gains."[67]

4. POLICY

The elimination or mitigation of the commercial cycle was not a leading problem for Mill. In the *Essays* it is not discussed and in the *Principles* there are few references to the question. The famous chapter on the "probable futurity of the labouring classes" is entirely silent on the issue. The question of mitigation of fluctuations and the related problem of unemployment arises only at three points: in connection with Thomas Attwood's proposals, the French Revolution of 1848, and the Bank Act of 1844.

Mill's treatment of the problem probably arose in part from his conception of the commercial cycle. In the quiescent state, business was normal and there was, presumably, no unemployment problem. Nor was the period of speculation viewed as any improvement. First, the speculative state seems to have been associated with a general delusion, so that, if exertion, employment, and output were greater, this was not in itself particularly desirable. Second, since the speculative state led into commercial crisis or revulsion, it was a positive evil, for the latter had adverse effects upon most classes of society. Third, speculative periods in themselves, since they involved high prices which wiped out fixed money income groups, were unjust and unfair. Thus there was little to be said in favor of measures designed to create speculative activity.[68] Commercial revulsion, on the other hand, was clearly undesirable. But here the problem appeared relatively unimportant because such periods were probably short, merging quickly into the quiescent state. Thus, whatever the drawbacks of revulsion, they were not a serious social problem.

From the point of view of the tendency of profits, Mill could indeed have argued, though he did not, that the cycle had some desirable aspects. In its absence, one factor permitting the continuance of economic growth would be eliminated. Although Mill was not impressed by the horrors of the stationary state, his remarks on its merits were somewhat tentative.

It is not surprising that Mill viewed the proposals of the Birmingham School with little enthusiasm. As a fellow reformer, Mill was, if anything, disposed to think well of Attwood, particularly for his role in the struggle for Reform in 1832. He laid down also the general principle that squabbles among the reformers were undesirable, but went on to point out that particularly pernicious and dangerous errors required criticism despite the general principle. Thus Attwood's doctrines were attacked in 1833 in "The Currency Juggle,"[69] and were once again considered, no more favorably, in the *Principles*.

In the 1833 article Mill apparently accepted the argument that the rise in prices prior to the crisis of 1825 had involved increased employment and production. But Mill took the same kind of position that had been adopted in the *Essays*:

Mr. Attwood's error is that of supposing that a depreciation of the currency *really* increases the demand for all articles, and consequently their production, because, under some circumstances, it may create a *false opinion* of an increase in demand; which false opinion leads, as the reality would do, to an increase in production, followed, however, by a fatal revulsion as soon as the delusion ceases.[70]

Thus an attempt to achieve "full employment" through issue of currency was rejected as futile. Two other differences were involved. First, Attwood started his expansion from a state of mass unemployment, so that the desirability and necessity of some action seemed obvious to him. To Mill on the other hand, expansion or speculation did not start from such a state, but rather from what he later called the quiescent state, without unemployment other than that which was voluntary. As a result, Mill naturally found himself unmoved by Attwood's impassioned pleas for higher prices, employment, and output. Second, Mill viewed the whole operation as sheer robbery, involving the expropriation of creditor classes.

In the *Principles* Mill distinguished between two cases involving the issue of notes. The first case, which he attributed to Attwood, assumed that "all prices . . . rise equally." The second, which was attributed to David Hume, assumed that "all commodities would not rise in price simultaneously." In both cases an inconvertible paper currency was assumed so that there would be no international check to issues.[71]

The first case seemed completely erroneous to Mill:

Mr. Attwood maintained that a rise in prices . . . stimulates every producer to his utmost exertions, and brings all the capital and labour of the country into complete employment; and that this has invariably happened in all periods of rising prices, when the rise was on a sufficiently great scale. I presume, however, that the inducement which, according to Mr. Attwood, excited this unusual ardour in all persons engaged in production, must have been the expectation of getting more commodities generally, more real wealth, in exchange for the produce of their labour.[72]

Mill failed at this point to endorse explicitly the view that rising prices would stimulate production.[73] In any case such an increase seemed to have no merit. The whole expansion is a delusion:

> It calculates on finding the whole world persisting for ever in the belief that more pieces of paper are more riches, and never discovering that, with all their paper, they cannot buy more of anything than they could before.[74]

Moreover, no such mistake is made in actual speculative periods, for then speculation is based on the expectation of realizing gains before prices fall. Even if enough notes were issued to sustain prices, speculators would be disappointed, the delusion would disappear, and with it, presumably, any increase in production.

Hume's argument was based on the assumption that "all commodities would not rise in price simultaneously," so that some persons would gain and some would lose from the price rise. Mill argues that this is correct. First of all, the issuer of the notes gains, with all holders of currency losing through the rise in prices what the issuer gains. Part of the gain goes to the producers and dealers who receive the new notes as loans. Second, there is a benefit reaped by all debtors and a corresponding loss by all creditors.

> On a superficial view it may be imagined that this is an advantage to industry; since the productive classes are great borrowers, and generally owe larger debts to the unproductive (if we include among the latter all persons not actually in business) than the unproductive classes owe to them; especially if the national debt is included.[75]

In effect then Mill seems to accept the view that a rise in prices will stimulate industry as Attwood and Hume had claimed. His objection to a program of this sort does not at this point seem to derive from empirical disagreement, but rather from a value judgment:

> And this might be accounted an advantage, if integrity and good faith were of no importance to the world, and to industry and commerce in particular.[76]

But again his ground seems to shift and a doubt arises as to whether any stimulus to industry does occur, for the next sentence says:

Not many, however, have been found to say that the currency ought to be depreciated on the simple ground of its being desirable to rob the national creditor and the private creditors of a part of what is in their bond.[77]

This may be merely the introduction of a transition to his discussion of the price drop after the war, or it may mean that the "superficial view" is erroneous and that no stimulus to industry, meaning production, occurs.

On balance Mill's attitude was probably based on several lines of thought. One line seemed to question the possibility of increasing production through inflation. A second suggested that such increases were undesirable in terms of the exertion involved. A third found that the injustices resulting from inflation outweighed the benefits that might result from an increase in production obtained by such means.

Moreover, there was another point which seemed of vital importance to Mill. Under convertibility there was a definite check to a rise in prices. With an inconvertible paper currency, a state of affairs which Mill associated with Attwood's argument, there was no such limit. The temptation, Mill believed, would prove too much for the issuers

who have at any rate a strong interest in issuing as much as possible, each issue being in itself a source of profit. Not to add, that the issuers may have, and in the case of a government paper, always have, a direct interest in lowering the value of the currency, because it is the medium in which their own debts are computed.[78]

While Attwood was confident that the government commissioners would act in the public interest, and did not care very much if this did involve inflation, Mill doubted that the government would act to stabilize prices, and, moreover, viewed inflation with alarm.

Mill's attitude toward the *droit au travail* pledge, made by the

Provisional Government during the French Revolution of 1848, casts further light on his views with respect to full employment proposals. The pledge and the *ateliers nationaux* that were its implementation arose out of the "great falling-off of employment through industrial stagnation," resulting either from the revolution or from the threat of socialism—it is impossible to tell which, on the basis of Mill's statements.

Its scheme was, that, when there was notoriously a deficiency of employment, the state should disburse sufficient funds to create the amount of productive employment which was wanting. But it gave no pledge that the State should find work for A or B. It reserved in its own hands the choice of its work-people. It relieved no individual from the responsibility of finding an employer, and proving his willingness to exert himself. What it undertook was, that there should always be employment to be found.[79]

Mill notes:

It is needless to enlarge on the incomparably less injurious influence of this intervention of the government in favour of labour collectively, than of the intervention of the parish to find employment individually for every able-bodied man who has not honesty or activity to seek and find it for himself.[80]

Thus the system differed from the English parochial system which gave to every pauper a right to demand work, or support without work, as an individual. The French government contemplated no such right, but only "action on the general labour market, not alms to the individual." The goal of the scheme, so strikingly similar to some of Attwood's pronouncements, was wholeheartedly endorsed by Mill as a moral principle. But for the existence of another consideration he could see no objection.

Mill's criticism of the *droit au travail* is based on its conflict with the principle of population. The argument involves a consideration of the reasons why unemployment can exist:

The rate of wages which results from competition distributes the whole existing wages-fund among the whole labouring population; if law or opinion succeeds in fixing wages above this rate, some labourers are kept out of employment.[81]

Thus it appears that while the unemployment in France, in 1848, may have originated from the disturbance of the revolution, its continuance depended upon the rigidity of wages. The unemployed would then starve unless the wages fund were increased. What the supporters of the *droit au travail* apparently intended was that through taxation a fund would be raised to finance the hire of the unemployed.[82] The taxation would fall upon both consumption and savings, so that on balance the size of the wages fund would increase.

However, the whole operation raises wages in the aggregate, and therefore tends to stimulate population, so that the Malthusian race between production and population becomes an issue. The difficulty arises even if the unemployed are employed productively:

But let them work ever so efficiently, the increasing population could not, as we have so often shown, increase the produce proportionally: the surplus, after all were fed, would bear a less and less proportion to the whole produce, and to the population: and the increase of people going on in a constant ratio, while the increase of produce went on in a diminishing ratio, the surplus would in time be wholly absorbed; taxation for the support of the poor would engross the whole income of the country; the payers and the receivers would be melted down into one mass. The check to population, either by death or prudence, could not than be staved off any longer.[83]

Despite this criticism Mill accepted the fact that after any revolution some such measures would be necessary.[84] From this to an endorsement of similar measures in other emergencies would seem to be a short step. Mill never took the step, either because he considered that serious unemployment, if it existed at any time, was too short-lived to warrant such measures, or because he feared, from experience, that such measures would become permanent features of the economy and thus subject to the argument based on the principle of population.

While neither the proposals of Attwood, nor those of Hume, nor those advanced in France met with a favorable response,

JOHN STUART MILL

Mill was inclined to look sympathetically on more modest attempts to mitigate commercial crisis:

> The frequent recurrence during the last half century of the painful series of phenomena called a commercial crisis, has directed much of the attention both of economists and of practical politicians to the contriving of expedients for averting, or, at the least, mitigating its evils.[85]

In this connection Mill felt that the excessive issue of bank notes aggravated gold drains in the later stages of speculation. The result was a contraction of credit by banks that was sharper than would otherwise have been required. The avoidance of this delay in contraction and the resulting sharpness of the contraction was, Mill felt, the real purpose of the Bank Act of 1844.[86]

The act, Mill thought, had both good and bad results. He believed that the limits placed upon the ability of the Bank of England to issue notes had a desirable effect in checking the extent of speculation and hence in limiting the violence of the recoil. On the system in operation before the passage of the act, a gold drain might lead not to a contraction of the note issue but rather to reissue, through new advances to the public:

> As long therefore, as the Bank of England and the other banks persevered in this course, so long gold continued to flow out, until so little was left that the Bank of England, being in danger of suspension of payments, was compelled at last to contract its discounts so greatly and suddenly as to produce a much more extreme variation in the rate of interest, inflict much greater loss and stress on individuals, and destroy a much greater amount of the ordinary credit of the country, than any real necessity required.[87]

Such reissues could not take place under the act. Mill ruled out the possibility that the same results would follow from advances in the form of deposits: the check to note issues would also limit deposit creation. The quicker action under the act slowed the gold outflow sooner and prevented the sudden and violent contractions that had characterized the years before 1844.

On the other hand, Mill saw two drawbacks in the act. First, when the recoil did come, the Bank was unable to act to mitigate the severity of the collapse.

Antecedently to 1844, if the Bank of England occasionally aggravated the severity of a commercial revulsion by rendering the collapse of credit more tardy and hence more violent than necessary, it in return rendered invaluable services during the revulsion itself, by coming forward with advances to support solvent firms, at a time when all other paper and almost all mercantile credit had become comparatively valueless.[88]

This is precluded through the limitation on note issues in the Bank Act. Mill predicted that suspension of the provisions of the act would be necessary in every great commercial difficulty, just as in 1847

The other drawback arose from the fact that the act made no distinction between those drains of gold which stemmed from general price increases and drains arising from other causes. In the first case there was no difficulty, but in the second the act created a contraction where none was required. As examples Mill cited government expenditures abroad during the Napoleonic Wars; large exportations of capital prior to the crises of 1825 and 1839; and crop failures either at home or abroad. Mill argued that in such instances the reserves of the Bank should be used without contraction of the currency, since the drains in many cases would cease of themselves. Here the act created a difficulty, for reserves that would be adequate if the Bank had one department became inadequate when two departments existed. Cessation of this type of drain might be achieved much more smoothly through a rise in interest rates which would attract foreign capital. The drain might also be corrected through income effects abroad:

The extra gains made by dealers and producers in foreign countries through the extra payments they receive from this country, are very likely to be partly expended in increased purchases of English commodities, either for consumption or speculation, though the effect may not manifest itself with sufficient rapidity to enable the transmission of gold to be dispensed with in the first instance.[89]

JOHN STUART MILL

Thus Mill argued that contractions of credit were likely to be more frequent under the act.

Although Mill usually favored the avoidance of speculative excesses as a means of preventing severe revulsions, there was one exception based upon the tendency of profits. Just as he argued that a quicker application of restraints to speculation would mitigate the subsequent reaction, so he argued at one point that a quicker onset of speculation might mitigate subsequent speculation:

The railway gambling of 1844 and 1845 probably saved the country from a depression of profits and interest, and a rise of all public and private securities, which would have engendered still wilder speculations, and when the effects came afterwards to be complicated by the scarcity of food, would have ended in a still more formidable crisis than was experienced in the years immediately following.[90]

5. CONCLUSION

The commercial cycle, as Mill saw it, differed in at least one respect from the cycle that seemed to be implicit in the writings of his contemporaries. In most of the other writers an expansion phase and a contraction phase can be distinguished. In Mill however, there are three phases. The cycle starts off with a speculative period in which both prices and production increase. This leads inevitably into crisis and revulsion in which prices and production fall. But the period of revulsion is short-lived and merges quickly and somewhat mysteriously into the quiescent state. Mill directs his attention to the turning points leading from speculation to revulsion and from quiescence to speculation, but ignores altogether the transition from revulsion to quiescence.

The quiescent state is essential to Mill's whole position. Mill could hardly have neglected the problems of unemployment during the cycle so easily but for the fact that the revulsion is quickly followed by a state of affairs characterized by full employment. Apparently the economic system tended to spring back rapidly to full employment, rapidly enough as a rule to make the problem of cyclical unemployment unimportant.

This also explains the distaste with which Mill generally views periods of speculation. The point of view which he adopted in the *Essays* seems to continue, though somewhat less explicitly, in the *Principles*. Such increases in production as take place during speculative periods are largely a result of that "general delusion" which leads producers to mistake money gains for real gains; to the extent that real increases in production do occur they are out of line with the extra effort that is exerted.

The quiescent state, it should be noted, is not characterized by constant aggregate production. It is rather a state of affairs in which capital is being accumulated, in which production is growing as the result of the normal, more or less routine, activities of the economy. Thus the whole cycle, as Mill sees it, is superimposed upon an upward secular trend of production. The combination of cycle and secular trend is not, however, mechanical. The cycle exists primarily because of the secular trend, and the secular trend is in turn influenced by the cycle. The trend, in itself, tends to lead to a decline in the rate of profit, which at a certain level would usher in the stationary state in which economic growth through accumulation would cease. The outbursts of speculation are a response to the falling profit rate: presumably during the quiescent periods the other factors working against a falling rate of profit are inadequate to offset the decline that results from accumulation. Low profits lead to risky investments that promise a larger return. Thus there arises the speculative period, marked and driven forward by investment in inventories and by the conversion of circulating capital into fixed capital. While such speculative periods may arise from the kind of exogenous event stressed by Tooke, Mill tends to view the effects of the falling rate of profit in routine operations as more fundamental. The speculative period is marked by the usual phenomena of expansion: rising prices, rising production, inventory investment, fixed capital formation.

The revulsion may arise for several reasons. First, inventory investment may come to an end when prices have risen so far as to lead to expectations of a fall in prices. This is stressed as long as Mill ignores fixed capital formation. Second, the rise in prices may lead to an external drain of gold and contraction in credit; while this is a normal phenomenon in every revulsion, Mill does not feel that it is essential to the downturn. Third, the conversion of circulating into fixed capital tends to drive up the rate of interest as circulating capital shrinks, and the higher rate of interest creates difficulties that precipitate the downturn. Mill's eclecticism is nowhere better illustrated than in this treatment of the onset of revulsion: these three different explanations had each been stressed by some contemporary.

It is the revulsion itself that creates the greatest difficulties in Mill's theory of the cycle. Characterized by falling prices and contraction of credit, it seems also to involve reduced production and unemployment. Most striking, however, is the fact that revulsion is rapidly replaced by the quiescent state, though why and how is obscure.

Mill's conception of the cycle is probably a leading reason for his neglect of depression as a social problem. Though other considerations played a role in his attitude, the belief that depression was very brief and that the normal state of affairs was a state of full employment was certainly most important. The remedies proposed by writers like Attwood had no attraction for Mill.

Conclusion

EACH OF the six writers discussed was concerned with economic fluctuations. These fluctuations were conceived to be general, that is to say, the writers recognized "the basic feature of business cycles," the "substantial agreement among many activities in the timing of their expansions and of their contractions."[1]

It may be useful to go further and consider six questions: First, what were the characteristics of expansions and contractions that impressed these writers most strongly? Second, how did they explain cumulative movements? Third, how did they treat turning points? Fourth, were these writers largely concerned only with crises and intervals between crises? Fifth, what measures of policy did they recommend to eliminate or mitigate fluctuations? Sixth, what were the methods used to derive generalizations about fluctuations?

Characteristics. There was quite general agreement that periods of expansion were marked by increases in aggregate production, in employment, in the prices both of commodities and factors of production, in money supply, and in investment and consumption; periods of contraction were marked by declines in the same variables.

Attwood, Malthus, Joplin, Wilson, and Tooke were, in varying degree, certain that expansion involved increased production and employment, although Mill at times seems to have had doubts about the matter. In contraction both production and employment moved down; again there is some difficulty in fitting Mill into this position, partly because of his treatment of the transi-

CONCLUSION

tion from revulsion to the quiescent state. Since statistics on this subject were almost totally nonexistent, there was a good deal of uncertainty and difference of opinion concerning the magnitude of the movements of production and employment.

There was no doubt, however, about the congruence of movements of commodity prices and money supply with expansions and contractions. Here statistics were available. The emphasis upon price movements was so marked in some writers, Tooke especially, that one is tempted to say that fluctuations in prices were the basic feature of the cycle. The concentration upon prices was one factor that led to the neglect of several cycles that are recognized today.

Interest rates rose during expansions, especially in the later stages, and fell in contraction, although the early stages of contraction might be marked by high interest rates. Money wage rates and money profits, it was agreed, rose during expansion and fell in contraction, but real wage rates received little attention. Wilson applied the generalization concerning profits only to the nonagricultural sector; profits in agriculture might follow an opposite course. Tooke stressed expected profits, seeing expansion as a period in which profit expectations became increasingly optimistic; eventually, however, this led to disappointment and hence to the pessimistic expectations of the contraction period.

Emphasis upon the instability of investment was characteristic of thinking at the time. Attwood, Tooke, and Mill particularly emphasized the instability of inventory investment. For Tooke, fluctuations in inventory investment were the most important factor in general expansions and contractions. Fixed capital formation played a relatively minor role in the literature before the 1840s. In Wilson's book on the agricultural cycle, fixed capital formation was considered, but it was only with his articles on the railroad boom of the 1840s that it became all-important. The same influence operated upon Mill, so that at the end of the period fluctuations in fixed capital formation received a good deal of attention.

Economic fluctuations were, for the most part, conceived of as national phenomena. The onset of expansion or contraction was often attributed to events overseas, but usually no attempt was made to suggest that expansions and contractions were worldwide. Only Wilson argued, notably in his agricultural theory, that contractions and expansions on the continent had the same timing as in England.

Cumulative Movements. The mechanism by which expansions and contractions took place was usually discussed in terms of interactions between incomes and expenditures. Increases in incomes led to increased expenditures, particularly expenditures on consumer goods, which in turn created income and further consumption expenditures. Attwood argued that inventory investment increased along with increased sales. Wilson introduced induced investment in fixed capital goods as a part of the process by which business reacted to increased expenditures upon consumer goods. In contraction the income-expenditure interaction worked in reverse. Tooke and Mill represented a somewhat different view, placing more stress on the speculative fever that, created by higher prices for one commodity, spreads to other commodities, thereby generalizing the expansion.

Turning Points. The explanation of turning points is closely related to the question: is there a business cycle? Cumulative movements may be set off by exogenous events completely unrelated to the state of business activity; and these events may even occur in such a way as to give an appearance of periodicity or of regular recurrence. If such were the case, there would be no need to do more than note at each turn the exogenous event or events that reversed the cumulative process. In contrast, explanation may be endogenous, so that, for instance, expansion itself creates forces that act to bring about the end of expansion and the onset of contraction. Reality is complicated by the fact that exogenous events do influence the course of business activity, so that in interpreting historical cycles it would be impossible to throw out exogenous explanations altogether.

In all of these writers there is recognition of exogenous events that influence turning points in business activity. Thus there are references to reduced government expenditures (Malthus, Attwood, Joplin), opening of new foreign markets (Tooke, Mill), harvest variations attributed to weather or left unexplained (Joplin, Tooke), variations in "enterprise" or saving (Joplin), corn laws (Wilson). In two writers, Malthus and Joplin, exogenous explanations play so large a role that relatively little stress is placed on endogenous forces working to reverse expansions or contractions.

The other four writers employed some type of endogenous explanation in their theorizing on economic fluctuations. A favorite mechanism, emphasized by Attwood, involved international gold flows: starting with expansion, the causal argument proceeded to higher commodity prices, to gold exports, and hence, by way of incorrect monetary policies, to recession. The agricultural theory of Wilson was also, to some degree, an endogenous theory of turning points. The overinvestment theory, used by both Wilson and Mill, provided an endogenous explanation of the upper turning point, though not of the lower turning point. Somewhat vaguer ideas concerning the effect of high prices on consumption (Tooke), on inventory investment (Mill), and on excessive stocks of commodities in relation to "necessary wants" (Attwood) were also used as endogenous explanations of upper turning points.

Essentially the same range of explanations appeared when the end of contraction was considered: international flows of gold, high corn output, and low prices were all used to explain how contractions turned into revival. Mill added his conception of gradually falling profits on routine operations as an explanation for the onset of speculation, but failed to explain how the transition from the revulsion to the quiescent state took place.

Crises and Intervals Between Crises. In the introductory chapter "economic fluctuations" were defined to include two types of fluctuation, "business cycles" and "changes in business conditions which occur between the dates of 'crises.' "[2] Wesley C. Mitchell expressed the following opinion:

CONCLUSION

To the early workers in our field the pressing problem was to account for the dramatic events which they called "commercial crises."[3]

Mitchell went on to state that these early workers confined their attention, for the most part, to this single phase of the business cycle; connected with this emphasis was the tendency to ignore those transitions from prosperity to depression that were mild, with the result that the intervals between crises might contain more than one business cycle.[4]

These generalizations are only partially valid for the six writers studied. It is true that the milder transitions from prosperity to depression were ignored: no writer identified all of the recessions and all of the business cycles that have been recognized in later investigations of the period. On the other hand, it is not true that these six writers ignored either expansions and contractions, or the process by which recession arose out of prosperity, or revival out of contraction.

Remedies. In addition to disagreement about the nature of economic fluctuations, disagreement about the relative importance of various goals influenced writers to differ about the remedies that would be appropriate. Attwood's enthusiasm for full employment outweighed any slight doubts he might have had about the undesirability of inflation, while Mill, at the other extreme, stressed the evils of inflation and showed, on the whole, little interest in policies designed to ensure full employment. It is hard to tell, however, whether the disagreement rested fundamentally upon goals, or whether there was an underlying difference as to the extent and duration of unemployment. Another type of disagreement involved the issue of international versus domestic stability. Attwood would willingly have sacrificed the gold standard, Joplin vacillated on the issue, and Tooke was outraged at the mere suggestion of such a sacrifice.

Attwood, and sometimes Joplin, advocated an easy money policy as a means of combating depression, while others placed little trust in such methods. Malthus favored unproductive consumption. Wilson advocated repeal of the corn laws, or deplored the excessive investments of the 1840s, while Tooke and Mill discussed measures that would mitigate the excesses of speculation and thus reduce the severity of revulsion.

Methods. The empirical evidence that was used to support generalizations concerning economic fluctuations was not, in the main, quantitative. The statistical materials available were very limited in coverage: time series relating to Bank of England accounts, to interest rates, to imports and exports, and to the prices of particular commodities were commonly used. But there was almost no use of series related, even remotely, to physical quantity of production or consumption, to employment, or to investment, and no use of series on national income or national wealth, savings, consumption, or profits; all of the latter series would have been difficult or impossible to obtain.

Qualitative material of two sorts substituted for statistics. First, there were "historical" data about which no disagreement was possible. Thus explanations that depended upon the enactment of laws, upon overseas political events, or upon the railroad boom of the 1840s had the same kind of objectivity as did those which could be grounded upon statistics. Such events were a matter of common knowledge.

Second, qualitative material of a different sort was involved in the use of concepts upon which no common knowledge was possible. Explanations in terms of expenditures, income, investment, consumption, or savings could not be a matter of everyday knowledge, and even the special knowledge of the theorists who used these concepts might be legitimately questioned. These explanations were based upon an extremely shaky foundation.

The absence of statistical data on such variables aroused no great dissatisfaction. While these concepts were used and even examined quite carefully (Malthus, Joplin, Wilson), suggestions that statistics should be collected were rare. Attwood, despite his emphasis on the level of employment, did not suggest the collection of employment statistics; he did, however, argue that statistics on the price of agricultural labor should be collected to provide a criterion for currency management. Wilson called for statistics on production and inventories, not with a view to scientific use, but on the ground that such data would directly mitigate fluctuations. The use of concepts such as income and investment did not do much, in this period, to stimulate the growth of empirical knowledge.

Conclusion. If we compare the theories of the six writers of 1815-48 with more modern theories, the differences are not striking. Consider, for example, the major types of theory identified by G. Haberler.[5] The purely monetary theory, as represented by R. G. Hawtrey, finds its analogue in the speculations of Thomas Attwood. Overinvestment theory, as set forth in the writings of F. A. Hayek, finds precursors in James Wilson and John Stuart Mill. The underconsumption theory of J. A. Hobson has some similarities to the doctrines of Thomas Malthus. Psychological theories emphasizing expectations and the infectious nature of optimism and pessimism suggest immediately the similar emphasis in the works of Thomas Tooke and John Stuart Mill. The less modern harvest theory of W. S. Jevons has a close affinity to the agricultural theory of James Wilson. Haberler's chapter on "recent discussions," largely concerned with the controversies arising out of the work of J. M. Keynes, is less clearly related to business cycles; but there are important points of similarity, as already seen, between Keynes and both Thomas Joplin and Thomas Malthus. Exact parallels are naturally impossible, but the rough congruence between the theories of the early nineteenth century and the theories current in recent times is notable.

In other respects there are great differences between the two periods. In general the modern writer is far more addicted to the use of quantitative data; more data are available and the emphasis upon empirical research is greater. Another difference is indicated by the very existence of an area of economics labeled "business cycles" or "economic fluctuations"; such an area was not recognized in the first half of the nineteenth century. There was no continuing tradition; writers were relatively isolated from one another. At the same time, the early writer was not primarily interested in scientific knowledge, but rather in reform: discussions of economic fluctuations were, for the most part, a byproduct of the public controversies of the day—currency reform, banking reform, repeal of the corn laws. The absence of a scientific tradition tended to reduce the clarity of thought and expression; while the modern theorist is not always clear, continuous inspection of the literature tends to minimize, even if it does not entirely eliminate, the kinds of confusion that plagued the writers of 1815-48.

Much of the theorizing during the period was obscure and illogical. The factual basis was thin. Publications that were explicitly concerned with economic fluctuations were the exception. There was little real attention devoted to what other writers said. Yet despite all these weaknesses, economic fluctuations were discussed, a conception of the business cycle began to take form, and attempts were made to explain why such fluctuations occurred.

Notes

INTRODUCTION

1. W. C. Mitchell, *Business Cycles* (New York, 1927), p. 468. The question of the relationship between business cycles and economic fluctuations as viewed by the writers considered in this study must be postponed until the Conclusion.

2. See especially J. W. Angell, *The Theory of International Prices* (Cambridge, Massachusetts, 1926); A. W. Marget, *The Theory of Prices* (2 vols., New York, 1938-42); L. W. Mints, *A History of Banking Theory* (Chicago, 1945); K. H. Niebyl, *Studies in the Classical Theories of Money* (New York, 1946); J. Viner, *Studies in the Theory of International Trade* (New York, 1937); E. Wood, *English Theories of Central Banking Control, 1819-1858* (Cambridge, Massachusetts, 1939).

3. The following works contain discussions of the literature on economic fluctuations during this period: E. v. Bergmann, *Geschichte der nationalökonomischen Krisentheorien* (Stuttgart, 1895); A. Gourvitch, *Survey of Economic Change and Employment* (Philadelphia, 1940); A. H. Hansen, *Business Cycles and National Income* (New York, 1951); J. Lescure, *Des Crises générales et périodique de surproduction* (4th ed., Paris, 1932).

4. See in this connection the following works: Mitchell, *Business Cycles*; W. L. Thorp, *Business Annals* (New York, 1926); W. Hoffmann, *Wachstum und Wachstumsformen der englischen Industriewirtschaft von 1700 bis zur Gegenwart* (Jena, 1940), translated by W. H. Chaloner and W. O. Henderson as *British Industry, 1700-1950* (Oxford, 1955); W. W. Rostow, *British Economy of the Nineteenth Century* (Oxford, 1948); J. A. Schumpeter, *Business Cycles* (2 vols., New York, 1939); N. J. Silberling, "British Prices and Business Cycles, 1779-1850," *Review of Economic Statistics* (1923).

5. See especially S. G. Checkland, "The Birmingham Economists, 1815-1850," *Economic History Review* (1948); R. S. Sayers, "The Question of the Standard, 1815-44," *Economic History* (1935).

6. J. M. Keynes, "Robert Malthus," *Essays in Biography* (New York, 1933), and *The General Theory of Employment, Interest, and Money* (New York, 1936).

7. See Viner, *Studies in the Theory of International Trade*, p. 221.

THOMAS ATTWOOD

1. Biographical material can be found in C. M. Wakefield, *Life of Thomas Attwood* (London, 1885); G. D. H. Cole, "Thomas Attwood," in *Chartist Portraits* (London, 1941).

2. Francis Place is quoted in Graham Wallas, *The Life of Francis Place, 1771-1854* (London, 1898), p. 251. Mill's description appears in his article "The Currency Juggle," *Tait's Edinburgh Magazine* (1833), reprinted in *Dissertations and Discussions* (Boston, 1865), I, 68-81.

3. J. S. Mill, *Principles of Political Economy*, ed. by W. J. Ashley (London, 1909), p. 550.

4. David Ricardo, *Letters of David Ricardo to Hutches Trower and Others, 1811-1823*, ed. by J. Bonar and J. H. Hollander (Oxford, 1899), p. 48; or P. Sraffa, ed., *The Works and Correspondence of David Ricardo* (10 vols., Cambridge, 1951-55), VIII, 370.

5. *Economist*, September 9, 1843, p. 18.

6. Wakefield, *Life*, p. ix.

7. Thomas Attwood, *Prosperity Restored; or, Reflections on the Cause of the Public Distresses, and on the Only Means of Relieving Them* (London, 1817), p. 196. This work is hereafter cited as *Prosperity Restored*.

8. The Chartist movement set forth its program in 1838 in a six-point "Charter" demanding universal manhood suffrage, annually elected Parliaments, vote by secret ballot, no property qualifications for members of Parliament, payment of members of Parliament, and equal electoral districts. See R. G. Gammage, *History of the Chartist Movement, 1837-1854* (London, 1894), p. 6.

9. Wakefield, *Life*, pp. 350, 360.

10. *Ibid.*, pp. 350-65; also Cole, *Chartist Portraits*, pp. 129-30.

11. Among the better known were his brother Matthias Attwood, George Frederick Muntz, Sir John Sinclair, Charles Callis Western,

John Rooke, Charles Jones, Henry James, Edwin and Frederick Hill, and the Reverend Richard Cruttwell. See R. S. Sayers, "The Question of the Standard," *Economic History* (1935), and S. G. Checkland, "The Birmingham Economists," *Economic History Review* (1948).

12. Thomas Attwood, *The Remedy; or, Thoughts on the Present Distresses* (London, 1816) (first edition ?), hereafter cited as *Remedy*. Thomas Attwood, *A Letter to the Right Honorable Nicholas Vansittart, on the Creation of Money and on Its Action upon National Prosperity* (Birmingham, 1817), hereafter cited as *Letter to Vansittart*. Also Attwood, *Prosperity Restored*.

13. Thomas Attwood, *Observations on Currency, Population, and Pauperism in Two Letters to Arthur Young, Esq.* (Birmingham, 1818), p. 8. This work is hereafter cited as *Observations*.

14. Attwood, *Prosperity Restored*, p. 39.

15. See pp. 13-14 on the reasons for the 1813 decline in expenditures.

16. Attwood, *Prosperity Restored*, pp. 28-29.

17. Attwood, *Remedy*, p. 11.

18. Attwood, *Observations*, pp. 194-95.

19. Attwood, *Prosperity Restored*, p. 36.

20. Attwood, *Letter to Vansittart*, p. 99.

21. *Report from the Committee of Secrecy on the Bank of England Charter with the Minutes of Evidence, Appendix and Index* (1832), Q. 5675, pp. 459-60. This report is hereafter cited as *Evidence 1832*.

22. *Ibid.*, Q. 5663-64, p. 459.

23. Attwood, *Prosperity Restored*, pp. 78-79.

24. Attwood, *Observations*, p. 204.

25. Attwood, *Letter to Vansittart*, p. 99.

26. Attwood, *Remedy*, pp. 11-12.

27. Attwood, *Prosperity Restored*, p. 38.

28. *Evidence 1832*, Q. 5651-59. By 1832 Attwood had lost interest in natural remedies.

29. Attwood, *Prosperity Restored*, p. 38.

30. Attwood, *Letter to Vansittart*, p. 100.

31. Attwood, *Remedy*, p. 12.

32. Attwood, *Prosperity Restored*, p. 154.

33. *Ibid.*, p. 140.

34. Attwood, *Remedy*, p. 26.

35. *Ibid.*, p. 5.

36. Attwood, *Prosperity Restored*, p. 10.

37. Attwood, *Observations*, pp. 110-11.
38. Attwood, *Prosperity Restored*, p. 49.
39. Attwood, *Letter to Vansittart*, p. 13; *Observations*, pp. 62-63.
40. Attwood, *Observations*, p. 241.
41. *Ibid.*, pp. 59-60; the same mechanism is described in *Prosperity Restored*, p. 132, and in *Letter to Vansittart*, pp. 39-41.
42. In 1817 and 1818 the Bank of England was still operating under the Restriction Act of 1797; this act had suspended specie payments on Bank of England notes. In November, 1816, however, the Bank, utilizing a provision of the Act, began to redeem certain categories of notes in gold, on demand, at the old par of £3 17s. 10½d. per ounce of gold. This practice continued until outlawed by Parliament in 1819. A. W. Acworth, *Financial Reconstruction in England, 1815-1822* (London, 1925), pp. 73-74; J. Viner, *Studies in the Theory of International Trade* (New York, 1937), p. 172.
43. Attwood, *Observations*, pp. 121, 210, 227.
44. *Ibid.*, p. 210.
45. *Ibid.*, p. 211.
46. *Ibid.*, p. 174.
47. *Reports Respecting the Bank of England Resuming Cash Payments viz. The First and Second Reports of the Lords Committees, Appointed a Secret Committee to Inquire into the State of the Bank of England with Respect to the Expediency of the Resumption of Cash Payments;—with Minutes of Evidence and an Appendix* (1819), p. 88. See also *Report from the Select Committee to Whom the Several Petitions Complaining of the Depressed State of the Agriculture of the United Kingdom Were Referred* (1821), p. 252.
48. Acworth, *Financial Reconstruction in England*, p. 93; Viner, *Studies in the Theory of International Trade*, p. 173.
49. Thomas Attwood, *A Second Letter to the Earl of Liverpool, on the Bank Reports, as Occasioning the National Dangers and Distresses* (Birmingham, 1819), p. 100. This work is hereafter cited as *Second Letter to Liverpool*.
50. *Ibid., passim*. Also Thomas Attwood, *An Exposition of the Cause and Remedy of the Agricultural Distress* (Hertford, 1828), written in 1821, *passim*.
51. Thomas Attwood (and Sir John Sinclair), *The Late Prosperity, and the Present Adversity of the Country, Explained; the Proper Remedies Considered, and the Comparative Merits of the English and Scottish Systems of Banking Discussed, in a Correspondence between Sir John Sinclair and Mr.*

Thomas Attwood (London, 1826), pp. 8-10, 110-11. This work is hereafter cited as *Late Prosperity*.

52. Attwood rejected explanations based on speculation in joint stock companies, which he regarded as sound, or on actions of country bankers, who, he claimed, only followed the Bank of England. *Ibid.*, pp. 112, 122-23.

53. *Ibid.*, p. 121.

54. *Ibid.*, pp. 24-26, 121.

55. After *The Scotch Banker* (London, 1828), and the testimony given in 1832, there are no extensive discussions of the causes of economic fluctuations. In Parliament Attwood confined himself to rather general statements which repeated his earlier published opinions. The date of the upturn is therefore unclear.

56. Attwood, *The Scotch Banker*, pp. 44-45.

57. *Evidence 1832*, Q. 5724-25, p. 464. See pp. 27-28 in this chapter.

58. Thomas Attwood, *The Distressed State of the Country* (Birmingham, 1829), p. 11.

59. Attwood, *Observations*, pp. 45-46.

60. *Ibid.*, p. 39. Elsewhere Attwood indicated that he preferred public to private relief, *ibid.*, pp. 42-43, and proposed government cotton factories as a solution for the problem presented by "Juvenile Delinquents" in London, *ibid.*, pp. 48-50.

61. *Ibid.*, p. 39.

62. *Ibid.*, pp. 39-40.

63. *Ibid.*, pp. 39-50.

64. See J. H. Clapham, *An Economic History of Modern Britain* (3 vols., Cambridge, England, 1930-38), I, 357-61.

65. Attwood, *Observations*, p. 43.

66. *Ibid.*, p. 95. Attwood also favored National Savings Banks which would provide "the means and inducement" to save for old age, *ibid.*, p. 96.

67. Attwood, *Prosperity Restored*, p. 105.

68. Attwood, *Observations*, p. 23 footnote.

69. *Ibid.*, pp. 23-32. This passage highly praises the ancient Egyptians for using peacetime armies in building public works, both useful and magnificent. Attwood argues that such activity was better than activity that merely increased individual luxury.

70. Attwood, *Remedy*, p. 7.

194 NOTES: ATTWOOD

71. Attwood, *Letter to Vansittart*, pp. 20-22. In the *Remedy*, pp. 28-29, Attwood had argued that government issues of exchequer bills would not be so effective since such bills did not circulate. But circulating exchequer bills were given all the characteristics of money, *Observations*, p. 130.
72. Attwood, *Second Letter to Liverpool*, pp. 46-47.
73. Attwood, *Observations*, pp. 141-45.
74. *Ibid.*, p. 171.
75. Attwood, *Remedy*, p. 20.
76. Attwood, *Prosperity Restored*, pp. 137-38.
77. Attwood, *Remedy*, pp. 22-24.
78. Attwood, *Prosperity Restored*, p. 131.
79. *Ibid.*, pp. 134-35; *Letter to Vansittart*, pp. 53-58.
80. Attwood, *Remedy*, pp. 28-29.
81. Attwood, *Prosperity Restored*, pp. 129-30.
82. *Ibid.*, pp. 130-31; *Letter to Vansittart*, pp. 53-58.
83. Attwood, *Observations*, pp. 126-27.
84. Attwood, *Remedy*, pp. 23-24.
85. Attwood, *Second Letter to Liverpool*, p. 28; see also the preface to *The Scotch Banker*.
86. Attwood, *Letter to Vansittart*, pp. 20-22.
87. *Ibid.*, p. 27. It was never clear what statistics, if any, formed the basis for these estimates.
88. See pp. 28-31.
89. *Mansell & Co's. Report of the Important Discussion Held in Birmingham, August the 28th and 29th, 1832, between William Cobbett, Thomas Attwood, and Charles Jones, Esqrs.* (2d ed., Birmingham, 1832), p. 30; see also Attwood, *Prosperity Restored*, p. 131.
90. *Evidence 1832*, Q. 5648, pp. 457-58.
91. See Asa Briggs, "Thomas Attwood and the Economic Background of the Birmingham Political Union," *Cambridge Historical Journal* (1948).
92. *Evidence 1832*, Q. 5724-26, p. 464.
93. Attwood, *The Scotch Banker*, p. 48.
94. *Ibid.*, p. 17.
95. Attwood, *Prosperity Restored*, pp. 135-36. In choosing a price of 15 shillings per bushel, Attwood was taking a price that was close to the peak annual average of the war years. The annual average in 1812, the peak year, was approximately 15.7 shillings. In 1816, when Attwood

was writing, the annual average was approximately 9.5 shillings. See W. W. Rostow, *British Economy of the Nineteenth Century* (Oxford, 1948), p. 125; and similar figures in D. G. Barnes, *A History of the English Corn Laws, from 1660-1846* (London, 1930), p. 298.

96. Attwood, *Prosperity Restored*, p. 193. The 18 shilling par was apparently based on the high wages of the war period. Though wages fell after the war, it is extremely difficult to say anything more exact on the subject, partly because of the variations from county to county. See, however, Clapham, *An Economic History of Modern Britain*, I, 125-26, and A. C. Bowley, "The Statistics of Wages in the United Kingdom during the Last Hundred Years," *Journal of the Royal Statistical Society* (1898 and 1899).

97. Attwood, *Observations*, pp. 166-67.

98. *Ibid.*, p. 204.

99. *Ibid.*, pp. 204-5.

100. *Ibid.* J. H. Clapham points out that the usury law limit of 5 per cent had all but killed ordinary mortgage business by 1816, but that roundabout borrowing from insurance companies was still carried on at rates of 10 per cent and upwards. See Clapham, *An Economic History of Modern Britain*, I, 348.

101. Attwood, *Observations*, p. 205. A further difficulty arises from Attwood's view that low interest rates were not necessarily an indication of abundant currency, but merely might indicate that few people would borrow for lack of confidence, while, for the same reason, many would be willing to lend. See Attwood, *Second Letter to Liverpool*, p. 30. And see p. 19 earlier in this chapter.

102. See, for example, the second quotation on page 29. Also *Evidence 1832*, Q. 5781, p. 468. See pp. 169-72, for the views of John Stuart Mill on Attwood.

103. Compare pp. 10-11.

104. *Evidence 1832*, Q. 5759, p. 467.

105. *Ibid.*, Q. 4781, p. 468.

106. Attwood, *Prosperity Restored*, pp. 71-73.

107. *Evidence 1832*, Q. 5627, p. 456; see also Attwood, *Prosperity Restored*, pp. 167-68.

108. Attwood, *Second Letter to Liverpool*, p. 43; also *Late Prosperity*, pp. 35-36, and *Evidence 1832*, Q. 5639, p. 457.

109. Attwood, *Late Prosperity*, pp. 29-31.

110. *Ibid.*, p. 34; also *Evidence 1832*, Q. 5637, p. 457.

111. Attwood, *Observations*, pp. 243-44.
112. On this point see Elmer Wood, *English Theories of Central Banking Control, 1819-1858* (Cambridge, Mass., 1939), p. 51.
113. Attwood, *Observations*, p. 39.
114. Sir W. H. Beveridge, *Full Employment in a Free Society* (New York, 1945), p. 20.
115. See, e.g., N. S. Buck, *The Development of the Organization of Anglo-American Trade* (New Haven, 1925).
116. Note J. S. Mill's disagreement, pp. 169-72.

THOMAS ROBERT MALTHUS

1. For biographical material see James Bonar, *Malthus and His Work* (New York, 1924); J. M. Keynes, "Robert Malthus," *Essays in Biography* (New York, 1933).
2. Thomas Robert Malthus, *Principles of Political Economy* (New York, 1951). This work is hereafter cited as *Principles*. This edition is a reprint of the second edition, published in 1836; the first edition was published in 1820.
3. Adam Smith, *The Wealth of Nations* (New York, 1937), pp. lvii-lx.
4. Malthus, *Principles*, p. 33.
5. *Ibid.*
6. *Ibid.*, p. 23.
7. *Ibid.*, p. 27.
8. *Ibid.*, p. 300.
9. *Ibid.*, p. 304.
10. *Ibid.*, pp. 304-5.
11. *Ibid.*, p. 301.
12. *Ibid.*
13. See, e.g., James J. O'Leary, "Malthus and Keynes," *Journal of Political Economy* (1942).
14. Malthus, *Principles*, p. 277.
15. *Ibid.*, p. 328.
16. See pp. 65-66.
17. Malthus, *Principles*, p. 326.
18. But see pp. 66-67.
19. David Ricardo, *Notes on Malthus' "Principles of Political Economy,"* ed. by J. H. Hollander and T. E. Gregory (London and Baltimore,

NOTES: MALTHUS

1928), p. 138 (this edition is hereafter cited as *Notes on Malthus*); or P. Sraffa, ed., *The Works and Correspondence of David Ricardo* (10 vols., Cambridge, England, 1951-55), II, 260.

20. David Ricardo, *Letters of David Ricardo to Thomas Robert Malthus, 1810-1823*, ed. by James Bonar (London, 1887), p. 190 (this edition is hereafter cited as *Letters to Malthus*); or Sraffa, ed., *The Works and Correspondence of David Ricardo*, IX, 25-26. A part of the relevant quotation appears on p. 66, later in this chapter. The views expressed by Ricardo in his *Principles of Political Economy* (Everyman's ed., London and New York, 1911), p. 176 (or Sraffa, ed., *The Works and Correspondence of David Ricardo*, I, 265) concerning the possible duration of unemployment seem to be in conflict with the passage cited.

21. See the preceding note.
22. Malthus, *Principles*, pp. 413-14.
23. *Ibid.*, p. 404.
24. *Ibid.*, p. 178.
25. This procedure foreshadowed the use of "wage units" by J. M. Keynes.
26. Malthus, *Principles*, p. 314.
27. *Ibid.*, p. 315.
28. Ricardo, *Notes on Malthus*, p. 169; or Sraffa, ed., *The Works and Correspondence of David Ricardo*, II, 319-21.
29. Oscar Lange, "Say's Law: A Restatement and Criticism," in *Studies in Mathematical Economics and Econometrics*, ed. by Lange, McIntyre, and Yntema (Chicago, 1942), pp. 59-61.
30. Malthus, *Principles*, p. 324.
31. *Ibid.*, p. 365.
32. *Ibid.*, pp. 363-64.
33. *Ibid.*, p. 374.
34. *Ibid.*
35. See pp. 56-59.
36. Malthus, *Principles*, p. 374.
37. *Ibid.*, p. 384.
38. *Ibid.*, p. 380.
39. See p. 47.
40. Malthus, *Principles*, p. 400.
41. *Ibid.*
42. [Thomas Robert Malthus], "Depreciation of Paper Currency," *Edinburgh Review* (1811), p. 364.

43. *Ibid.*
44. *Ibid.*, pp. 365-66.
45. [Thomas Robert Malthus], "Tooke—on High and Low Prices," *Quarterly Review* (1823), p. 216.
46. *Ibid.*, p. 223.
47. *Ibid.*
48. *Ibid.*, p. 228.
49. Malthus, *Principles*, p. 329.
50. *Ibid.*, p. 409.
51. *Ibid.*, p. 420.
52. *Ibid.*, p. 421.
53. *Ibid.*, pp. 416-17.
54. *Ibid.*, p. 413, reprinted unchanged from the first edition of the *Principles*, which came out in 1820.
55. *Ibid.*, p. 424.
56. *Ibid.*, p. 232.
57. Ricardo, *Letters to Malthus*, p. 190; or Sraffa, ed., *The Works and Correspondence of David Ricardo*, IX, 25.
58. Malthus, *Principles*, p. 393.
59. *Ibid.*, p. 387.
60. See the chapter on Thomas Attwood.
61. Malthus, *Principles*, p. 431.
62. *Ibid.*, pp. 431-32.
63. *Ibid.*, p. 432.
64. At the time "public works" meant works used by the public; the term was not confined to government-financed projects.
65. Malthus, *Principles*, pp. 429-30.
66. Railroad building in the 1830s and 1840s seems to have first attracted attention, on a major scale, to the role of investment in fixed capital goods. See the chapter on James Wilson.
67. Malthus, *Principles*, p. 430.
68. Ricardo, *Notes on Malthus*, editor's introduction.

THOMAS JOPLIN

1. For biographical material see "Thomas Joplin," *Dictionary of National Biography* (London, 1921-22), and his obituary in *The Gentleman's Magazine* (1848).

2. Thomas Joplin, *An Analysis and History of the Currency Question* (London, 1832), p. 73. This work is hereafter cited as *Analysis*. See also *Outlines of a System of Political Economy* (London, 1823), pp. 154-56. This work is hereafter cited as *Political Economy*.

3. Joplin, *Analysis*, p. 101.

4. Joplin, *Political Economy*, p. 44; also, *Analysis*, p. 102.

5. Thomas Joplin, *Views on the Currency* (London, 1828), p. 52. This work is hereafter cited as *Views 1828*.

6. Joplin, *Political Economy*, pp. 44-45.

7. Thomas Joplin, *Currency Reform* (London, 1844), pp. 36-37.

8. Joplin, *Political Economy*, p. 164; also *Views 1828*, p. 53.

9. Compare Joplin, *Political Economy*, p. 59, and *Analysis*, p. 106.

10. Joplin, *Analysis*, p. 106.

11. *Ibid.*

12. Joplin, *Political Economy*, pp. 61-62.

13. Joplin, *Analysis*, pp. 105-6; also *Political Economy*, p. 62.

14. Joplin, *Analysis*, p. 104.

15. Joplin, *Currency Reform*, p. 47.

16. *Ibid.*, p. 116.

17. Joplin, *Views 1828*, p. 165.

18. Joplin, *Analysis*, pp. 139-40.

19. Joplin, *Currency Reform*, p. 47; see also the quotation from David Hume's *Essay on Money* in *Analysis*, pp. 148-49.

20. Joplin, *Analysis*, p. 123.

21. Joplin, *Views 1828*, p. 165.

22. Figures 3 and 4, as well as Figures 5 and 6, are an adaptation of the graphical presentation of the Keynesian system used by I. O. Scott, Jr., "An Exposition of the Keynesian System," *Review of Economic Studies* (1950-51).

23. Joplin, *Currency Reform*, p. 31.

24. *Ibid.*, pp. 28-29.

25. *Ibid.*, p. 85.

26. *Ibid.*, p. 55.

27. Joplin, *Analysis*, p. 168.

28. *Ibid.*, pp. 166-68.

29. Arthur F. Burns and Wesley C. Mitchell, *Measuring Business Cycles* (New York, 1946), p. 79.

30. Joplin, *Analysis*, p. 123.

31. *Ibid.*

32. Joplin, *Views 1828*, p. 164. Joplin had three theories of the manner in which harvests affected economic activity. Taken individually these theories may be intelligible; as a group they are not intelligible. In practice he made little use of harvests in explaining economic fluctuations.
33. Joplin, *Analysis*, p. 125.
34. Joplin, *Views 1828*, p. 165.
35. Joplin, *Analysis*, pp. 139-40.
36. Thomas Joplin, *Articles on Banking and Currency* (London, 1838), p. 107. This work is hereafter cited as *Articles*.
37. Joplin, *Analysis*, p. 223.
38. Joplin, *Currency Reform*, p. 6.
39. *Ibid.*, p. 80.
40. Joplin, *Articles*, p. 65.
41. *Ibid.*, p. 67.
42. Joplin, *Currency Reform*, p. 77.
43. *Ibid.*, pp. 77-78.
44. *Ibid.*, pp. 78-79.
45. Thomas Joplin, *The Cause and Cure of Our Commercial Embarrassments* (London, 1841), p. 47. This work is hereafter cited as *Cause and Cure*.
46. *Ibid.*, p. 48.
47. Joplin, *Articles*, p. 89.
48. *Ibid.*
49. Joplin, *Political Economy*, p. 260.
50. Joplin preferred a paper to a metallic currency on grounds of greater convenience. *Ibid.*, p. 261.
51. The charter of the Bank of England prevented the formation of banks with more than six partners in England, and so made joint stock banks illegal. The existing banks in England were private banks, that is, banks with not more than six partners. Joplin, *An Essay on Banking*, pp. 8 and 18; this publication is bound with Joplin, *Political Economy*, but the pagination is separate.
52. Joplin, *Political Economy*, pp. 266-67.
53. *Ibid.*, pp. 269-70.
54. *Ibid.*, pp. 271-77.
55. Thomas Joplin, *An Illustration of Mr. Joplin's Views on Currency* (London, 1825), p. 17.
56. After 1826 note-issuing joint stock banks were permitted if lo-

cated more than 65 miles from London. See J. H. Clapham, *An Economic History of Modern Britain* (Cambridge, England, 1930-38), I, 275.

57. Joplin, *Analysis*, pp. 148-49; also *Views 1828*, p. 168.

58. Joplin, *Analysis*, pp. 149-50.

59. *Ibid.*, p. 173.

60. The growth of note-issuing joint stock banking outside of London had been rapid after the legalization of such institutions in 1826. See E. Wood, *English Theories of Central Banking Control, 1819-1858* (Cambridge, Mass., 1939), p. 14. The act renewing the Bank of England charter in 1833 permitted the establishment of nonissue joint stock banks in the London area. See Clapham, *An Economic History of Modern Britain*, I, 509-10.

61. Thomas Joplin, *On Our Monetary System* (London, 1839), pp. 53-57.

62. *Ibid.*, p. 58.

63. *Ibid.*

64. Joplin, *Cause and Cure*, pp. 41-46; also *Currency Reform*, p. 65.

65. Joplin, *Currency Reform*, p. 74.

66. *Ibid.*

67. Thomas Joplin, *An Examination of Sir Robert Peel's Currency Bill of 1844* (London, 1844), especially pp. 37-38.

68. *Ibid.*, p. 95.

JAMES WILSON

1. For biographical material see Walter Bagehot, "Memoir of the Right Hon. James Wilson," Supplement to the *Economist* (November 17, 1860); Bagehot was Wilson's son-in-law and his successor as editor of the *Economist*. See also "James Wilson," *Dictionary of National Biography* (London, 1921-22).

2. James Wilson, *Influences of the Corn Laws as Affecting All Classes of the Community and Particularly the Landed Interests* (London, 1839), p. 10. This work is hereafter cited as *Influences*. Mark Lane was the London corn market, dealing in all grains, both home-grown and imported; see C. R. Fay, *The Corn Laws and Social England* (Cambridge, England, 1932), pp. 56-57 and p. 115. Wilson devoted most of his attention to wheat, though he attempted to extend his argument to include barley rye, and oats.

3. Wilson, *Influences*, p. 129.
4. *Ibid.*, p. 16.
5. Wilson's analysis here, as well as in his rejection of monetary influences (shifts in demand), is hardly borne out by either his own or by more recent statistics. He ignored the peak in wheat prices in 1825, which according to his own statistics was almost as high as that in 1829. A recent series shows the 1825 price higher than 1829, 1830, or 1831; see W. W. Rostow, *British Economy of the Nineteenth Century* (Oxford, 1948), p. 125.
6. Wilson, *Influences*, p. 33.
7. *Ibid.*, p. 34.
8. *Ibid.*, p. 35.
9. *Ibid.*, p. 36.
10. This relation, by which agricultural and nonagricultural prosperity move together, is exactly opposite to the theory advanced in Wilson's second work. See section two in this chapter.
11. Wilson, *Influences*, p. 48.
12. *Ibid.*, pp. 21-22.
13. *Ibid.*, p. 97.
14. *Ibid.*, p. 120.
15. *Ibid.*, p. 126.
16. James Wilson, *Fluctuations of Currency, Commerce, and Manufactures; Referable to the Corn Laws* (London, 1840), p. iii. This work is hereafter cited as *Fluctuations*.
17. Wilson was interested in showing the importance of wheat in the economy. To this end he presented estimates of the average annual expenditure on wheat as £41.6 million, an "enormous sum," which was not compared to any other magnitude. *Ibid.*, pp. 10-11. His estimates of fluctuations in such expenditure were based on the assumption of constant consumption, measured in quarters of wheat. *Ibid.*, p. 13. He also tried to bolster his argument by reference to other commodities necessary for subsistence.
18. *Ibid.*, p. 21.
19. *Ibid.*, p. 23.
20. *Ibid.*
21. *Ibid.*, p. 22.
22. *Ibid.*, p. 23.
23. *Ibid.*
24. Wilson also argued that high wheat prices had been a factor in

the French Revolution of 1830: "The great distress and consequent discontent which prevailed in France in the manufacturing districts during 1829-30 led to the disturbances, and at length to the revolution of the latter year." *Ibid.*, p. 122. A more detailed examination of this interpretation of French political disturbances appeared in 1850; see J. T. Danson, "On the Fluctuations of the Annual Supply and Average Price of Corn in France during the Last Seventy Years... with Particular Reference to the Political Periods of 1792, 1814, 1830, and 1848," *Journal of the Statistical Society* (1850), pp. 152-67.

25. Wilson, *Fluctuations*, pp. 24-25.
26. *Ibid.*, pp. 25-26.
27. *Ibid.*, pp. 26-27.
28. Bagehot reported that Wilson was almost wiped out in 1837 as the result of speculations in indigo. See Bagehot, "Memoir of the Right Hon. James Wilson," Supplement to the *Economist* (November 17, 1860), p. 1288.
29. Wilson, *Fluctuations*, p. 117; also p. 67.
30. *Ibid.*, pp. 29-30.
31. *Ibid.*, p. 75.
32. *Ibid.*, pp. 75-76.
33. *Economist*, Preliminary Number and Prospectus (August, 1843), p. 5.
34. Wilson, *Fluctuations*, p. 45.
35. James Wilson, *Capital, Currency, and Banking; Being a Collection of a Series of Articles Published in the Economist in 1845, on the Principles of the Bank Act of 1844, and in 1847, on the Recent Monetarial and Commercial Crisis; Concluding with a Plan for a Secure and Economical Currency* (London, 1847). This work is hereafter cited as *Capital, Currency, and Banking*. Roughly one half of the volume is devoted to the Bank Act of 1844. Neither the banking system, nor the Bank Act, play a part of much importance in Wilson's theories of general fluctuations.
36. David Ricardo, *The Principles of Political Economy and Taxation* (London and New York, 1911), Chapter XXXI. See also John Barton, *Observations on the Circumstances Which Influence the Condition of the Labouring Classes of Society* (London, 1817).
37. Wilson, *Capital, Currency, and Banking*, pp. 119-21.
38. *Ibid.*, p. 121.
39. *Ibid.*, pp. 122 ff.
40. *Ibid.*

41. *Ibid.*, p. 125.
42. *Ibid.*, p. 143.
43. *Ibid.*
44. *Ibid.*, pp. 150-51.
45. *Ibid.*, p. 128.
46. *Ibid.*
47. *Ibid.*, p. xvii.
48. *Ibid.*, pp. xiii-xiv. Later Wilson admitted that to the extent that expenditures involved only an exchange of railroad securities for land rights, the expenditure was of no importance. *Ibid.*, p. xxviii.
49. Other results are the rise of imports in price and value, and the fall of exports, resulting in the export of bullion.
50. Wilson, *Capital, Currency, and Banking*, pp. 147-48.
51. *Ibid.*, p. 153.
52. *Ibid.* In part the reduction in the production of food and other consumables seems to be independent of the diversion of labor to railroad construction; possibly this argument presupposes a backward-sloping labor supply curve.
53. *Ibid.*, p. 148.
54. According to H. G. Lewin, additional railroad mileage authorized by Parliament reached a peak in 1846 and new railroad mileage actually opened for use reached a peak in 1848. See H. G. Lewin, *The Railway Mania and Its Aftermath* (London, 1936), p. 473, for the 1845-52 statistics; for earlier statistics see H. G. Lewin, *Early British Railways* (London, 1925), p. 186. See also W. Hoffmann, *Wachstum und Wachstumsformen der englischen Industriewirtschaft von 1700 bis zur Gegenwart* (Jena, 1940), table opposite p. 284 and pp. 224-26; translated by W. H. Chaloner and W. O. Henderson as *British Industry, 1700-1950* (Oxford, 1955).
55. Wilson, *Capital, Currency, and Banking*, pp. 168-69.
56. This third type of crisis is described on pp. 111-12 and 114.
57. Wilson, *Fluctuations*, p. 32.
58. *Ibid.*, p. 122.
59. *Ibid.*, p. 39.
60. *Ibid.*, p. 90.
61. The third type of crisis is referred to on pp. 119-20.
62. Wilson, *Fluctuations*, pp. 29-30; also Wilson, *Capital, Currency, and Banking*, p. 173.
63. Wilson, *Capital, Currency, and Banking*, pp. vi-viii, xvi.

64. *Ibid.*, p. 162.
65. See pp. 106-7.
66. Wilson, *Capital, Currency, and Banking*, p. 199.
67. Mordecai Ezekiel, "The Cobweb Theorem," *Quarterly Journal of Economics* (1938), reprinted in *Readings in Business Cycle Theory* (Philadelphia, 1944).
68. See Walter Bagehot, *Lombard Street* (New York, 1873), pp. 127-28; A. and M. P. Marshall, *Economics of Industry* (London, 1879), p. 152.
69. W. S. Jevons, "The Periodicity of Commercial Crises and Its Physical Explanation," *Journal of the Statistical and Social Inquiry Society of Ireland* (1878), reprinted in *Investigations in Currency and Finance* (London, 1884), p. 217.
70. Rostow, *British Economy of the Nineteenth Century*, pp. 50-51.
71. Hyde Clarke, e.g., argued that dire predictions of the Wilson type were without justification in view of the existing unemployment. See Hyde Clarke, *Theory of Investment in Railway Companies* (London, 1846), especially p. 9.
72. F. A. Hayek, *Prices and Production* (2d ed., London, 1935), p. 102.
73. W. S. Jevons, "A Serious Fall in the Value of Gold Ascertained and Its Social Effects Set Forth," *Investigations in Currency and Finance* (London, 1884), p. 28.

THOMAS TOOKE

1. For biographical material see "Thomas Tooke," *Dictionary of National Biorgaphy* (London, 1921-22).
2. Thomas Tooke, *A History of Prices and of the State of the Circulation from 1792 to 1856* (6 vols., London, 1838-57). William Newmarch collaborated on Vols. V and VI. This work is hereafter cited as *History*.
3. Thomas Tooke, *An Inquiry into the Currency Principle* (London, 1844). This work is hereafter cited as *Inquiry*.
4. Tooke, *History*, I, 175.
5. A. F. Burns and W. C. Mitchell, *Measuring Business Cycles* (New York, 1946), p. 79.
6. W. Hoffmann, *Wachstum und Wachstumsformen der englischen Industriewirtschaft von 1700 bis zur Gegenwart* (Jena, 1940), p. 261; translated by W. H. Chaloner and W. O. Henderson as *British Industry, 1700-1950* (Oxford, 1955).

NOTES: TOOKE

7. W. W. Rostow, *British Economy of the Nineteenth Century* (Oxford, 1948), p. 125.
8. Tooke, *History*, I, 276.
9. *Ibid.*, II, 25.
10. *Ibid.*, II, 214.
11. *Ibid.*, II, 77-78.
12. *Ibid.*, II, 147 and 270.
13. *First Report from the Secret Committee on Commercial Distress* (1848), Q. 5306, p. 411.
14. Tooke, *History*, I, 277-78.
15. *Ibid.*, II, 5-6.
16. *Ibid.*, II, 145.
17. *Ibid.*, II, 147.
18. *Ibid.*, II, 251.
19. *Ibid.*, II, 254.
20. *Ibid.*, II, 155, footnote.
21. *Ibid.*, IV, 182.
22. Tooke, *Inquiry*, p. 71.
23. *Ibid.*, p. 123. See also *Report from the Committee of Secrecy on the Bank of England Charter; with Minutes of Evidence, Appendix and Index* (1832), Q. 5449, p. 441, and *Report from the Select Committee on Banks of Issue; with Minutes of Evidence, Appendix, and Index* (1840), Q. 3296-99, pp. 298-99.
24. Tooke, *Inquiry*, pp. 69-70.
25. Tooke, *History*, IV, 183-97.
26. See pp. 137-38.
27. Tooke, *Inquiry*, p. 158, footnote, added in the second edition.
28. *Ibid.*, p. 79.
29. *Ibid.*, p. 82.
30. *Ibid.*, p. 85.
31. Tooke, *History*, IV, 294-95.
32. *Ibid.*, IV, 332.
33. Tooke, *Inquiry*, p. 103.
34. *Ibid.*, p. 124, footnote, added in the second edition. See also *Report from the Select Committee on Banks of Issue; with Minutes of Evidence, Appendix, and Index* (1840), Q. 3625-36, pp. 341-42.
35. Tooke, *History*, III, 158.
36. *Ibid.*

37. *Ibid.*, IV, 402.
38. S. J. Loyd (Lord Overstone), *Reflections Suggested by a Perusal of Mr. J. Horsley Palmer's Pamphlet on the Causes and Consequences of the Pressure on the Money Market* (London, 1837), p. 34.
39. S. J. Loyd (Lord Overstone), *Thoughts on the Separation of the Departments of the Bank of England* (London, 1844), p. 240.
40. Tooke, *Inquiry*, p. 105.
41. *Ibid.*, p. 108.
42. Cf. J. Viner, *Studies in the Theory of International Trade* (New York, 1937), pp. 229-30.

JOHN STUART MILL

1. For biographical material see John Stuart Mill, *Autobiography* (London, 1873); Alexander Bain, *John Stuart Mill* (London, 1882); Michael St. John Packe, *The Life of John Stuart Mill* (London, 1954); Herbert Spencer (and others), *John Stuart Mill, His Life and Works* (Boston, 1873); Sir Leslie Stephen, *The English Utilitarians*, Vol. III (London, 1900).
2. John Stuart Mill, *Principles of Political Economy*, ed. by W. J. Ashley (London, 1909). All references, unless otherwise noted, are to passages included in the first (1848) edition. The work is hereafter cited as *Principles*.
3. John Stuart Mill, *Essays on Some Unsettled Questions of Political Economy* (London, 1844), written in 1829 and 1830. This work is hereafter cited as *Essays*.
4. *Ibid.*, p. 47.
5. *Ibid.*, p. 55.
6. *Ibid.*, p. 67.
7. *Ibid.*
8. *Ibid.*
9. Compare Mill, *Principles*, p. 87.
10. Mill, *Essays*, p. 68.
11. *Ibid.*
12. *Ibid.*
13. *Ibid.*, p. 69.
14. *Ibid.*, p. 70; but contrast J. S. Mill, "War Expenditure,"

Westminster Review (1824), a review of William Blake's *Observations on the Effects Produced by the Expenditure of Government during the Restriction of Cash Payments* (London, 1823).

15. Mill, *Essays*, p. 71.
16. *Ibid.*, p. 73.
17. Mill, *Principles*, p. 561.
18. *Ibid.*
19. The chief chapters containing material relevant to periodic fluctuations in the *Principles* are as follows: in Book III—Ch. XII, Influences of Credit on Prices; Ch. XIII, Of an Inconvertible Paper Currency; Ch. XIV, Of Excess of Supply; Ch. XXIII, Of the Rate of Interest; Ch. XXIV, Of the Regulation of a Convertible Paper Currency; and in Book IV—Ch. IV, Of the Tendency of Profits to a Minimum; Ch. V, Consequences of the Tendency of Profits to a Minimum.
20. Mill himself tends to neglect fixed capital formation in Book III of the *Principles*, stressing its role only in Book IV.
21. Mill, *Principles*, p. 653.
22. In this connection see the reference to "short periods of transition," *Essays*, p. 68, quoted on p. 151. See also p. 167, later in this chapter.
23. Mill, *Principles*, p. 653.
24. *Ibid.*, pp. 654-55.
25. See section three in this chapter. The general tone of Book III suggests that speculation arises as the result of exogenous events, while the description in Book IV suggests an endogenous explanation.
26. Mill, *Principles*, p. 526.
27. *Ibid.*
28. *Ibid.*, p. 527.
29. *Ibid.*, p. 526.
30. See especially *ibid.*, Book III, Chapter XII.
31. *Ibid.*, pp. 655-56.
32. See the last quotation; also *ibid.*, p. 491.
33. *Ibid.*, p. 528.
34. *Ibid.*, p. 550.
35. *Ibid.*, p. 528.
36. *Ibid.*, p. 656.
37. *Ibid.*, p. 636.
38. *Ibid.*, p. 527.
39. *Ibid.*, p. 528.

40. *Ibid.*
41. *Ibid.*, p. 641.
42. *Ibid.*, p. 528.
43. See pp. 166-67.
44. Mill, *Principles*, p. 638.
45. Section three tends to support this interpretation.
46. Mill, *Principles*, p. 732.
47. *Ibid.*
48. *Ibid.*, p. 728.
49. *Ibid.*, pp. 728-29.
50. *Ibid.*, p. 731.
51. *Ibid.*, p. 743.
52. *Ibid.*, p. 734.
53. *Ibid.*, p. 744.
54. *Ibid.*, p. 529.
55. Elsewhere Mill recognized the "temporary" influence of money upon interest rates. *Ibid.*, p. 646.
56. *Ibid.*, p. 529.
57. See p. 159.
58. Mill, *Principles*, pp. 733-35. The other agencies working againts the tendency of profits to decline were improvements in production, the export of capital, and new foreign sources of cheap imports. None of these were specifically related to the cycle.
59. *Ibid.*, p. 734.
60. *Ibid.*
61. *Ibid.*, p. 744.
62. *Ibid.*, p. 734.
63. *Ibid.*
64. *Ibid.*, p. 641.
65. *Ibid.*, p. 734.
66. *Ibid.*
67. *Ibid.*, p. 709.
68. See, however, p. 177.
69. J. S. Mill, "The Currency Juggle," *Tait's Edinburgh Magazine* (1833), reprinted in *Dissertations and Discussions*, Vol. I (Boston, 1864).
70. *Ibid.*, p. 79.
71. Mill, *Principles*, pp. 550-51.
72. *Ibid.*, p. 550.
73. See, however, pp. 156-57.

74. Mill, *Principles*, p. 550.
75. *Ibid.*, p. 552.
76. *Ibid.*
77. *Ibid.*
78. *Ibid.*, p. 544.
79. J. S. Mill, "The French Revolution of 1848 and Its Assailants," *Westminster Review* (1849), p. 32.
80. *Ibid.*
81. Mill, *Principles*, p. 362.
82. *Ibid.*, pp. 363-64, first appearing in the second edition (1849).
83. *Ibid.*, p. 364.
84. Mill, "The French Revolution of 1848 and Its Assailants", *Westminster Review* (1849), p. 33.
85. Mill, *Principles*, p. 651.
86. *Ibid.*, pp. 656-57.
87. *Ibid.*, p. 661.
88. *Ibid.* pp. 662-63.
89. *Ibid.* p. 673.
90. *Ibid.*, p. 743.

CONCLUSION

1. W. C. Mitchell, *What Happens during Business Cycles* (New York, 1951), p. 51.
2. See p. 1.
3. W. C. Mitchell, *Business Cycles* (New York, 1927), p. 451.
4. *Ibid.*, pp. 378-81, 451-53, and 468. These generalizations were **not** based on the same group of writers that is considered here.
5. G. Haberler, *Prosperity and Depression* (3d ed., Geneva, 1941).

Bibliography

WORKS BY THE SIX WRITERS STUDIED

ATTWOOD, THOMAS

The Currency. (From Aris's Birmingham *Gazette*, January 30.) Observations on the Letters of the Right Honorable Sir Robert Peel, Baronet, to the Birmingham Chamber of Commerce, as Printed in the *Times* Newspaper of January the 20th, 1843. Birmingham, 1843.

The Distressed State of the Country. Birmingham, 1829.

An Exposition of the Cause and Remedy of the Agricultural Distress. Hertford, 1828.

With Sir John Sinclair. The Late Prosperity, and the Present Adversity of the Country, Explained; the Proper Remedies Considered, and the Comparative Merits of the English and Scottish Systems of Banking Discussed, in a Correspondence between Sir John Sinclair and Mr. Thomas Attwood. London, 1826.

Letter of Mr. Thomas Attwood to the Right Hon. Sir Robert Peel, Bart. London, 1837.

A Letter to the Earl of Liverpool on the Reports of the Committees of the Two Houses of Parliament on the Question of the Bank Restriction Act. Birmingham, 1819.

A Letter to the Right Honorable Nicholas Vansittart, on the Creation of Money and on Its Action upon National Prosperity. Birmingham, 1817.

Mansell & Co's. Report of the Important Discussion Held in Birmingham, August the 28th and 29th, 1832, between William Cobbett,

Thomas Attwood, and Charles Jones, Esqrs. 2d ed. Birmingham, 1832.

Observations on Currency, Population, and Pauperism in Two Letters to Arthur Young, Esq. Birmingham, 1818.

Prosperity Restored; or, Reflections on the Cause of the Public Distresses, and on the Only Means of Relieving Them. London, 1817.

The Remedy; or, Thoughts on the Present Distresses. London, 1816. (First edition?)

The Scotch Banker. London, 1828.

A Second Letter to the Earl of Liverpool, on the Bank Reports, as Occasioning the National Dangers and Distresses. Birmingham, 1819.

JOPLIN, THOMAS

An Analysis and History of the Currency Question. London, 1832.

Articles on Banking and Currency. London, 1838.

The Cause and Cure of Our Commercial Embarrassments. London, 1841.

Currency Reform. London, 1844.

An Essay on the General Principles and Present Practice of Banking in England and Scotland. London, 1822.

An Examination of Sir Robert Peel's Currency Bill of 1844. London, 1844.

An Illustration of Mr. Joplin's Views on Currency. London, 1825.

On Our Monetary System. London, 1839.

Outlines of a System of Political Economy. London, 1823.

Views on the Currency. London, 1828.

Views on the Subject of Corn and Currency. London, 1826.

MALTHUS, THOMAS ROBERT

Definitions in Political Economy. London, 1827.

"Depreciation of Paper Currency," *Edinburgh Review*, 1811.

An Inquiry into the Nature and Progress of Rent. London, 1815.

Observations on the Effects of the Corn Laws. 3d ed. London, 1815.

Principles of Political Economy. 2d ed. New York, 1951.

"Tooke—on High and Low Prices," *Quarterly Review*, 1823.

MILL, JOHN STUART

Autobiography. London, 1873.

"The Currency Juggle," *Tait's Edinburgh Magazine*, 1833. Reprinted in Dissertations and Discussions, Vol. I. Boston, 1865.

Essays on Some Unsettled Questions of Political Economy. London, 1844.

"The French Revolution of 1848 and Its Assailants," *Westminster Review*, 1849.

"An Inquiry into the Currency Principle by Thomas Tooke," *Westminster Review*, 1844.

Principles of Political Economy. Edited by W. J. Ashley. London, 1909.

"War Expenditure," *Westminster Review*, 1824.

TOOKE, THOMAS

Considerations on the State of the Currency. London, 1826.

A History of Prices and of the State of the Circulation from 1792 to 1856. 6 vols. London, 1838-57. William Newmarch collaborated on Vols. V and VI.

An Inquiry into the Currency Principle. London, 1844.

A Letter to Lord Grenville, on the Effects Ascribed to the Resumption of Cash Payments on the Value of the Currency. London, 1829.

On the Bank Charter Act of 1844. London, 1856.

On the Currency in Connexion with the Corn Trade. London, 1829.

Thoughts and Details on the High and Low Prices of the Last Thirty Years. London, 1823.

WILSON, JAMES

Capital, Currency, and Banking; Being a Collection of a Series of Articles Published in the *Economist* in 1845, on the Principles of the Bank Act of 1844, and in 1847, on the Recent Monetarial and Commercial Crisis; Concluding with a Plan for a Secure and Economical Currency. London, 1847.

The Cause of the Present Commercial Distress, and Its Bearings on the Interests of Ship-Owners. Liverpool, 1843.

Editor. *Economist* (London), 1843-50.

Fluctuations of Currency, Commerce, and Manufactures; Referable to the Corn Laws. London, 1840.

Influences of the Corn Laws as Affecting All Classes of the Community and Particularly the Landed Interests. London, 1839.

The Revenue; or, What Should the Chancellor Do? London, 1841.

OTHER PRIMARY SOURCES

Barton, J. An Inquiry into the Expediency of the Existing Restrictions on the Importation of Foreign Corn: With Observations on the Present Social and Political Prospects of Great Britain. London, 1833.

—— Observations on the Circumstances Which Influence the Condition of the Labouring Classes of Society. London, 1817.

Bentham, J. The Rationale of Reward. London, 1825.

Blake, W. Observations on the Effects Produced by the Expenditure of Government during the Restriction of Cash Payments. London, 1823.

Boyd, W. A Letter to the Right Honorable William Pitt, on the Influence of the Stoppage of Issues in Specie at the Bank of England; on the Prices of Provisions, and Other Commodities. London, 1801.

Bray, J. F. Labour's Wrongs and Labour's Remedy; or, The Age of Might and the Age of Right. Leeds, 1839.

Chalmers, T. On Political Economy. Glasgow, 1832.

Clarke, H. Theory of Investment in Railway Companies. London, 1846.

Cruttwell, R. Reform, without Revolution! London, 1839.

Danson, J. T. " . . . Investigation of the Changes in . . . the Condition of the People . . . from the Harvest of 1839 to the Harvest of 1847, and . . . the Connection (If Any) between the Changes Observed and the Variations . . . in the Prices of the Most Necessary Articles of Food," *Journal of the Statistical Society.* Vol. XI, 1848.

—— "On the Fluctuations of the Annual Supply and Average Price of Corn in France during the Last Seventy Years . . . with Particular Reference to the Political Periods of 1792, 1814, 1830, and 1848," *Journal of the Statistical Society.* Vol. XIII, 1850.

Evans, D. M. The Commercial Crisis of 1847-1848; Being Facts and Figures Illustrative of the Events of that Important Period, Considered in Relation to the Three Epochs of the Railway Mania, the Food and Money Panic, and the French Revolution. London, 1848.

Fullarton, J. On the Regulation of Currencies; Being an Examination of the Principles, on Which It Is Proposed to Restrict, within Certain Fixed Limits, the Future Issues on Credit of the Bank of England, and of the Other Banking Establishments throughout the Country. London, 1844.

BIBLIOGRAPHY

Graham, Sir J. Corn and Currency; in an Address to the Land Owners. A New Edition. 3d ed. London, 1827.

Gray, J. The Social System; a Treatise on the Principle of Exchange. Edinburgh, 1831.

Great Britain, Parliament, House of Commons. Reports from the Secret Committee on the Expediency of the Bank Resuming Cash Payments. 1819.

—— Report from the Select Committee to Whom the Several Petitions Complaining of the Distressed State of the Agriculture of the United Kingdom Were Referred. 1821.

—— Report from the Committee of Secrecy on the Bank of England Charter; with Minutes of Evidence, Appendix and Index. 1832.

—— Report from the Select Committee on Banks of Issue; with the Minutes of Evidence, Appendix, and Index. 1840..

—— First Report from the Secret Committee on Commercial Distress. 1848.

Great Britain, Parliament, House of Lords. Reports Respecting the Bank of England Resuming Cash Payments, viz. The First and Second Reports of the Lords Committees, Appointed a Secret Committee to Inquire into the State of the Bank of England with Respect to the Expediency of the Resumption of Cash Payments;—with Minutes of Evidence and an Appendix. 1819.

—— Report from the Secret Committee of the House of Lords, Appointed to Inquire into the Causes of the Distress Which Has for Some Time Prevailed among the Commercial Classes and How Far It Has Been Affected by the Laws for Regulating the Issue of Bank Notes Payable on Demand, together with the Minutes of Evidence, and an Appendix. 1848.

Hume, D. Political Discourses. Edinburgh, 1752.

James, H. Essays on Money, Exchanges, and Political Economy, Showing the Cause of the Fluctuation in Prices and the Depreciation in the Value of Property of Late Years; also Explaining the Cause of the Deranged and Distressed State of the Country since the Peace in 1814, and Pointing Out the Safest, Speediest, and Easiest Method of Removing the Same. London, 1820.

—— State of the Nation. Causes and Effects of the Rise and Fall in Value of Property and Commodities from the Year 1790 to the Present Time. London, 1835.

Lauderdale, Earl of. An Inquiry into the Nature and Origin of Public Wealth, and into the Means and Causes of Its Increase. Edinburgh, 1804.
―― Three Letters to the Duke of Wellington. London, 1829.
Loyd, S. J. (Lord Overstone). Reflections Suggested by a Perusal of Mr. J. Horsley Palmer's Pamphlet on the Causes and Consequences of the Pressure on the Money Market. London, 1837.
―― Remarks on the Management of the Circulation; and on the Condition and Conduct of the Bank of England and of the Country Issuers, during the Year 1839. London, 1840.
―― Thoughts on the Separation of the Departments of the Bank of England. London, 1844.
McCulloch, J. R. Letters of John Ramsey McCulloch to David Ricardo 1813-1823. Edited by J. H. Hollander. Baltimore, 1931.
―― Principles of Political Economy. 3d ed. Edinburgh, 1843.
Mill, James. Commerce Defended. An Answer to the Arguments by Which Mr. Spence, Mr. Cobbett and Others, have Attempted to Prove That Commerce Is Not a Source of National Wealth. 2d ed. London, 1808.
―― Elements of Political Economy. 3d ed. London, 1826.
Ricardo, D. Letters of David Ricardo to Hutches Trower and Others 1811-1823. Edited by J. Bonar and J. H. Hollander. Oxford, 1899.
―― Letters of David Ricardo to Thomas Robert Malthus, 1810-1823. Edited by J. Bonar. London, 1887.
―― Notes on Malthus' "Principles of Political Economy." Edited by J. H. Hollander and T. E. Gregory. London and Baltimore, 1928.
―― The Principles of Political Economy and Taxation. London and New York, 1911.
―― The Works and Correspondence of David Ricardo. Edited by P. Sraffa. 10 vols. Cambridge, England, 1951-55.
Rooke, J. An Inquiry into the Principles of National Wealth, Illustrated by the Political Economy of the British Empire. Edinburgh, 1824.
Say, J. B. Letters to Thomas Robert Malthus on Political Economy and Stagnation of Commerce. London, 1821.
Scrope, G. P. The Currency Question Freed from Mystery, in a Letter to Mr. Peel, Showing How the Distress May Be Relieved without Altering the Standard. London, 1830.

―― Principles of Political Economy. London, 1833.
Senior, N. W. Political Economy. 2d ed. rev. London, 1850.
Smith, A. An Inquiry in the Nature and Causes of the Wealth of Nations. New York, 1937.
Thompson, W. An Inquiry into the Principles of the Distribution of Wealth. London, 1824.
Thornton, H. An Enquiry into the Nature and Effects of the Paper Credit of Great Britain. London, 1802.
Torrens, R. An Essay on Money and Paper Currency. London, 1812.
―― The Principles and Practical Operation of Sir Robert Peel's Bill of 1844 Explained, and Defended against the Objections of Tooke, Fullarton, and Wilson. London, 1848.
Wade, J. History of the Middle and Working Classes. 3d ed. London, 1835.
West, Sir E. Price of Corn and Wages of Labour with Observations upon Dr. Smith's, Mr. Ricardo's, and Mr. Malthus' Doctrines upon Those Subjects; and an Attempt at an Exposition of the Causes of the Fluctuation of the Price of Corn during the Last Thirty Years. London, 1826.

SECONDARY SOURCES

Acworth, A. W. Financial Reconstruction in England, 1815-1822. London, 1925.
Andreades, A. M. A History of the Bank of England. London, 1909.
Angell, J. W. The Theory of International Prices. Cambridge, Massachusetts, 1926.
Ashton, T. S. The Industrial Revolution, 1760-1830. London, 1948.
―― "The Standard of Life of the Workers in England, 1790-1830," *The Tasks of Economic History*, 1949.
Bagehot, W. Lombard Street: A Description of the Money Market. New York, 1873.
―― "Memoir of the Right Hon. James Wilson," in Supplement to *Economist* (London), November 17, 1860.
Bain, A. John Stuart Mill. London, 1882.
Barnes, D. G. A History of the English Corn Laws, from 1660-1846. London, 1930.
Bergmann, E. v. Geschichte der nationalökonomischen Krisentheorien. Stuttgart, 1895.

Beveridge, Sir W. H. Full Employment in a Free Society. New York, 1945.
—— "The Trade Cycle in Britain before 1850," *Oxford Economic Papers*, 1940.
Bonar, J. Malthus and His Work. New York, 1924.
Bouniatian, M. Geschichte der Handelskrisen in England, 1640-1840. Munich, 1908.
Bowen, I. "Country Banking, the Note Issues and Banking Controversies in 1825," *Economic History*, 1938.
Bowley, A. C. "The Statistics of Wages in the United Kingdom during the Last Hundred Years," *Journal of the Royal Statistical Society*, 1898 and 1899.
Briggs, A. "Thomas Attwood and the Economic Background of the Birmingham Political Union," *Cambridge Historical Journal*, 1948.
Buck, N. S. The Development of the Organization of Anglo-American Trade, New Haven, 1925.
Burns, A. F., and W. C. Mitchell. Measuring Business Cycles. New York, 1946.
Cairncross, A. K. "The Victorians and Investment," *Economic History*, 1936. Reprinted in A. K. Cairncross, Home and Foreign Investment, 1870-1913. Cambridge, England, 1953.
Cannan, E. The Paper Pound, 1797-1821. London, 1919.
Carpenter, C. C. "The English Specie Resumption of 1821," *Southern Economic Journal*, 1938-39.
Checkland, S. G. "The Birmingham Economists, 1815-1850," *Economic History Review*, 1948.
Clapham, J. H. An Economic History of Modern Britain. 3 vols. Cambridge, England, 1930-38.
Cole, G. D. H. Chartist Portraits. London, 1941.
Daugherty, M. R. "The Currency-Banking Controversy," *Southern Economic Journal*, 1942-43.
Dempsey, B. W. "The Historical Emergence of Quantity Theory," *Quarterly Journal of Economics*, 1935.
Dorfman, J. The Economic Mind in American Civilization, 1606-1865. New York, 1946.
Ezekiel, M. "The Cobweb Theorem," *Quarterly Journal of Economics*, 1938.
Fay, C. R. The Corn Laws and Social England. Cambridge, England, 1932.

BIBLIOGRAPHY

Feavearyear, A. E. The Pound Sterling: A History of English Money. London, 1931.

Fetter, F. A. "Lauderdale's Oversaving Theory," *American Economic Review*, 1945.

Gammage, R. G. History of the Chartist Movement, 1837-1854. London, 1894.

Gourvitch, A. Survey of Economic Theory on Technological Change and Employment. Philadelphia, 1940.

Gregory, T. E. Select Statutes, Documents and Reports Relating to British Banking, 1832-1928. 2 vols. London, 1929.

Haberler, G. Prosperity and Depression. 3d ed. Geneva, 1941.

Halévy, E. The Growth of Philosophic Radicalism. New York, 1950.

—— A History of the English People in the Nineteenth Century. 2d ed., 6 vols. London, 1949-52.

Hansen, A. H. Business Cycles and National Income. New York, 1951.

—— Monetary Theory and Fiscal Policy. New York, 1949.

Hawtrey, R. G. The Art of Central Banking. London, 1932.

—— Currency and Credit. 3d ed. New York, 1928.

—— "Inflationism," Trade and Credit. New York, 1928.

Hayek, F. A. "The Development of the Doctrine of Forced Saving," *Quarterly Journal of Economics*, 1932.

—— Prices and Production. 2d ed. London, 1935.

Hobson, J. A. The Economics of Unemployment. London, 1922.

Hoffmann, W. Wachstum und Wachstumsformen der englischen Industriewirtschaft von 1700 bis zur Gegenwart. Jena, 1940. Translated by W. H. Chaloner and W. O. Henderson as British Industry, 1700-1950. Oxford, 1955.

Hollander, J. H. "The Development of the Theory of Money from Adam Smith to David Ricardo," *Quarterly Journal of Economics*, 1911.

Horsefield, J. K. "The Origins of the Bank Charter Act, 1844," *Economica*, 1944.

Hyndman, H. M. *Commercial Crises of the Nineteenth Century*. London and New York, 1892. 3d ed., 1908.

Imlah, A. H. "Real Values in British Foreign Trade, 1798-1853," *Journal of Economic History*, 1948.

—— "The Terms of Trade of the United Kingdom, 1798-1913," *Journal of Economic History*, 1950.

Jenks, L. H. The Migration of British Capital to 1875. New York, 1927.

Jevons, W. S. Investigations in Currency and Finance. London, 1884.
Kepper, G. Die Konjunkturlehren der Banking- und der Currencyschule. Leipzig, 1933.
Keynes, J. M. The General Theory of Employment, Interest, and Money. New York, 1936.
—— "Robert Malthus," Essays in Biography. New York, 1933.
Kimball, J. The Economic Doctrines of John Gray—1799-1883. Washington, 1948.
King, W. T. C. History of the London Discount Market. London, 1936.
Klein, L. R. The Keynesian Revolution. New York, 1947.
Kuznets, S. "Equilibrium Economics and Business Cycle Theory," *Quarterly Journal of Economics*, 1930.
Labrousse, C.-E. La Crise de l'économie française à la fin de l'ancien régime et au début de la révolution. Vol. I. Paris, 1944.
Lange, O. "Say's Law: A Restatement and Criticism," in Studies in Mathematical Economics and Econometrics. Edited by Lange, McIntyre, and Yntema. Chicago, 1942.
Lescure, J. Des Crises générales et périodique de surproduction. 4th ed. Paris, 1932.
Lewin, H. G. Early British Railways. London, 1925.
—— The Railway Mania and Its Aftermath. London, 1936.
Lowenthal, E. The Ricardian Socialists. New York, 1911.
Marget, A. W. The Theory of Prices. 2 vols. New York, 1938-42.
Marshall, A., and M. P. Marshall. Economics of Industry. London, 1879.
Meek, R. L. "Thomas Joplin and the Theory of Interest," *Review of Economic Studies*, 1950-51.
Miller, H. E. Banking Theories in the United States before 1860. Cambridge, Massachusetts, 1927.
Mints, L. W. A History of Banking Theory. Chicago, 1945.
Mitchell, W. C. Business Cycles. New York, 1927.
—— What Happens during Business Cycles. New York, 1951.
Morgan, E. V. "Railway Investment, Bank of England Policy and Interest Rates, 1844-1848," *Economic History*, 1940.
—— "Some Aspects of the Bank Restriction Period, 1797-1821," *Economic History*, 1939.
Myint, H. *Theories of Welfare Economics*. Cambridge, Massachusetts, 1948.

Niebyl, K. H. Studies in the Classical Theories of Money. New York, 1946.

O'Leary, J. J. "Malthus and Keynes," *Journal of Political Economy*, 1942.

—— "Malthus' General Theory of Employment and the Post-Napoleonic Depressions," *Journal of Economic History*, 1943.

Opie, R. "A Neglected English Economist: George Poulett Scrope," *Quarterly Journal of Economics*, 1930.

Packe, M. St. J. The Life of John Stuart Mill. London, 1954.

Pigou, A. C. Industrial Fluctuations. 2d ed. London, 1929.

—— "Mill and the Wages Fund," *Economic Journal*, 1949.

Roll, E. A History of Economic Thought. New York, 1942.

Rostow, W. W. British Economy of the Nineteenth Century. Oxford, 1948.

Sayers, R. S. "The Question of the Standard, 1815-44," *Economic History*, 1935.

—— "The Question of the Standard in the Eighteen-Fifties," *Economic History*, 1933.

Schlote, W. British Overseas Trade from 1700 to the 1930's. Oxford, 1952.

Schumpeter, E. B. "English Prices and Public Finance, 1660-1822," *Review of Economic Statistics*, 1938.

Schumpeter, J. A. Business Cycles. 2 vols. New York., 1939.

Scott, I. O., Jr. "An Exposition of the Keynesian System," *Review of Economic Studies*, 1950-51.

Shannon, H. A. "Bricks: A Trade Index, 1785-1849," *Economica*, 1934.

Silberling, N. J. "British Financial Experience, 1790-1830," *Review of Economic Statistics*, 1919.

—— "British Prices and Business Cycles, 1779-1850," *Review of Economic Statistics*, 1923.

—— "Financial and Monetary Policy of Great Britain during the Napoleonic Wars," *Quarterly Journal of Economics*, 1924.

Smart, W. Economic Annals of the Nineteenth Century. 2 vols. London, 1910-17.

Smith, V. E. "The Classicists' Use of 'Demand,' " *Journal of Political Economy*, 1951.

Sotiroff, G. "John Barton (1789-1852)," *Economic Journal*, 1952.

Spencer, H., and others. John Stuart Mill, His Life and Works. Boston, 1873.

Stephen, L. The English Utilitarians. 3 vols. London, 1900.

Thorp, W. L. Business Annals. New York, 1926.
Trautmann, F. E. Das Problem der Wirtschaftskrisen in der klassischen Nationaloekonomie. n.p. 1928.
Tucker, R. S. "Real Wages of Artisans in London, 1729-1935," *Journal of the American Statistical Association*, 1936.
Veblen, T. "The Overproduction Fallacy," *Quarterly Journal of Economics*, 1892. Reprinted in Essays in Our Changing Order. New York, 1934.
Viner, J. Studies in the Theory of International Trade. New York, 1937.
Wakefield, C. M. Life of Thomas Attwood. London, 1885.
Wallas, G. The Life of Francis Place, 1771-1854. London, 1898.
Ward-Perkins, C. N. "The Commercial Crisis of 1847," *Oxford Economic Papers*, 1950.
Wicksell, K. Lectures on Political Economy. 2 vols. London, 1935.
Wood, E. English Theories of Central Banking Control, 1819-1858. Cambridge, Massachusetts, 1939.
Wood, G. H. "Course of Average Wages, 1790-1860," *Economic Journal*, 1899.

Index

Agricultural theory of fluctuations, 4, 104-14, 119-21, 123-26, 186; *see also* Agriculture; Cobweb theorem
Agriculture: Attwood on, 11-14, 23, 28-30, 34; Joplin on, 87, 90, 92-93, 97, 183; Malthus on, 39, 68; Mill on, 176; Wilson on, 4, 106, 107-14, 119-26 *passim*, 149, 181, 183, 186; *see also* Corn laws; Wheat, price of
Aristocracy, landed, 56
Attwood, Matthias, 74
Attwood, Thomas, 2, 3, 6-35, 180-87; Joplin and, 73, 74, 88, 93; Malthus and, 67-68; Mill and, 5, 6, 149, 158, 168, 169-70, 171, 172, 179; Tooke and, 74, 142

Balance of payments, *see* Exchange rates; Gold standard; International trade
Bank Act of 1844, 99, 128, 137, 143-45, 147, 168, 175-77, 203
Bank of England, 185, 200-1; Attwood on, 8, 13, 22-23, 27, 29, 31-32; Joplin on, 74, 83-85, 88-89, 92-93, 99; Mill on, 168, 175-77; Tooke on, 128, 137, 141-45 147; Wilson on, 121-22, 203; *see also* Bank Act of 1844; Gold standard
Barton, J., 124
Benthamites, 35
Beveridge, W. H., 34
Bills of exchange, 9, 98-99, 137, 138-39, 155, 156
Birmingham, 27

Birmingham Political Union, 6
Birmingham School, 3, 67-68, 142, 169, 190-91
Bullion Committee, report of, 14, 74, 89
Business cycles, concept of, 1, 72, 177-79, 182-84, 186

Capitalists, 14-15, 17, 21, 23-24, 43, 46-53 *passim*, 57, 115-16
Chartist movement, 7, 191
China, trade with, 131
Cobbett, William, 26
Cobweb theorem, 4, 104-7, 123
Consumption, 180, 183-85; Attwood on, 8-10; Joplin on, 75-76, 80, 82; Keynes on, 71-72; Malthus on, 41, 54, 56-57, 184; Mill on, 149-53; Wilson on, 118-19, 124-25
Consumption goods industries, 118-19
Corn laws, 2, 4, 73, 104-7, 121-22, 123, 149, 183, 184-85, 187
Country banks, 74, 77-79, 83, 87, 94, 101
Currency, 2, 3, 187; Attwood on, 6, 7, 9, 12, 14-18, 22-23, 25-27, 31-33; Joplin on, 73-74, 83-85, 89, 92-99, 101; Malthus on, 60-68 *passim*; Mill on, 150-51, 155-58, 170-72, 175; Tooke on, 127, 136-42, 144; Wilson on, 111, 114, 122-23
Currency School, 3, 137, 147

Distribution, means of, 53-59
Droit au travail, 172-74

Economist (London), 4, 6, 103, 113, 114
Effectual demand, 53-59, 71-72
Enterprise, 78-80, 82, 91, 100
Exchange rates, 31-35, 93, 101-2; *see also* Gold standard
Exchequer bills, 15, 18, 24
Ezekiel, Mordecai, 123

Fiscal policy, *see* Government spending; Taxation
Fixed capital formation, 181-83, 185; Attwood on, 11, 33; Joplin on, 76, 90; Malthus on, 62, 69, 71-72; Mill on, 148-49, 154, 160-68, 177-79; Tooke on, 133-36; 140, 146; Wilson on, 4, 104, 109-19, 121, 124-26; *see also* Public works; Railroad investment
France, 120-21; *see also* French Revolution; Napoleonic Wars
French Revolution of 1830, 120, 204
French Revolution of 1848, 168, 173, 174

Glut theory: Malthus on, 36-37, 41-72; Mill on, 148, 151-53
Gold discoveries, 3
Gold standard, 183-84; Attwood on, 8, 15-19, 25, 31-35; Joplin on, 83-85, 88-99, 101-2; Malthus on, 61; Mill on, 158, 160, 172, 175-76, 179; Tooke on, 140-42, 144-45, 147; Wilson on, 120-23; *see also* Bank Act of 1844; Bank of England; Exchange rates; International trade
Government spending, 14, 21-22, 34, 36, 62-64, 68-72, 79-82, 86, 117, 138, 173-74, 183; *see also* Taxation

Haberler, G., 186
Hawtrey, R. G., 33, 186
Hayek, F. A., 125, 186
Hobson, J. A., 186
Hoffmann, W., 131
Hollander, J. H., 70
Hume, David, 170, 171
Huskisson, W., 6

Income, concept of, 37-41, 45
Inflationary gap, 116-18, 124
Interest rates, 181, 185; Attwood on, 15, 28, 33, 34; Joplin on, 4, 74-78, 80, 82-84, 87, 92, 94, 95, 99-102; Malthus on, 72; Mill on, 159, 165, 167, 176, 179; Tooke on, 127, 136-47 *passim;* Wilson on, 108-12 *passim,* 116, 125, 126
International fluctuations, 31, 119-21, 182
International trade, 15, 18, 31, 33, 35, 88-89, 106-7, 119-21, 129, 131-34, 146, 176, 183, 185; *see also* Gold standard
Inventory investment, 181-83; Attwood on, 9, 11-13, 33; Joplin on, 76; Mill on, 5, 153-60, 178-79; Tooke on, 4, 131-32; 134-36, 146
Investment, 4, 181-83, 185; Joplin on, 79-83, 99, 100-1; Malthus on, 42, 51, 69-72; Mill on, 178-79; *see for greater detail* Fixed capital formation; Inventory investment

Jevons, W. S., 1, 123-26, 186
Joint stock banks, 73, 94-96, 97, 111
Joplin, Thomas, 2, 3-4, 73-102, 180-87
Juglar, C., 1

Keynes, J. M.: Attwood and, 34; Joplin and, 4, 100, 186; Malthus and, 3, 4, 70, 71, 186; on Ricardo, 70

Landowners, 17-18, 23-24, 36, 46-53 *passim,* 57-59, 71, 76-77
Lange, Oscar, 52
Lauderdale, Earl of, 38
Leisure, 54-57, 67
Liverpool, Earl of, 22, 25, 32
Loans, *see* Interest rates; Monetary policy; Monetary theory of fluctuations
London banks, 83-85
London money market, 24, 30, 84, 90, 94, 97, 98
Loyd, Samuel Jones (Lord Overstone), 143

INDEX

Malthus, Thomas Robert, 2, 3, 36-72, 180-87; Joplin and, 73; Mill and, 149, 174; Ricardo and, 36, 37, 41, 42-43, 49-51, 66
Manufacturers, 16, 18, 23-24, 135, 157
Manufacturing, 11, 12-13, 46, 90, 106, 108-14, 121
Merchants, 18, 23-24, 67, 76, 77, 135-36, 157
Mill, James, 36
Mill, John Stuart, 2, 3, 4-5, 148-79, 180-87; on Attwood, 6
Mitchell, Wesley C., 1, 183-84
Monetary policy, 183-85, 187; Attwood on, 8, 13-35, 183; Joplin on, 92-99; Malthus on, 67-68; Mill on, 169-72, 175-77; Tooke on, 142-45; Wilson on, 122-23
Monetary theory of fluctuations, 1-3, 33-34, 83-85, 88-91, 179, 183
Money illusion, 150-51, 178

Napoleonic Wars, 3, 131, 145, 176
National Bureau of Economic Research, 85-86, 130
Natural rate of interest, 4, 78, 82-83, 100
Natural remedies, 8-13, 14, 33
Newmarch, William, 128

Overinvestment theory of fluctuations, 4, 5, 103, 114-19, 122, 124-26, 164-67, 179, 183, 186

Peel, Sir Robert, 16, 17
Personal services, 40-41, 46, 54, 55, 58-59
Physiocrats, 38
Place, Francis, 6
Poor Laws, 21, 173
Population, theory of, 14, 15, 36, 41, 43-44, 64-65, 161-62, 163, 173, 174
Prices, 180, 181, 183, 185; Attwood on, 9-15, 18, 19, 23, 25-31, 74; Joplin on, 83, 97; Malthus on, 45-46, 60; Mill on, 150-51, 155, 157, 159, 171, 172, 179; Tooke on, 127, 129-36, 140-41, 143, 146; Wilson on, 104, 120

Psychological theories of fluctuations, 186
Public works, 22, 68-70, 71, 72, 193, 198

Quantity theory, 26, 68, 72-73, 85, 100-1, 136-42, 146-47

Railroad investment, 33, 90, 181, 185, 204; Mill on, 165-66, 177; Tooke on, 133, 135, 140; Wilson on, 4, 103, 111-12, 114-19, 121, 124-26
Reform Bill of 1832, 6, 7, 169
Relief, 20-21
Rents, 46-47, 74-75
Restriction Act of 1797, 15, 192
Resumption Act of 1819, 16, 17
Ricardo, David, 3; quoted on Attwood 6; Malthus and, 36, 37, 41, 42-43, 49-51, 66; Mill and, 148, 154, 161-63; Wilson and, 114, 124
Rostow, W. W., 131

Savings: Joplin on, 3, 73-83, 85-101, 185; Malthus on, 41-53, 62-67, 69; Malthusian and Keynesian, compared, 70-72; Mill on, 162, 163, 164, 166; Wilson on, 114-19; *see also* Glut theory; Inflationary gap
Say's Law, 149, 152-53; *see also* Glut theory
Smith, Adam, 38
South America, trade with, 17, 131, 145
Speculation, 5, 90, 182, 185; Mill on, 149, 153-60, 166, 167, 169, 171, 175, 177, 178; Tooke on, 131, 133-34, 135, 139-40, 141, 145, 146, 147, 157; Wilson on, 112, 114, 119, 120, 124
Statistics, use of, 28, 34, 127, 129-31, 181, 185-86

Taxation, 13-14, 19, 21, 28, 34, 62-67, 72, 174; *see also* Government spending
Thornton, Henry 89
Tooke, Thomas, 2, 4, 127-47, 180-87; Joplin and, 74; Malthus and, 61, 63; Mill and, 5, 6, 149, 154

INDEX

Underconsumption theory, 3, 186; *see also* Savings
Unemployment: Attwood on, 11, 14, 17, 20-22, 184; Joplin on, 78, 88, 90; Malthus on, 37, 44-59, 65-70; Mill on, 160, 168-70, 177, 179, 184; Tooke on, 135; Wilson on, 106
Unproductive labor, *see* Personal services

Vansittart, Nicholas, 22

Wages, 181; Attwood on, 10-11, 25-27, 29-30, 34, 195; Joplin on, 74-75; Malthus on, 39-40, 42-53, 65-67, 72; Mill on, 161-64, 173-74; Tooke on, 133; Wilson on, 118
War, effects of, on economic fluctuations, 3, 44, 59-65, 131, 145, 176
Wealth, concept of, 37-41, 45
Wellington, Duke of, 7
Wheat, price of, 28-29, 34, 74, 103, 104-14, 123, 129, 194-95, 202
Wilson, James, 2, 4, 103-26, 180-87; Jevons and, 186; Mill and, 148, 149, 154, 165